The Church and the Liberal Society

THE CHURCH AND THE LIBERAL SOCIETY

By Emmet John Hughes

UNIVERSITY OF NOTRE DAME PRESS
NOTRE DAME, INDIANA

To the memory of
my uncle

THE REVEREND JAMES HUGHES, O.M.I.

Friend, Teacher and Soldier of Justice
and for

MY FATHER

who carries on the fight

INTRODUCTION TO THE NEW EDITION

I was a university student when I wrote *The Church and the Liberal Society*, and World War II was only beginning to be fought. In the life of one who is only 40 years of age today, the two decades intervening between then and now loom large. And, across that span of time, the backward look upon the youthful work can be made only with many frowns—and a little fear. Will not the seeming profundities of yesterday strike the eye and the mind of today as shallow and superficial? One's manner of speech, surely, has changed. And may there not be even graver change in one's manner of thought?

I have survived the retrospective ordeal with less wincing, less intellectual pain, than I might have feared. Many a word from the past summons a wiser choice today. Many a phrase strikes the ear of its author with an odd and disturbing ring. And many a simplification would be shunned.

Yet time, on the whole, has been kind. The true essence, the substance of the historical argument, stays and stands—not too much mocked by later events. To the perceptions and convictions, whatever their final worth, here voiced with such youthful certitude, the older man finds himself, for better or for worse, still wed.

II

They have been stunning decades, those between now and then. The home of the Third Reich, stirred with monstrous passion to rule the earth even as it shamed humankind, has become the split-nation of Germany today—its Western half a newly built bastion of the hopes of Western freedom. Across the globe, the Japan then threatening to make the vast Pacific a lake along whose Asian shores a titanic empire would rise in menace—now practises democracy at home and, in the world of nations, towers as America's most powerful ally in the Eastern world. And between these two foes of such recent ferocity stands the Soviet Union, presiding over the vastly extended Communist Empire: the valiant ally of *then*, the imposing and tenacious challenge to all the West *now*.

Yet the revolutionary forces and furies of our age strike to levels deeper than even these colossal caprices of the shifting, surface alignments of national powers. Not mere nations but whole continents are, in one sense or another, being born, for the first time or anew. All Africa seethes with new freedom—and with its historic demand that a West, once the colonial master, now prove itself the compassionate minister to the wants and hungers of the millions. One political cycle ahead, Latin America, technically sovereign for generations, proclaims a birth of pride as well as need, as it scorns to play any longer the role of clown or pauper on the great stage of world affairs. And Far East meets West in an intimacy of contact, a common bond of destiny, never known to any previous age of man. And all the while, the revolution of science and technology—unmatched in the story of man since first he ceased to be the nomad and learned to till the soil—suddenly endows him with power to conquer space and to destroy himself.

As the West has struggled and stumbled through these years since the relatively simple issues of World War II were fought to their resolution, the political days have been marked by a phenomenon, in Western Europe, of which there was hardly an outward sign as the 1930's ended. Then there was no Christian Democracy ready to preside over the turbulent politics of Italy. There was no sign or hint of such leadership as has appeared under Adenauer in Germany. And even in the over-populated jungle of French domestic politics there was no force comparable to the MRP that would emerge from war's havoc. Such forces simply did not exist in significant strength—when these pages were written.

It is easy to debate how much Christian Democracy brought to the saving of Europe after World War II. It has been no unblemished force. Often enough, its leaders have vacillated or fallen. Its policies, at times, have lacked vision. Its tactics have often lacked skill.

Yet there is no denying that one cannot know how the story of Western Europe's return to strength would have been written without this force, insurgent almost everywhere and ranging powerfully across old national frontiers. As war ended and the dubious peace began, Europe was on the edge of desperation. Old forms and moulds and fashions had been shattered. And the continent, scarcely able to fill its belly, was famished more than physically. There was hunger in its soul.

For this feeding, it turned to the Christian tradition. The diet that mind and spirit received—let it be acknowledged again—was no miracle of nutrition. Sometimes it lacked balance. Sometimes it lacked iron. But it sufficed—savingly. And there was nowhere else to find such food.

<h1 style="text-align:center">III</h1>

All this (I dare argue so briefly) suggests deeper truths. They are the truths that the following pages—written in the darkness of other shadows, now passed and gone—strove, quite haltingly and even clumsily, to discern and to define.

It suggests that the democratic idea of man is vitally rooted in the Christian idea of man—and, torn from this soil, it must starve and wither.

It suggests that a society's or a civilization's idea of man—its definition of what matters to him because of *who* he is—is the crucial fact of life, around which political and economic formulas and devices must cluster and cohere.

It suggests, therefore, that a civilization unsure of *who* man is can be sure of only one thing: its own mortal peril. For how is it conceivable to be committed to the *rights* of man without first being committed to a definition of his *nature?* And without some such commitment, the world struggle for "freedom" can be little more than a gigantic joust for power, with mere and senseless sound-effects provided by the trumpets and drums of righteous rhetoric. It was so in the contest with Naziism. It is no less so with the challenge of Communism.

It suggests, further, that the historic struggle is not really waged *against* something but *for* something—in this instance, something as precious and grand and difficult as a world of men and nations respectful of the dignity of man. In the world of nations, then, the strong are summoned to help the weak, the rich are called to share with the poor, not because it is expedient but because it is right. The supreme task—for all the clatter of conflict from rice paddies in Southeast Asia to a divided city in the heart of a divided Europe—is not to battle, but to build. And faith, not fear, must be the spur.

And it suggests—finally—that only as the ends are clearly perceived can the means be wisely chosen. Only as the realm of *values* takes its proper place in men's awareness of what confronts them can the realm of *politics* assume *its* proper place. Only thus can the baleful confusion of morals and politics be escaped. Only thus can each choice or crisis be met for what it is—one more testing of will and wisdom—rather than the fateful, final issue on which all must blindly be staked. Only *within* such a framework of faith—of clear definitions and explicit purposes—is it possible truly to practise the pragmatism of politics. For when these absolute values, telling *who* man is and *what* makes his dignity, are denied their proper place, they merely invade the lower realm of politics and (in the minds of men) proclaim a spurious sovereignty. Then no matter can be truly met, no issue fairly judged, for each decision struts as the supreme challenge, and each day wears the inscrutable mask of the eternal.

The heart of the matter, then, is not very complex.

In this age when men and nations are thrusting so audaciously toward stars and planets, the great decisions will be made in *inner* space. Here—in the brain and conscience of man—will be answered the question of *who* he is. And from that knowledge alone can come the commitment to live as he must: free—because bound to Him Who made him so.

So I believed then. And so I believe now.

E.J.H.

New York, July 14, 1961

PREFACE

THE summer of 1943 has come and where great armies of the world are joined in battle the earth has hardened for the swifter rush of men and machines, surging forward to bring to final decision the greatest war which has come to pass since beings nobler than beasts came to live upon this planet. Instruments of mutual annihilation have become ever more refined and ingenious. The impact of war leaves no part of man's world to pursue the even tenor of its way. The battle lines flame with a conflagration that even twenty-five years ago would have seemed beyond belief or fear.

Yet, through all the riotous rush of change, the firm fact stands that the great issues now joined will be decided where they have ever been decided throughout man's history: in the minds of men. This is a fact, however, which brings little solace to men of the West, men fighting in the name of democracy. These men are troubled. Much more profoundly than by military adversity, or economic maladjustments, they are troubled by a disintegration of faith—not someone else's, but their own faith. Lack of sureness of purpose, absence of moral conviction, insistent sense of doubt, demoralizing lack of intellectual certitude—these afflict the mind of Western man.

What has happened to the Liberal Heritage? What has befallen the Liberal Society?

A study of Liberalism and Catholicism signifies a study of the dominant, life-giving creed of the Western world for the last five centuries—and that creed's most uncompromising and virile critic, also guardian and propagator of another faith: the Catholic Church. The nature of such a study almost automatically dictates certain emphases. It is necessary, on the one hand, to focus attention on the implicit social gospel of the Catholic faith and, on the other hand, to stress the philosophical premises and precepts of Liberalism. The reason for this is clear. To allow each to meet face to face, as it were, on the plane of social philosophy, it has been necessary to underscore the common denominators to both, thus revealing in clear, comparable lines the conflict between the two faiths. This does not constitute merely pressing facts into any preconceived interpretive mold. For in the final analysis any politico-economic theory (including Liberalism) must rest on a specific conception of man and his true destiny. And any religious conception of the nature of man and his true destiny (including Catholicism) must be capable of translation into a guide for man in his life in human society on this earth.

The issue of precise emphasis in a study of such scope is one upon which no two historians could agree. To make clear the clash of principles arising at certain points in the narrative, there follows an inevitable failure to signify the constant historic continuity which is operative even in times of profoundest stress and revolution. To touch on vital courses of historic development has demanded selection of focal events or evolutions (as, for example, in centering the discussion of the disintegration of the medieval world almost entirely on the rise of the cities). To convey more than a surface picture and to lend some depth and sense of reality to the narrative has demanded what amounts to dramatization of certain events which seem to have a representative or symbolic significance (as with the Cult of Reason Festival, the ceremonies attending the Vatican Council, and the Congress of Versailles). Such devices yield results which cannot but seem badly proportioned to the historian of any given period or specific problem touched on in these pages. The only justification can be that degree of integration and coherence which the work, as a unity, should achieve.

Essentially a critical review of the Liberal tradition, this work is not an exercise in defense of a religious institution. The ultimate validity of any church's claims to men's allegiance rests on issues almost completely independent of those here discussed. We are concerned with the institution of the Catholic Church as an historic force of enormous potential power in shaping the future of the West. And we are concerned with certain political and social principles which, it happens, have been consistently defended only by the Church or are ineradicably implicit in the faith of the Church—and in that faith alone.

Throughout the following pages certain basic ideas will find reiteration, indirectly or explicitly—not *a priori* axioms but conceptions which constitute the central substance of the work, principles whose validity seems to be supported by the story of the Liberal tradition. Some of these can be stated simply at the outset.

1. The intimate relevancy of religious ethics to politics and economics—the dependence of a nation's political and economic strength on the moral health and vigor of the people. Men who witnessed the fall of France in 1940 know the meaning of this.

2. The tragic implications of the confusion of the terms, democracy and representative government. In 1931 the nations of the West, witnessing Japan's assault on China, could not understand how a nation with what seemed a representative form of government could fundamentally menace the principles of democracy. Men of the West could not clearly distinguish between the democratic faith and the political machinery of representative government which they had developed to implement that faith. Because of such confusion, such an inexact amalgam of ends and means, many who believed in democracy were not awake to reality until after December 7, 1941.

3. The logical emergence of Fascism from an era of degenerate Liberalism. However violent and revolutionary be the meaning of Fascism, it is the grossest sort of historical perversion to assume that it arose in a vacuum of barbarism. It found nurture in an era saturated with the Liberal faith's aversion to fixed moral values, its essential contempt for ab-

solute ethical standards prescribed by any religious creed. The first territorial annexation of Nazi Germany came with the plebiscite in the Saar region; modern history's first application of the plebiscite principle to territorial demands was provided by the French Revolutionary government's annexation of the papal enclave of Avignon. That, in a simple symbolic way, merely suggests the flourishing of Fascism through its exploitation of techniques and its absorption of principles whose historic origin is in the Liberal tradition.

4. The need for clearer perception of the meaning of the democratic faith is accentuated by the danger of the implication of democracy in the discrediting and disintegration of the substance of the Liberal tradition. The immediate future of the West will not be governed by the success with which a specific social or economic blueprint is imposed on society. That future will largely be dictated by the relative clearness of vision with which the ultimate ideals of democracy are perceived by men, and the understanding which men possess in defending those principles—to themselves as much as to others, against their own doubts as well as against the more vocal challenges of their opponents. Should the precepts which constitute the democratic faith remain nothing more than inherited persuasions, casual and unreasoned regard for them will prove mortal. If democracy is to survive its hour of trial, men who believe in it must be unafraid of it. They must be unafraid of striking back to democracy's true intellectual roots and also unafraid of carrying out the logical conclusions of democracy's meaning, however much those conclusions may invalidate long-cherished economic inhibitions.

5. Men eager to affirm the positive content of democracy must be prepared to reorient their educational ideas and system to that end. If they believe in democracy, men must be unafraid to propagate their faith, to instill the basic principles of their faith in the hearts and minds of their children. Sane tolerance is the logical practice of Christian humility, but it can be a corrosive force if allowed to become merely a lazy, vacuous latitudinarianism afraid either to affirm or de-

nounce. An invertebrate educational system cannot support the body of the democratic faith.

Immediately necessary, as a corollary to this, is a critical review of the uncritically revered Liberal historiography. Unafraid reassessment of the Liberal hagiography can cleanse minds of some of the most unreasoned superstitions which plague men. It is fair time to review in detail the economic credo which underlay the philosophizings of Voltaire and other philosophes—to print the fact that the Bastille, when stormed, did not release hundreds of incarcerated peasants and intellectuals but five criminals and two madmen. Should matters like these be handled in capricious, sneering fashion, any resultant reassessment will be as untruthful as perpetuation of Liberal myths themselves. But soberly and conscientiously the historian can begin to clean house—and this would be the first intelligent step in the construction of a stronger intellectual edifice for the democratic faith.

Recognition of some of these facts and action along some of these lines can reasonably be expected to atone for some of the historic sins of Western man. . . . He who has propagated and practiced racism in Asia for more than a century only to find himself threatened with destruction by a force exploiting the same dreadful lie. . . . He who witnessed for seven years the barbarisms inflicted on the Jewish people of Nazi Germany but whose atrophied conscience reacted with violence only when the territorial integrity of the British Empire was placed in serious jeopardy by those persecutors. . . . He who so frankly and repetitiously confesses his own lack of community sense—the absence of firmly founded and universally respected ideals and aspirations— by his ever vocal fear of disunity within his own ranks. . . . He whose cause derives the bulk of its moral energy and spiritual strength not from his own tradition but from the outraged and oppressed millions fighting off enslavement in the Orient. . . . He who—in the midst of a world falling apart—insists on perpetuating imperial dominion over hundreds of millions of the people of the East, while sophistic rhetoric and mischievous equivocation fail to disguise rank, rampant acquisitiveness. . . . He whose Liberal Society faces annihilation by a revolution violent in its denial of the Christian tradition—but was itself born of progressive abandonment of Christian social ethics.

The task of the generation born to fight Fascism is nothing less than the historic salvation of this man of the West.

Four years—and one world—ago, this book was begun at Princeton University. It has been revised and completed in varying environments: at Columbia University, where I was enrolled in the Graduate School of Political Science in the fall of 1941; in Washington, D.C., during a period of five months when I was employed in the office of the Coordinator of Information; and at my home in Summit, New Jersey, in the late spring and early summer of 1942. These last lines are being written at the American Embassy in Madrid as the summer of 1943 begins.

During these years my debt to others, for advice and encouragement, has mounted at a pace that defies curt acknowledgment in a few lines here. To a few, however, I must try to express my profound gratitude.

At Princeton University, this book was started under the impetus of the unforgettable encouragement and infectious enthusiasm of Professor Walter P. Hall. A more gracious, sympathetic, and invigorating teacher, no student ever had. Also at Princeton, in the spring of 1941, when the prospects of finishing this work seemed to have faded, Professor Harris Harbison entered the scene. With him he brought clear thought and a generous, sustained interest in this project without which it is doubtful if it ever would have been completed.

My sincerest thanks go also to Mr. Datus C. Smith, Jr., Mrs. Douglas Stuart, and Mrs. E. Harris Harbison of the Princeton University Press, who successfully converted what could have been but a business relationship into a most pleasant and rewarding association by their patient, perceptive, and friendly advice.

Responsibility for any flaws or errors in the work is, of course, entirely my own.

What this book—as well as all else—owes to my mother and to Betty successfully challenges description. They know, I know, and that will suffice.

EMMET JOHN HUGHES

Madrid, June 4, 1943

CONTENTS

INTRODUCTION TO THE NEW EDITION   IX

Preface   XIII

PART I • THE GENESIS OF THE LIBERAL SOCIETY

   I. The Revolution of the Times   3
  II. Death Mask of a Society   5
 III. The Revolt of Economics   16
 IV. The Caldron of the Sixteenth Century   28

PART II • THE MAKING OF THE LIBERAL SOCIETY

   V. Philosophers in Arms: The New World of Ideas   55
  VI. The Liberal Faith: *Civitas Hominis*   77
 VII. Men in Arms: The New World of Facts   102
VIII. The Mountains Made Level   127

PART III • LIBERAL SOCIETY AND CHURCH MILITANT

  IX. The Rationale of the New Order   145
   X. The Titan of Industrialism   161
  XI. The Great Liberal Adventure   180
 XII. The Church Militant   203

PART IV • THE CRISIS OF THE WEST

XIII. Weimar, Versailles, and Munich   225
XIV. Liberalism: An Autopsy   234
 XV. The Faith of Democracy   258

Notes   278

Bibliography   290

Index   303

Part I · The Genesis of the Liberal Society

O God! that one might read the book
    of fate,
And see the revolution of the times
Make mountains level, and the
        continent,
Weary of solid firmness, melt itself
Into the sea!

KING HENRY IV.

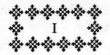

The Revolution of the Times

THE instruments were many with which men fashioned the Liberal Society. The pen of Voltaire, the sword of Cromwell, the telescope of Galileo; the mysticism of Luther and the logic of Calvin, the optimism of Rousseau and the realism of Machiavelli—a vast and strange congeries of factors were these, assailing the world of the past and, with the levers of the present, pushing to the surface the world of the future.

Yet more decisive may have been those forces which, by their very character, were never consciously devised or purposefully employed by men: forces that matured in eventualities no one could foresee. For the Liberal Society was the final product of the elements—all the elements—constituting the titanic social revolution that spanned the period from the Protestant Reformation to the French Revolution: splintering of Christian unity—spiritual as well as territorial, decay of feudal economy, erection of national states, geographical discoveries, and scientific renaissance. All those streams were here which formed the tide bearing men into modern times.

A revolution it was which pressed its militant way into every sphere of society. The commercial and industrial class—the "middle" class of businessmen—rose to power, and with them came urban dominion over the countryside. The national state signified at once the coalescence of myriad feudal provinces and the disintegration of the quasi-universal Christian society: the capitulation of the medieval dichotomy of *jus divinum* and *jus naturale* to the mundane and militant might of national sovereignty. In economic life, movable capital supplanted tenure of land as the supreme arbiter of economic distinction; and the static agrarianism of the medieval economy was forged into the dynamic, expansive capitalism of the modern world.

But the ultimately decisive change was born of the revolution in men's conception of their own nature and of their place in society and in the universe. The issue involved much more than the institutional changes implicit in the multiplication of the Christian churches, or in the substitution of state for church as the preeminent institutional arbiter of man's destiny in the West. These factors signify the result, but they neither constitute nor explain the basic revolution—the revolution in men's understanding of their relationship to their God, their universe, and their neighbor.

It was of this revolution that the faith and the fact of the Liberal Society were born, and in this context alone can they be comprehended. To view Liberalism as an innocuous political attitude to which most educated and civilized people generously subscribe is to stare unknowingly at a shell drained of its substance. The philosophical pillars of Liberalism constitute a succession of specific postulates, each of which possesses individual and explicit meaning, each of which was erected on the debris of demolished pillars of past ages and past societies. A specialized philosophical technique was utilized in the construction of those pillars, and the social edifice erected upon them was perpetuated by a specialized institutional technique. The completed structure of Liberalism embodies an autonomous, self-sustaining conception of man's relationship to his God, his universe, his society.

In this sense is Liberalism a faith, and by virtue of this fact has it been forced to fight other faiths. It has, in particular, fought the Catholic faith. To follow the course of this struggle of contradictory creeds, from its roots to its resolution: to analyze the solemn and meaningful character of this centuries-spanning conflict . . . this is to see clearly the forces which went into the making of the faith, the will, and the reason of the Liberal Society . . . and this is to approach an

[4]

understanding of the forces which, in the twentieth century, were to darken that reason, weaken that will, and uproot that faith.

II

Death Mask of a Society

"BETWEEN the conception of society as a community of unequal classes with varying functions, organized for a common end, and that which regards it as a mechanism adjusting itself through the play of economic motives to the supply of economic needs; between the idea that a man must not take advantage of his neighbor's necessity, and the doctrine that 'man's self-love is God's providence'; between the attitude which appeals to a religious standard to repress economic appetites, and that which regards expediency as the final criterion—there is a chasm which no theory of the permanence and ubiquity of economic interests can bridge, and which deserves at least to be explored."[1]

In these terms has an historian of the twentieth century—disregarding the maxim that history must be written of, by and for the survivors—reflected upon the clash of social philosophies attending the emergence of the modern economy from the ruins of the medieval world. To allow the birth of the new the old world had to perish: the roots of the Liberal creed sprang from the soil of history where lay buried the medieval faith. The issue was one not merely of disparate economic environments, but of divergent—if not contradictory—assessments of the function and character of economics.

The matter can be most simply stated in the terms of an assimile persistently recurrent in medieval theological writings. Man, in the thought and the words of medieval times, was conceived as the spiritual coin of God's realm, for his worth derived from his bearing of the image of the King.* To the Liberal this currency was to be counterfeit; for he denied there was such an image. And it was superfluous; for the coin of Caesar was, in the broadest sense, sufficient for the purchase of the good society. It was this change of standards (and not the simple passage from a natural economy to a money economy) which signalized the transition from the medieval to the modern world.

At the apex of the medieval hierarchy of values there stood the faith not only in an after-life, but also in the worth and the necessity of institutional mediation between man's God and man. This signified the mediation of the Church. It was characteristically described in these words of John of Salisbury: "And therefore those who preside over the practice of religion should be looked up to and venerated as the soul of the body [i.e. the body politic]. . . . Furthermore, since the soul is, as it were, the prince of the body, and has rulership over the whole thereof, so those whom our author calls the prefects of religion preside over the entire body."[2]

Such a faith did more than to lean all things of this world toward the next. It endowed, in varying degree, all things of this world with the spiritual quality of the next. The Church signified only the institutional embodiment of the eternally valid and immutable harmony of the natural and the supernatural, the conjunctive unity of philosophy and theology, the inevitable correspondence between the conclusions of reason and the foundations of faith. So conceived, this world was an image of, a testimony to, the glory of the Creator —a world in which man alone had capacity to know and to love, capacities which must lead him to ascribe all things of this world to their ultimate origin and end. Upon all things of this world were imprinted *vestigia* of the divine; and all

---

* For a characteristic statement along this line, cf. Gratian's *Decretum* (*Patrologiae Latinae Tomus* CLXXXVII), 1861: *Pars Prima, Distinctio* LXXXVIII, c. XI: "Pecunia spiritualiter homines intelliguntur, quia sicut nummus habet charagma Caesaris, sic homo habet charagma Dei."

man's activities and techniques—his arts, his sciences, his technical skills—served to represent on a lower plane the perfection of divine art and divine knowledge. And the function of man in all this was to make articulate and real all things in creation, which, without him, would be but dumb and potential. For of the things of nature it can be said that "each of them *is* a word, while man alone can *say* it."[3]

In a world of values so constructed, there existed no expedient distinction to be drawn between the esoteric world of the individual soul, viewed as the only province where spiritual values can exercise dominion; and the world of the affairs of society, to be exalted by a later age as a sanctuary for the acquisitive instincts of men—a sanctuary from which all dictates of religion could be expelled. Individual piety could not be disassociated from fidelity to the Christian social discipline. To medieval thinkers ethical precepts were as vitally operative in the market place as in the monastery. "To know the truth about God, and to live in society" was the phrase of St. Thomas Aquinas:[4] to direct one's supreme regard toward one's God and one's neighbor—this was the ideal which touched men's daily lives at all sensitive points. Ideally conceived, society itself—not subdivided into parallel independent spheres, but the total organism—represented a reflection of the celestial order in the mirror of this life.*

Upon this foundation rose logically the functional conception of man's society—after otherworldliness, the second pillar of medieval social thought.† All facts of social existence were reviewed in their relation to the moral purpose with which social organization was endowed—the fulfillment of the spiritual destiny of man. Man's advance toward the

* Von Gierke (*The Development of Political Theory*, p. 71) states the issue thus: "The universe is one organism (macrocosmus) animated by one Spirit and molded by one Law in which, by virtue of the all-pervading divinely ordained harmony, every partial unity (microcosmus) presents an image of the universal whole."

† Here Von Gierke (*ibid.*, p. 149) summarizes the issue in these words: "The essence of the State consists in the unity of a common life which, as in the case of natural organisms, results from the harmonious coherence of the parts, which are properly differentiated, disposed and vested with special functions."

realization of that purpose could not be conceived as a discordant march, made perilous by the persistent warfare of self-aggrandizement and sheer greed, lest humanity turn and prey on itself. If the purpose and goal were unitary, the advance, ideally conceived, must be harmonious.

This way of thinking was easily translatable into the organic analogy of society. It was in such terms that John of Salisbury wrote. "The place of the head in the body of the commonwealth," he proclaimed, "is filled by the prince, who is subject only to God and to those who exercise His office and represent Him on earth. . . . The place of the heart is filled by the Senate, from which proceeds the initiation of good works and ill. The duties of eyes, ears and tongue are proclaimed by the governors of provinces. Officials and soldiers correspond to the hands. Those who always attend upon the prince are likened to the sides. Financial officers and keepers . . . may be compared with the stomach and intestines, which, if they become congested through excessive avidity, and retain too tenaciously their accumulations, generate innumerable and incurable diseases, so that through their ailment the whole body is threatened with destruction. The husbandmen correspond to the feet, which always cleave to the soil, and need the more especially the care and foresight of the head, since while they walk upon the earth doing service with their bodies, they meet the more often with stones of stumbling, and therefore deserve aid and protection all the more justly since it is they who raise, sustain and move forward the weight of the entire body.* Take away the support of the feet from the strongest body, and it cannot move forward by its own power, but must creep painfully and shamefully on its hands, or else be moved by means of brute animals."[5]

Functional unity was thus designated as the primary axiom governing social organization in man's world. It signified,

---

* Compare with Leo XIII's *Rerum Novarum*, seven centuries later: "It is only by the labor of the working man that states grow rich." (Cf. below, Part III, Chapter XII, p. 215.)

however, neither the unity which was to be sanctified as an end in itself, nor the unity of force, born of oppression and matured in slavery. It was, in the first instance, a unity sought only as a translation into social forms of the immanent harmony of the universe flowing from its Maker—and as the only social means by which the spiritual harmony of society could be preserved. In the second place, it meant unity by force no more than organic unity of the body can be secured through the "oppression" of subsidiary members by the head. It was a unity born of conscious and free cooperation, deliberate and sustained harmony of purpose and method.

In its operation, then, the functional conception of social organization maintained the immutable priority of the spiritual purpose of society—yet held liberty to be an equally immutable prerequisite for the realization of that purpose: "for slavery is as it were the image of death, and liberty is the assured certainty of life."[6] As the *Policraticus* stated the issue, "nothing but virtue is more splendid than liberty, if indeed liberty can ever properly be severed from virtue. . . . Virtue can never be fully attained without liberty, and the absence of liberty proves that virtue in its full perfection is wanting. Therefore a man is free in proportion to the measure of his virtues, and the extent to which he is free determines what his virtues can accomplish."[7]

Translated into less abstract terms, this doctrine necessarily asserted the moral right of popular rebellion and even tyrannicide. Such was John of Salisbury's open profession: "If it [the power of the ruler] resists and opposes the divine commandments, and makes me share in its war against God; then with unrestrained voice I answer back that God must be preferred before any man on earth."[8]

Not only, therefore, was the spiritual purpose with which social organization was endowed not antithetical to human liberty: it was the enduring and unchanging foundation for the assertion of that liberty. What stamped the medieval conception of freedom as something distinct from that entertained by a later age was this fact: it sought freedom for the individual to achieve a self-gratifying material goal less than it sought freedom for the community to realize what it regarded as a divinely ordained spiritual objective. Freedom was conceived to be a dynamic and divine potential. It was spiritual in genesis and ultimately spiritual in fulfillment. That it be spiritual in practice—in the affairs of human society—was essential for that fulfillment. Hence freedom could not be disengaged from truth or, as John of Salisbury pointed out, from virtue. It is this thought which is infused in that discussion of St. Thomas Aquinas which defines the proper field of philosophical speculation by circumscribing it with the dictates of theology. By this delimitation, the Thomist would say, philosophy's freedom to err is restricted—but its freedom to attain truth is correspondingly safeguarded.[9] Medieval man's conception of liberty, in short, sought less to lead life away from obstruction than to guide it toward a purpose—thought less in terms of emancipation than in terms of fulfillment.

To realize a social order so conceived, the key implement was the third great pillar of medieval social thought: assertion of the sovereignty of religious ethics over economic activity. The compelling reason for such assertion is clear. For a religious philosophy—unless it is through ignorance or weakness to surrender the major part of human conduct to the riotous forces of acquisitiveness—cannot embrace the doctrine of a world of economic and business relations that is autonomous and completely severed from ethics and religion.

The medieval thinker had a well-stocked arsenal from which to choose his weapons in attacking the acquisitive impulse. In all intellectual history it is doubtful if any more slashing assault was hurled at the cold pursuit of profit than that launched by the early Christian fathers. To St. Jerome, "Opulence is always the result of theft, if not committed by the actual possessor, then by his predecessors."* No less blunt

* Medieval treatises followed this line of thought with little variation. References to private property were virtually always to be found under the heading of the sin of theft or its equivalent. For example, cf. St. Thomas

was St. John Chrysostom: "Behold the idea we have of the rich and covetous: they are truly as robbers, who, standing in the public highways, despoil the passersby. They convert their chambers into caverns, in which they bury the goods of others." St. Basil the Great assailed the very foundations of private ownership: "You cover with tapestry the bareness of your walls—and you do not clothe the nakedness of men. . . . You will say to me: 'What wrong do I commit if I hoard that which is mine?' And I ask you: 'Which are the things you think belong to you? From whom did you receive them?' " St. Ambrose continued in a similar vein of inquiry: "The soil was given to the rich and poor in common. Wherefore, O ye rich! do you unjustly claim it for yourselves alone?"[10] And unsurpassed in sharp, searing eloquence was the Catholic Epistle of St. James: "Go to, now, ye rich men, weep and howl in your miseries, which shall come upon you. Your riches are corrupted and your garments are moth-eaten. Your gold and silver is cankered, and the rust of them shall be for a testimony against you, and shall eat your flesh like fire. You have stored up to yourselves wrath against the last days. Behold the hire of the laborers who have reaped down your fields, which by fraud has been kept back by you, crieth, and the cry of them hath entered into the ears of the Lord of Saboath. You have feasted upon earth, and in riotousness you have nourished your hearts in the day of slaughter."[11]

Perorations such as these, be they from early Church fathers or from medieval authorities, were not capricious flashes of vituperation. They were terse statements of doctrine which followed logically from a single and constant basic principle: the moral and social necessity of ruling economic appetites by ethical precepts. To medieval man, there could be no splintering of society into several autonomous spheres. There could exist, then, no final end for man to be sought in an isolated economic sphere, because the totality of economic activity was itself subordinate to other principles,

Aquinas, *Summa Theologica*, Part II, Second Part, Second Number, Question LXVI: "Theft and Robbery."

secondary to other considerations. "The art of acquiring money," as St. Thomas Aquinas argued, "is subordinate to the art of using money, not so much by way of providing material for it as by way of providing tools for it. For money and every kind of wealth are merely economic tools."[12] And St. Antonio, in the *Summa Moralis*, set forth the logical implications of this concept: "The object of gain is that by its means man may provide for himself and others according to their state. The object of providing for himself and others is that they may be able to live virtuously. The object of a virtuous life is the attainment of everlasting glory."[13]

All economic activity was thus regarded as amenable to the final criterion of purpose. In itself to attach to economic pursuits a sovereign purpose was to circumscribe the art of money-making: a preconceived end was the equivalent of a preestablished cessation point. And conversely, what made the self-sustaining pursuit of profit so dangerous was the fact that, with no moral purpose to harness it, there existed no rational cause for men to stop or even to moderate the pace of sheer accumulation. Acquisitiveness, literally and inevitably, became infinite. Such was the reasoning followed by the *Summa Theologica* in its condemnation of exchange for profit. "Considered in itself," St. Thomas concluded, "it satisfies the greed for gain, which knows no limit and tends to infinity. Hence trading, considered in itself, has a certain debasement attaching thereto, in so far as, by its very nature, it does not imply a virtuous or necessary end."[14]

Social evaluations implicit in these theories were inversions of the standards of technically enlightened ages yet to come. Not profit but consumption—distributed and sustained consumption—was the immediate criterion of prosperity. The commendation of society, furthermore, was extended to those walks of life which are walks, and not racetracks, for economic activity. Hence the hierarchy of business occupations passed in descending order from labor through trade to finance: the reverse of the gradation to be inaugurated by industrial capitalism.

When they turned to the task of converting piously pronounced social ideals into tangible social results, medieval leaders found their efforts to hinge on two operations: the invocation of the just price, and the ban on usury. The former issue was succinctly stated by Gratian. "Whosoever buys an article," the *Decretum* asserted, "not that he may sell it whole and unchanged, but that it may serve as a material for fashioning something, he is not a merchant; but the man who purchases it in order that he may profit by selling it again unchanged and whole, that man is of the buyers and sellers cast forth from the temple of God."[15] It is with reference to this doctrine that it has been said that St. Thomas Aquinas was the father of the labor theory of value.[16] Was Karl Marx the last of the Schoolmen? . . .

Gratian quickly follows his remarks on the just price with the statement that "super omnes mercatores plus maledictus est usurarius."[17] It was a sentiment shared by almost all his brethren, for the prohibition of usury was a pillar at once supporting and symbolizing the whole edifice of medieval social philosophy. The time was not long in coming when men would attack that prohibition: when that time had come, the whole structure of medieval thought was falling apart. . . . The time was to come, too, when that social order which succeeded the medieval was itself to weaken: when that time had come and the wheel had turned full circle, men looked ahead and prophesied that "in the near future anti-usury laws will be the common sign of a doomed capitalism."[18]

Medieval doctrine on usury was more than a general effort to implement the abstract philosophical sovereignty of ethics over economics. Its specific purpose was protection of the economically frail from exploitation by the economically powerful. For peasant and craftsman the doctrine was proclaimed. It was the negative edge of the weapon by which the Church sought to save ill-equipped humanity from oppression and destruction. Positive action was undertaken by agencies of the Church—guilds and fraternities, parishes and monasteries—which advanced cheap capital to the needy.

[13]

The whole was a gigantic movement that supplemented purely charitable institutions, fanning out from Italy, through France, the Low Countries, and Germany: a long, strong line of economic barricades against the attacks of poverty and famine.

Conditioning this entire program of economic guarantees was the medieval conception of private property. As a *de facto* institution, it was accepted but not applauded—tolerated but not venerated. "Community of goods," explained St. Thomas, "is ascribed to the natural law . . . The division of possessions is not according to the natural law, but rather arose from human agreement which belongs to positive law. . . . Hence the ownership of possessions is not contrary to the natural law, but an addition thereto devised by human reason."[19] The established doctrine was cogent: conditional private ownership of the means of production, and communal use of the same instruments.

Like all other economic factors in the composition of society, private property was regarded as an instrument, not an end—and an instrument subject to the most refined regulation of its use. Property was "held," not "owned," by king or vassal. Extending through society was an elaborate pattern of subinfeudation, by virtue of which all tenure was contingent upon the fulfillment of social obligations. For failure to fulfill these obligations the king could be deposed, vassals stripped of their holdings. It would have been impossible for the medieval mind to understand what a nineteenth-century Liberal would mean by "undue interference" with the autonomous province of private property. For the term, "interference," would presuppose two or more unrelated spheres in society, with no valid nexus. To the medieval thinker, society was a single cohesive entity, its myriad functions properly interlocking in a harmony of purpose attainable only through vigilant regulation. Clearly then, with such a basic conception governing private property, the condition for the latter's existence was its obeisance to ethical sanctions.

These ethical sanctions, in turn, prescribed what was

equivalent to the communal use of all means of production. If human frailty indicated that private tenure was the most practicable adjustment, immutable moral right ordained communal use. Lest private property become the instrument snapping the bonds that bind man to man, let all recognize that "the first claim upon it was not that of the man who made it but that of the man who needed it."[20] With this issue in mind, St. Clement infused most of the spirit of medieval social thought into these words which fairly embody the era's social creed: "The *communis vita* is essential for all men, and especially for those who wish to be called soldiers of Christ, and long to imitate the lives of the Apostles and their disciples. Communal use of all the things of this world should be the way of life of all men. But, pursuing iniquity, one man calls this 'his,' and another calls that 'his,' and thus is humanity divided against itself."[21]

Such were the threads from which was woven the fabric of medieval social thought: an integral part of that yet vaster pattern to be known by a later age as the medieval synthesis, that philosophical experiment which essayed to assimilate the myriad parts of man's knowledge and man's experience into a single Christian whole. Society was regarded as endowed with a moral purpose, necessarily—because of the nature of its human substance—governed by clearly articulated ethical precepts, these principles to define the functions of men and classes to the end that man not trample man: that society not be stripped of its moral purpose and become a bare mechanism for the operation of competing cupidities: that this living mirror of the next life be not broken, nor even dulled, but be clear and bright.

That ofttimes, between the ideal and the reality, there fell a shadow; that ofttimes an awesome chasm separated purpose and practice—this does not alter the truly basic fact: there *was* a transcendent ideal, there *was* a moral purpose. And so R. H. Tawney has concluded: "When the distinction between that which is permissible in private life and that which is permissible in business offers so plausible an escape from the judgment pronounced on covetousness, it is something to have insisted that the law of charity is binding on the second not less than on the first. When the austerity of principles can be evaded by treating them as applicable only to those relations of life in which their application is least exacting, it is something to have attempted to construct a system tough enough to stand against commercial unscrupulousness, but yet sufficiently elastic to admit any legitimate transaction. . . . Men . . . had not learned to persuade themselves that greed was enterprise and avarice economy. . . . So merciless is the tyranny of economic appetites, so prone to self-aggrandizement the empire of economic interests, that a doctrine which confines them to their proper sphere, as the servant, not the master of civilization, may reasonably be regarded as among the pregnant truisms which are a permanent element in any sane philosophy."[22]

It was, indeed, something to have done all this: something—but not enough. For restless men were about, moving through Europe, summoning again the latent energies of cities, breaking the shackles of the old order with hammers of silver and gold. Again, and with perhaps more vehemence than ever before, each man was to call this "his," or that "his": and so was humanity to be divided against itself. But for the first time the division was to be welcomed as a blessing, applauded as a philosophy, and finally consecrated as a faith by which all men might live.

III

The Revolt of Economics

THE medieval era, far from being a static period, was one of genuine and dramatic change in the history of the West. The onslaught of Islam and the resultant northward shift of the economic center of gravity, the swing westward from Constantinople of the axis of cultural and political power, the militant projection of the frontiers of Christianity, the grandiose energy and futility of the Crusades, the rush of the Norsemen from the northern seas driven by a spirit that ultimately was to bring Norman knights into the heart of the Mediterranean world to do battle with Byzantines and Moslems, the Norman invasion of England and consequent linking of the island realm to the cultural and commercial world of the continent—all this tumult of men and movements scarcely signifies a static epoch.

The Islamic irruption, which in half a century had beaten its path east to the China Sea and west to the Atlantic, by the ninth century had converted Europe into a closed economy. The Germanic tribes which had swept the Roman Empire centuries before had come not to destroy but to enjoy, and the world that had been built around the Mediterranean had lived on, albeit under new political auspices. The westward surge of Islam in the seventh and eighth centuries had signified something vastly different. For here an openly hostile and triumphant faith and force, with its own religion, its own law, and its own language, stood astride the Mediterranean. The Germanic kingdoms of the West were isolated from the Byzantine Empire. What had united East and West now became a barrier between them. What had been a Roman lake became a Moslem lake.

In a world thus economically sealed, where men turned to the soil as commercial frontiers fast receded, the expansive energies of cities had become purposeless and cities themselves had become still shadows of an economic life already dead. There was not even a perceptible increase in the area of cultivated land from the time of the Roman Empire to the eleventh century. The rhythm of the West's economic machine became slow and subdued.

In this milieu the economic ethics of the Church had taken natural root, measuring as they did the worth of man's work by a standard transcending the pace of business enterprise.

It was not an arduous task for men to govern to some degree their acquisitive instincts, when opportunity was limited for those instincts to become articulate. The land-locked Carolingian Empire, with its frontiers virtually coterminous with those of Christianity, had served as something of a laboratory designed for the application of the social ethics of the Church.

This had sufficed for awhile—for some centuries, in fact. But it could not suffice for all time. And it did not.

From the eleventh century could be heard the rumblings of a world yet to come. Cities of Europe were busy with new affairs. In the south, there was Venice—settled first by those who had fled before onrushing Huns, Goths and Lombards to seek refuge on the little islands of the lagoons at Dorsoduro, at Olivolo, at Spinalunga, at Rialto. Subsistence in the forbidding marshes had taxed Venetian ingenuity and inspired Venetian trade, while its insular position protected it from the conquerors who overran Italy and severed the peninsula's ties to Byzantium and the East. Capitalizing fully on its sustained movement in the narrowing commercial orbit of Constantinople, and unmoved by religious restrictions which its urban competitors felt more bound to observe, Venice by the eleventh century was rich and powerful. A contemporary's characterization was at least half-just: a city, said Guglielmo of Apuleia, "rich in money, rich in men."[1]

Trade, inherently contagious, spread out through Italy: all Lombardy, Naples and Amalfi, Pisa and Genoa. All these commercially active cities punctuated the eleventh century with military and naval assaults on accessible Moslem strongholds in the Mediterranean, and the launching of the First Crusade in 1096 marked the first definite recoil of Islam. At the same time, the routes to the north, Rhone, Rhine and Danube, were plied with mounting frequency—and dividends.

To the north lay the second great focus of the new commercial life. It was Flanders, capitalizing on both its location and its indigenous cloth industry, which dated back at least as far as the Roman Empire. After 1066 its expanding trade drew England ever more securely into the continental orbit. And—paralleling Venice in the south—it stretched from West to East in a great fan of trade that spread from the Caspian to the North Sea and pivoted on Bruges, Ghent, Lille, Ypres. At the same time, while the reach of Italian trade moved north, the scope of Flemish commerce extended correspondingly south, and, on the route from Bruges to Venice, the two movements finally came to touch and link with one another on the fields of Champagne.

Natural crystallization points for the new commerce were the cities, either the old fortified bourgs of the provincial nobility or the ecclesiastical towns. Here a modicum of security surrounded the practice of commerce. The traders traveled on routes formerly used by the invaders, and thus fortresses once erected as a protection against the latter served now to furnish shelter for the former.

In both bourg and town, the merchant, uninitiated into the medieval scale of social values and classes, was—at least in the regard of his fellow citizens—something of an extraneous adjunct to traditional civic life. He was compelled to settle outside the walls of the city, there erecting his "faubourg" or "portus." There was no more appropriate symbol of the bowing of the medieval world to the ascending world of trade and commerce than the manner in which these initially petty projections of the old towns slowly encircled the static nucleus, until the appendage finally won dominion over the entire body. Here operating, cast in their most elementary forms, were those forces which, in the not distant future, were to advance toward the erection of the Liberal Society.

Once established in the cities, the merchant class confronted an immediate problem: to define its own social status in such terms as to insure itself against the capricious interference of lay or ecclesiastical superiors, under whose nominal jurisdiction they resided. This was resolved by the merchant into a demand for personal liberty—the right to move freely and to transact business freely—entailing guarantees that villeins settled in the cities, plying their trade diligently, should not be subjected to forcible return to a manor from which they had escaped. Demands for this freedom were implemented by persistent communal revolts, which, through a slow, disjointed process, finally brought the desired results. "Freedom became the legal status of the bourgeoisie, so much so that it was no longer a personal privilege only, but a territorial one, inherent in urban soil just as serfdom was in manorial soil. In order to obtain it, it was enough to have resided for a year within the walls of the town. 'City air makes a man free' ('Stadtluft macht frei'), says the German proverb."[2]

With personal liberty soon came administrative and jurisdictional autonomy for the merchants of the cities, as they sought to secure their freedom by protecting themselves against arbitrary application of a formalized and somewhat inchoate ancient law. The creation of an independent *jus mercatorum* and (in England) the "piepowder" courts were testimonies to their success. The final consequence was that the cities became islands of privilege in the framework of society. In short, as it existed in the twelfth century, the city of the Middle Ages was "a commercial and industrial commune living in the shelter of a fortified enclosure and enjoying a law, an administration and a jurisprudence which made of it a collective, privileged personality."[3]

The age was feeling the surge of a peculiarly portentous undercurrent in the tide of history. Some have asserted even that possibly no period in all history was to have a more profound effect upon humanity.[4] Europe was now being socially equipped with that triple-class constitution which was so long to endure. The merchant class having established itself in the social hierarchy, its energies were being summoned and mobilized for yet greater gains. This mobilization, in the earliest stages, meant loose confederations of cities, dedicated to securing their members prosperity through prevention of mutually disadvantageous competition and through conquest and exploitation of new economic provinces. Finally was to come consultation by and representation in the great political assemblies of Europe—Cortes, Estates General, Parliament and Reichstag.*

The impending economic revolution was to assume unheralded proportions in its full and lucrative maturity. But already was born a new notion of wealth: liquid capital and mercantile wealth were successfully disputing the dominion which landed wealth had formerly exercised over men's minds and ambitions. That a financial class would rise to commandeer this new and puissant force was inevitable.

In terms of changing political forms, the national state could be seen germinating in the new economic realities. In spirit, the nationalism of a later age was the beneficiary of a political heritage easily traceable to the fierce avidity and jealous exclusiveness of the late medieval city, with its guarded privileges and bitter hostility toward all urban competitors. In a more tangible sense, the state—or, more precisely, the dynasty—was establishing itself in a position from which it might challenge the usurped powers and functions of the feudality. This came to pass largely because of the financial sinews of government furnished to the ambitious monarch by the not less ambitious merchant-financier—who anticipated with relish the advent of a unified state capable of enforcing order and guaranteeing the peaceful pursuit of business. At the same time, while the financial upheavals of the age were fortifying the monarchic position, the same developments undermined the value of landed wealth and the social status of the feudality which depended upon it. Thus did the political and social alignment of the era define itself: as the functions and status of the feudal order deteriorated, to the merchant class came the blessings of relative peace and order, along with representation in Cortes, Estates General and Parliament—these beneficently extended by grateful

* The starting points for middle class representation in the assemblies of Europe can be set at approximately these dates: 1189 for the Cortes, 1295 for the English Parliament, and 1302 for the Estates General. Bourgeois connection with the Reichstag remained for a long time in the more or less nebulous "consultative" stage.

dynasts as the *quid pro quo* for the financial support they so desperately needed. Persistent and sustained was to be the mutual reinforcement of the rise of the merchant class and the rise of the national state.

All these, however, were forces which drew their strength from yet something else—the slowly maturing revolution in men's conception of their own nature, their society, their universe, and the God who governed all three. By some historians, the simple increase in wealth has been advanced as the most fundamental development marking man's passage from medieval to modern times.[5] It can so be regarded only if full account be taken of the moral and ethical reorientation which attended that change. For, from its very initiation, that increase in wealth moved toward the day when it would demand ethical sanction—when it would seek a benediction not to be found within the medieval framework of economic ethics.

Already forming upon men's lips were the words of the hymn that was to bless the new order. A basically lay culture was assuming embryonic form. In terms of the business of daily life, production for profit was replacing medieval production for sustenance: not only in the cities but also in the surrounding countryside, which now found new and ever expanding markets for its foodstuffs in the populous urban islands of commercial activity. Within the cities, at the same time, initial steps in secular education were being taken. Commercial life demanded a modicum of literacy. And the merchants set themselves to the task of educating themselves and their sons in schools which, while still under ecclesiastical supervision, were operating on principles and for ends vastly different from the properly religious institutions of the past.

What was meaningful for the future in all this was not the bare issue of the existence of non-religious schools or an expanded economy. Rather the significant issue was the purpose—or the absence of purpose—to which new institutions could be harnessed. Implicit in the swift social changes of the period was this problem: were the rewards of the pursuit of wealth lucrative enough to be self-constituted ends in themselves? An enterprising merchant, it is certain, did not interrupt his day's work to convert the meaning of his occupation into any such abstract terms as these. But, like Francis Bacon years later, he was already perceptibly impatient of the labors of the Schoolmen, who "did, out of no great quantity of matter, and infinite agitation of wit, spin out unto us those laborious webs of learning which are extant in their books . . . but of no substance or profit."[6] In truth, that philosophy might be both correct and useful which argued that the business of life was business.

Along with this germination of secular thought, there stirred in the minds of the more contemplative bourgeoisie a yet dim conception of liberty. Its importance derives from the fact of its being the bare base upon which more refined expositions of the Liberal creed were to arise in the future. The cities and the merchant class, it will be recalled, were categorically privileged points in the social order. Personal freedom they had sought and won for themselves, but "nothing was further from the mind of the bourgeoisie than any idea of freedom as a natural right: in their eyes it was merely a useful one.[7] Freedom, as the middle class conceived it, was a monopoly."[8]

Here, graced with none of the rhetorical flourishes that were to dignify it in a later age, lay the essence of freedom as conceived by the middle class. Freedom was to be a *weapon*. It was to be kept in the private and closely guarded arsenal of the bourgeoisie. It was to be kept from the laboring masses, from the rural workers, and from as many urban—in a later age, national—competitors as might use it menacingly.

It was useful, this new freedom. It was catalogued in the ledgers of the bourgeoisie as an asset—a negotiable intellectual asset. It was not, of course, to be confused with the liberty of which John of Salisbury had written: "the assured certainty of life." It was, the industrious merchant perceived (and his vision was clear), something less concerned with metaphysics, more intimate with the visible realities of daily life: the assured certainty of profit.

Nor was this freedom only a nebulous pattern of political liberties, immunities, and privileges. Firm and strong was the hold of the bourgeois on economic power considerably before political rights and recognition were accorded him. Inverting the movement that was to be pursued by the nine-teenth-century proletariat, he had grasped the sword first—then demanded that society surrender also the sheath.

Despite the deliberate intent of the merchant class, how-ever, other hands reached for the weapon, for freedom was inherently as infectious as trade. The rural masses were stirred to action by the enviable spectacle of urban freedom. More than this, the cities furnished expanding markets which could absorb virtually as much as the peasant could produce. And since the feudal dues extracted by his seigneur were fixed by demesnial custom at a virtually immutable rate, the peasant's expanded productivity yielded profits directly to himself. In this fashion the exigencies of the new economic processes worked relentlessly toward establishing a new status for the tillers of the soil. Unknowingly and unwillingly, the merchant class stimulated the propagation of a concept of freedom. The ascending bourgeoisie "had not the power to arrest an evolution of which it was the cause and which it could not suppress save by itself vanishing."[9]

To the insurgent social, economic and political forces of the era, to the shifting foundations for men's beliefs and be-havior—to these the immediate, living monuments were the cities, now the province of a new social class. The degree to which they were memorable creative achievements was measured in the caustic meter of a sixteenth century poet:

> And this is a Citye
>   in name, but, in dede,
> It is a packe of people
>   that seke after mede;
> For officers and al
>   do seke their owne gaine,

And for the wealth of the commons
not one taketh paine.
An hell with out order
I maye it well call,
Where euerye man is for him selfe,
And no manne for all.[10]

The scaffolding of medieval thought was tottering. It was as yet a process only of attrition. But the foundations were going fast.

The two centuries that directly preceded the Reformation saw a world fall apart. This was a story of more than merely cities and money. There was the religious crisis of the fourteenth century, when the Babylonian Captivity and the Great Schism signified in unmistakable terms that the cycle of Church history which had begun with Gregory the Great was swiftly rushing to its close. Competing sacramental systems and rival systems of ecclesiastical taxation and administration at once inspired doubt as to both the validity of the spiritual functions of the Church, and the utility of its institutional operations. This, followed by the failure of the Conciliar movement for reform and the personal failure of the Papacy in the Renaissance period, made men ask if the rock had turned to sand.

There was more too than Church history to the period. Civil strife like the Wars of the Roses signified the suicide of the feudality, revealed its pretensions to the governance of social crder to be as dangerous as they were fatuous. Catastrophes of continental proportions came with the Hundred Years War and the Black Death, creating a chaos from which men emerged uncompromisingly intent upon a search for order and security to be achieved by any instrument or agency available.

Yet whatever the dramatic and meaningful events that appeared on the surface of the history of these centuries, the substance of their narrative is found in the decline and fall of the elaborate medieval scheme of values. The balance and integration of thought that was achieved by men like John of Salisbury and St. Thomas Aquinas did not survive. On the one hand Ockham and the nominalists and on the other the mystics: together they succeeded in toppling the Scholastic edifice. The first group—denying the integrity of universals and the notion of causality, their empiricism almost presaging the age of Hume—found their ethics interlocking remarkably with those of the ascendant bourgeoisie: both seeking an inexpensive and inobtrusive church; both seeking secular education; both satisfied with will rather than reason, power rather than thought, control over nature rather than understanding of nature; both accepting the universe as pliable chaos in which the only genuine power for good was the individual.

With the mystics, the tradition of Augustine, Tertullian, Anselm and Bonaventura was, in great measure, revived. The gestures of piety were accepted, sometimes welcomed, as a substitute for the substance of truth.* Impatience with philosophical speculation and dialectic became chronic and was manifest in individuals of widely disparate intellectual character. The thirteenth century Franciscan poet, Jacapone da Todi, complained metaphorically that Paris (the University of Paris) had detroyed Assisi (the simple purity of Christian life). Thomas à Kempis inquired, displaying evident irritation with the Scholastics: "What signifies making a great dispute about hidden and obscure things which for having been ignorant of we shall not be reproved in the judgment?"[11] Petrarch scorned the refinements of Aristotelian logic, and disposed of their originator by claiming that his conception of happiness was excelled by "the opinions upon this matter of any pious old woman, or devout fisherman, shepherd

* A telling example of this is the case of St. Bonaventura. In his discussion of the problem of grace and free will, he invokes the following flexible standard: "However much you ascribe to the grace of God, you will not harm piety by so doing. . . . If, on the contrary, you wrong grace by crediting nature with what belongs to grace, there is danger. . . . Even though that (the former) position were false, it would not harm piety or humility; it is therefore fitting and safe to hold it." (Cited by Gilson, E., *The Unity of Philosophical Experience*, pp. 51-52.)

or farmer."[12] It was a time, in short, when men proclaimed that they "would rather feel compunction, than know how to define it."[13]

Perhaps the reflections of two men can best signify what happened to the faith of all. There was Peter Abailard, who, long before, had written to Heloise a few words that read like an epitaph for medieval philosophy: "Sister Heloise, Dialectics has made me hateful to the world."[14] And there was Petrarch, who, as his letters narrate, fled in irritation "from the turmoil of the city," retiring with a long list of Cicero's books "to my Helicon across the Alps."[15] He was a figure representative of the flight of so many, humanist or mystic, who hastened from the confusion of theological disputation to the more secure refuge of a compelling, immediate authority—be it monetary or mystical.

Thus, while the merchants and men of the cities of Europe were building the foundations of a new society, the world of the Schoolmen met its end. In this era of transition between two societies, between two complete conceptions of the nature of man, man's universe and his God—here sounded echoes of the past, murmurs vestigial and insubstantial, yet audible; here were whispered words of the future, phrases unformed and inarticulate, real though nascent. Centuries after these shadows had passed, in an age of Western man's mind far removed from this, the poet would look upon a volume of Scholastic philosophy and, as he turned its leaves, ask of himself,

> What chilly cloister or what lattice dim
> Cast painted light upon this careful page?
> What thought compulsive held the patient sage
> Till sound of matin bell or evening hymn?
> Did visions of the Heavenly Lover swim
> Before his eyes in youth, or did stern rage
> Against rash heresy keep green his age?
> Had he seen God, to write so much of Him?

Then, suddenly conscious of the distance that stood between his mind and that whose inmost thoughts he sought to unveil. . . .

> Gone is that irrecoverable mind
> With all its phantoms, senseless to mankind
> As a dream's trouble or the speech of birds.
> The breath that stirred his lips he soon resigned
> To windy chaos, and we only find
> The garnered husks of his disused words.[16]

The garnered husks were trampled upon.

The Liberal advance and the secular advance, synchronizing in something more basic than time, were propelled as responses to the same demands of men: men eager to exploit to the fullest what lay before them, buoyantly confident that the harvest would be rich. The men who were builders of the Liberal faith set themselves to winning that initial victory without which nothing they conceived of would come to pass: the emancipation of economic appetites from the dominion of religious ethics.

IV

The Caldron of the Sixteenth Century

THE sixteenth century was the great crucible in the history of the West. Men's institutions and men's ideals passed through it as through a great furnace. The total legacy of the past was melted down, broken into its constituent elements, and recombined in strange new forms to produce the social substance of the world to come. For here three titanic revolutions interlocked.

The economic revolution was sweeping beyond the limits of control or calculation. The great arc formed by the axis of economic power as it swung from the Mediterranean to the Atlantic; the dramatic spectacle of the rise of the Spanish and Portuguese empires; the swift flourishing of new commercial companies, financial dynasties whose compulsive powers were already taking their places behind the thrones of Habsburg and Valois and Tudor—no longer local but international in scope and stature were these energetic economic units whose grasp was as firm as their reach was long; the total collapse of medieval rural society, its fabric ripped to shreds by the forces of insurgent commercial enterprise, price revolution, and peasant wars . . . all this came at a pace that defied man's perspective, taunted his comprehension. A man born at the time when Nicholas V secured papal triumph over the Councils might live to see the Diet of Worms declare Martin Luther an outlaw.

Accompanying and drawing its energy from the economic revolution came the revolution of the state and of political doctrine: a revolution propelled equally by theory and fact. Political doctrine—stimulated by the revival of Roman law and profiting from the lesson of papal triumph over the Conciliar movement—abandoned the conception of the king as a *dominus*, a *primus inter pares*, and, as embodied in the work of Bodin, established the monarch as *rex*. And this refinement of political theory derived its energy from a work that had appeared at the opening of the century—the work of Machiavelli. Therein was embodied in the most incisive form the whole of the Renaissance spirit: scorn for humility and lust for power, deprecation of piety and admiration of success, impatience with the prescriptions of religious ethics and delight in the course of expediency.

The furious pressure of events in the sixteenth century forced men a long way toward translation of Machiavellian theory into the Machiavellian state. The whole was an unparalleled pageant of hate and brutality, too sustained and all-pervasive to admit of adequate symbolic representation in even such a work as Dürer's *Melancholia*. There were Charles of France leading his armies across the Alps in the first tragic episode to mark Italy as the cockpit of Europe;

the Habsburg emperor sacking Rome with a finesse that would have put the *barbari* to shame; Suleiman's Turks surging across the plains of Hungary past Mohacs, till they were hammering the very gates of Venice. Metz, Toul and Verdun for the first time stepped forth as symbols of Europe's national hates. The Spanish ring of war stretched from distant Lepanto; through Portugal and the Netherlands, where Alva's legions performed their bidden duties; to the solemn rocks of the Scottish shores, where the great Armada was broken and died. All the while religious wars fastened Germany to the rack for a century, hurled the Moors from Spain back across the Strait, and converted France into a nation of pious, murdering men. Even on the seas, humanity fared no better: the work of Barbarossa's pirates was matched by the only slightly more refined activities of men like Drake and Hawkins. Small wonder, then, that the sharpest pen of the age wrote these words: "Of all birds, the eagle alone has seemed to wise men the type of royalty—not beautiful, not musical, not fit for food, but carnivorous, greedy, hateful to all, the curse of all, and with its great powers of doing harm, surpassing them in its desire of doing it."[1]

With the world about him bent on destroying itself and its humanity, poor vagabond Simplicissimus—tired, distracted symbol of an age that tired all men—dreamed, as he slept beneath the trees in his favorite grove. . . . "And as I looked methought all trees I saw were but one tree, at whose top sat the war god Mars, and which covered with its branches all Europe. It seemed to me that this tree could have overshadowed the whole world; but because it was blown about by envy and hate, by suspicion and unfairness, by pride and haughtiness and avarice, and other such fair virtues, as by bitter north winds, therefore it seemed thin and transparent; for which reason one had writ on its trunk these rhymes:

> By civil war within and brothers' deadly feud,
> All's topsy-turvy turned and misery hath ensued."[2]

To depose this tyranny of anarchy, men unwittingly walked

in the ways exalted by Machiavelli. They turned to the state, the several central powers, in a desperate effort to secure a semblance of order and stability.

They turned to the state; they did not turn to the Church. The third revolution, the religious revolution, made that impossible. For when men came to realize the compelling necessity for an institutional arbiter to govern the new economic and political forces—when that time had come, there existed no longer a single religious institution which could command men's allegiances, totally and harmoniously.

Dynamic changes in the structures of societies, such as these, cannot be arbitrarily categorized as exclusively religious or economic or political; all forces blend, synchronize and interlock to generate the new social realities. This was particularly manifest in the crucial instance of the era of the Protestant Reformation. For the Church which the Reformation assailed was the institutional backbone of a whole social order; to repudiate its religious authority was to make imperative substitutes for its social and economic principles. In this fashion the Protestant movement necessarily both reflected and reinforced the other great forces of its time, political, economic and intellectual—cradling nascent nationalism in the doctrine of the priority of temporal over spiritual power; endowing economic aspirations of the bourgeoisie with a spiritual benediction; and nourishing through the entire religious revolt an assertive, self-confident individualism which ultimately was to emancipate the business of daily life from the strict dominion of ethical principles enforced by the Church. The Reformation, in short, represented the battle of nationalism, capitalism and individualism carried into the religious arena.

Across the Liberal Society was to fall the shadow of the pen of a young Florentine bureaucrat. From Florence, in the young years of the sixteenth century, came the bold conception of the national state which coming events were to convert into yet bolder political fact. Stirred to fervent thought by the awful spectacle of shattered Italy, Machiavelli poured into the single mold of nationalism the main forces and ideals that were to dictate the making of modern mind and conscience.

The Prince to whom Machiavelli dedicated his work emerged as a daring, amoral sculptor who was to shape the national entity from that pliable and despised substance known as the people. To be fully capable of perfecting his art, he was conceived in the most absolute terms of individualism and was inspired with the ideal of *virtu*, by which the pagan legacy of Rome was invoked to arouse men to fight for the redemption of stricken Italy. The Prince thus stood forth as more than an omnipotent ruler in the usual sense: he was omnipotent, not merely in the exercise of positive political powers, but even more importantly in his exemption—his "emancipation"—from the rules of morality. "A man who wishes to make a profession of goodness in everything," Machiavelli explained, "must necessarily come to grief among so many who are not good. Therefore it is necessary for a prince, who wishes to maintain himself, to learn how not to be good, and to use this knowledge and not use it, according to the necessity of the case."[3] To avoid misunderstanding the same point is reiterated, this time in unequivocal terms: "There are two methods of fighting, the one by law, the other by force: the first method is that of men, the second of beasts; but as the first method is often insufficient, one must have recourse to the second. It is therefore necessary for a prince to know well how to use both the beast and the man."[4] The process of transfiguration thus extolled was one in which many princes of the future were to be proficient.

Herewith Machiavelli sketched the entire outline of "the conduct of a successful ruler" in the sharp, clear lines of expediency. Liberality and parsimony, cruelty and clemency, integrity and duplicity—all conceivable attributes of government and ruler were measured by the same standard—utility, committed to achieving the transcendent end of power. "It is not, therefore, necessary," Machiavelli elaborated, "for a prince to have all the above-named qualities, but it is very necessary to seem to have them. I would even be bold to say that to possess them and always to observe them is dangerous, but to appear to possess them is useful. Thus it is well to seem merciful, faithful, humane, sincere, religious, and also to be so; but you must have the mind so disposed that when it is needful to be otherwise you may be able to change to the opposite qualities. . . . A prince . . . therefore . . . must have a mind disposed to adapt itself according to the wind, and as the variations of fortune dictate."[5]

There was sound reason for the Prince to follow with precision this elaborate pattern of deceit. For humanity, whom he must govern, was conceived as an untutored herd. "It may be said of men in general that they are ungrateful, voluble, dissemblers, anxious to avoid danger, and covetous of gain. . . . As they are bad, and would not observe their faith with you, so you are not bound to keep faith with them. . . . Thus it comes about that all armed prophets have conquered and unarmed ones failed; for . . . the character of peoples varies, and it is easy to persuade them of a thing, but difficult to keep them in that persuasion. And so it is necessary to order things so that when they no longer believe, they can be made to believe by force."[6] And armed prophets, not least conspicuously in the twentieth century, were in ensuing ages to follow this advice.

Here was the blunt, total assault upon the principles of men like John of Salisbury—preferring to the goodness of Christ the stamina of Caesar; assailing at once the sovereignty of moral principles in the affairs of mankind, and the investiture of that sovereignty in the people. Was it merely coincidence that the same philosophy which converted religion into an instrument of the state also converted men into instruments of the state . . . that the same creed which dethroned morality dethroned humanity?

The new patriotism and the inexorable *raison d'etat* could tolerate no competing ideals; it must muster and command all the buoyant, puissant energies within men, energies that were chained by the ultra-sensitive Christian conscience. It was that conscience which "leads us to depreciate the love of the world and makes us mild . . . teaches men to be strong in enduring rather than in doing; and thus the world has become the prey of scoundrels who have found men willing, in order to gain Heaven, to endure injuries rather than to avenge them."[7] To Machiavelli, too, religion was the opiate of the people.

Yet here was no negation of faith; it was the negation of but one faith. There was to be another. "If . . . it was necessary in order that the power of Moses should be displayed that the people of Israel should be slaves in Egypt . . . so at the present time, in order that the might of an Italian genius might be recognized, it was necessary that Italy should be reduced to her present condition, and that she should be more enslaved than the Hebrews. . . . Behold how she prays God to send some one to redeem her from this barbarous cruelty and insolence."[8]

Here was a creed with a more captivating sense of immediacy than the soft, dim other-worldliness of Christianity. The old faith no longer commanded the imagination of men like Machiavelli. But what seemed to be the undying need of faith summoned forth this, first of the dramatic succession of non-Christian doctrines which were to anoint the new order: Blessed are the strong, for they shall rule men and build nations.

These were the political conceptions which, when projected into the turmoil of the Reformation, were infused with new energy. The assault on the supra-national character of the Church, and the positive necessity, born of religious wars and the denial of Church authority, of establishing a new institutional guarantor of social order—these factors, immanent in the Reformation, demanded the elevation of the state. And the demand was made articulate in every nation in which Protestantism assumed any important stature:

by Luther and von Hutten in Germany, by the Politiques in France, by Henry VIII and the English reformers.

It was not Machiavelli but Luther who proclaimed that "the princes of this world are gods, the common people are Satan, through whom God sometimes does what at other times he does directly through Satan."[9] Popular right to constrain regal authority thus dismissed, the German reformers at the same time challenged the competency of the spiritual power to dictate to the temporal—this exercise of Church authority over the rulers of nations being the first of Luther's famous Three Walls of the Romanists. The wall was breached by Luther's proclamation that priest and prince, pope and layman "are all one body . . . all because we have one baptism, one Gospel, one faith, are all alike Christians." Therefore the temporal sword, since it was "ordained of God to punish evil-doers and to protect them that do well," should be "left free to perform its office without hindrance through the whole body of Christendom, without respect of persons, whether it affect pope, bishops, priests, monks, nuns or anybody else."[10] The final basis for exaltation of the temporal power was the sweeping dictum that all men must accept the decrees of temporal authority even when "it does wrong," because "its power, whether it do right or wrong, cannot harm the soul, but only the body and property."[11] Thus did Luther's gospel bestow its blessing on a temporal power whose wrongs were trivial because they little affected man's ultimate destiny—but whose authority could be circumscribed by neither will nor right of either people or Church.

Recollecting the political and economic forces operative at this time, one might suspect that they were influencing such proclamations as these. The suspicion would not be without foundation. In Luther's own discussion of trading and usury, he paused to make a far from dispassionate digression. "God has cast us Germans off," he cried. "We have to throw our gold and silver into foreign lands and make the world rich while we ourselves remain beggars."[12] It was, however, another religious insurgent, one Ulrich von Hutten, who explored this state of affairs in great detail. "We see," he observed, "that there is no gold and almost no silver in our German land. . . . Would you know, dear Germans, what employment I have myself seen that they make at Rome of our money?. . . . Cunning hypocrites . . . under cover of the monk's cowl. . . . Now if all these who devastate Germany . . . might once be driven out . . . we should again have gold and silver in sufficiency. . . . God grant that we may soon cease to be the victims of foreigners."[13]

A cynical sixteenth-century commentator would not be in error if he observed that issues in the Reformation were deriving energy from realms other than that of decorous doctrinal disputation. Assertion of the priority of temporal power became political fact with the Peace of Augsburg in 1555, terminating for a time the German religious wars and pronouncing the principle of *cuius regio eius religio*. Each secular ruler in the German states was given the commission of dictating to his people the terms of the religious settlement. The matter of the spiritual life of a state was thus formally defined as an issue of political administration.

England witnessed a yet more precipitate flight of authority from the altar to the throne.[14] Seeds of nationalist revolt from Church dominion had been sown as long ago as the bitter time of the Hundred Years War—when it was, significantly, financial exigencies of war which impelled both belligerents to rebel from ecclesiastical exactions and regulations: these latter in the multiple forms of papal dues, appointment of foreigners to native benefices, and extended ecclesiastical jurisdiction. The new spirit was tersely indicated by the words of a distich chanted by English soldiers after the victory of Poitiers:

Now the Pope has become French and Jesus has become English,
You have seen which is greater, the Pope or Jesus.[15]

The combination of popular nationalism and economic grievances against the Church was galvanized into a national crisis when, in the reign of Henry VIII, England faced renewed civil war in the absence of a male heir to the throne. Issues of theology or dogma scarcely were debated.* When the Reformation parliaments had ended their labors, there was—excepting wider circulation of the Bible—only one change inaugurated: Parliament had issued a guarantee that all future popes would be English. Such was the meaning of the 1534 Act of Supremacy: ". . . The King, our sovereign lord, his heirs and successors, kings of this realm, shall be taken, accepted and reputed the only supreme head in earth of the Church of England, called the Anglicana Ecclesia. . . ."[16]

Dividends accruing to those who capitalized on the emancipation of the nation from Rome were summarily indicative of the character of the era's compelling political and economic forces. Church estates with a capital value—in terms of twentieth-century money—of from 15,000,000 to 20,000,000 pounds passed from ecclesiastical to state hands. Passage thence to the speculators was easily and quickly negotiated. It was the same kind of religious investment applauded on the continent by von Hutten.†

Finally, in France not many years later, one could observe the truculent movement of analogous forces. For long, Huguenot and Catholic had engaged in a sustained war of pamphlets and arms, fervent and bitter. Hostile as they had been, nonetheless, both sides had agreed on the persistent reference of their respective causes to ultimate spiritual objectives. Yet from the chaos of the civil wars neither of these parties emerged victorious, the single principle on which both had agreed was the cause of the failure of both, and a third faction—the Politiques—carried the day.

Tired of endless theological disputation and internecine strife, the Politiques argued triumphantly on the simple, level plane of utility. To them religious unity was, in a

* The Act of the Six Articles, in 1539, actually enforced, with stringent sanctions, the body of Catholic dogma.

† Significant in the same way and for the same reasons was the sequence of events in the course of the Reformation in the Scandinavian countries: expropriation of Church holdings in land antedated by some twenty years the consummation of any genuine religious change.

rather academic sense, desirable—but not at too high a cost: civil order came first. Dictates of religion or conscience must surrender their traditional priority to the transcendent ideal of national peace and the exigencies of personal security.

This victory of the Politiques signified much more than the isolated triumph of a single Gallic political faction, for its strength flowed from forces operative throughout the Western world. It signalized the triumph of the secular state. "It meant that the status of political right," in the words of Harold J. Laski, "no longer needed definition in terms of an ecclesiastical sanction. From the medieval angle, it put the worldly interests of men above what was regarded as their heavenly interest. It meant that the preservation of order was so much the highest political good, that the state would disregard any claim to its interference which would jeopardize the cause of order. Once that view was accepted, the self-sufficiency of the state had no longer to be argued."[7]

That this would be the political consequence of the Reformation was, in large measure, inevitable. Whatever had been the exact character of the pamphlets of Luther, the acts of the Reformation parliament, or the arguments of the Politiques, the final consequence could have been modified but little. For, in fact, the secular state evolved as a necessary institutional substitute for the Church whose authority the Reformation repudiated. It came into being as something more than a weapon in the hands of the reformers to be employed in upsetting the international structure of the Church—however conspicuous was its service in this respect. It came to fill the hiatus in social organization consequent upon the removal of Church sanctions. Interacting with the ascendent spirit of national self-consciousness, the Reformation propelled the advent of the secular, absolutist state through two synchronizing movements: emancipation of the state from its prior subordination to the spiritual power, and investiture of the state with the functions previously exercised by the Church. As Bossuet, two centuries later, justly observed, "what men accomplished in the Reformation through

[38]

rejecting the Pope as ecclesiastical successor to Saint Peter, was to surrender themselves to a lay pope, and to place in the hands of civil magistrates the authority of the apostles."[18] In more than a metaphorical sense was the state to be the great religious institution of the future.

"On pourrait presque dire, telle religion, tel système économique," a French historian has written. And if ever in the history of the West, this nexus between religion and economics were valid, it was so in the sixteenth century. As the religious revolution at once reflected and reinforced the political revolution, so it did the yet more vital economic revolution.

The issue can most clearly be delineated in its negative outlines. Directly in the capitalistic line of march, "a whole world of social relations stood in the way. And these established social relations found at once their supreme expression and their trusty support in one massive and puissant institution, the Catholic Church."[19] The sum of the labor of the sixteenth century was the discrediting of institutional control of men's daily affairs in the interest of religion.

That this was not the preconceived purpose of Protestant reformers does not modify the decisive character of the result. The simple event of the multiplication of the Christian churches was perhaps the most effective single solvent of the old order. In an era of intellectual disturbance, with vast new worlds springing to life from across the seas, from the dusty archives of antiquity, and from the wide expanse of the heavens—at a time when men first learned of myriad variations of religious belief and for the first time clearly understood that moral codes and intellectual allegiances could be established entirely independent of Christianity . . . it was in such an era and at such a time as this that the internal unity of Christianity was shattered by the Reformation. The entire intellectual outlook was made bloody—and, worse than that, incomprehensible to men—by the spectacle of competing religions within the single framework of the Christian tradition. Logically, then, the sixteenth century, on the negative side of its historical ledger, came to write this: undermining of the authority of the only institution in the history of the Western world which had been able to fasten men's aspirations and impulses to a single, cohesive structure of values, governing men, society and the universe.

The work of Luther was the concrete medium. Seeking to arraign what he regarded as a corrupt Church and degenerate civilization before the imposing bar of an untarnished primitive Christianity, he shook the foundations of the one institution which had given that past living form. No compromiser with the avidities of acquisitive merchants and financiers, he hurled his most piercing invective at the only institution which could conceivably tame the racing pulse of men's greed.

Not capricious hatred, but an immutable ingredient of his own creed, pointed the forensic weapons of Luther in this direction. For him it was repugnant to face the organized mediation, between man and his God, of a complex hierarchy of prelates or an elaborate pyramid of dogma. More even than this, to Luther the whole of man's worldly society seemed a dark, awful abyss which yawned threateningly in the way of the perilous passage of man's soul to its Maker—a direct passage, to be negotiated under the single impulse of faith. Thus the *Treatise on Christian Liberty* proclaimed that "one thing and one only is necessary for Christian life, righteousness and liberty. That one thing is the most holy Word of God, the Gospel of Christ. . . . Wherefore it ought to be the first concern of every Christian to lay aside all trust in works, and more and more to strengthen faith alone. . . . Faith alone, without works, justifies, makes free and saves."[20]

The only spiritual realities thus became three: man's soul, weak and depraved; God, distant and omnipotent; and divine grace, alone efficacious and omnicompetent. Not only did the institution of the Church fade as a mechanical elaboration of forms and gestures spiritually superfluous; but also the entire medieval conception of the social order as a spiritual organism of members and functions, all contributing to the final realization of a single spiritual purpose. Man's society was no longer an imperfectly mirrored reflection of the next world. It was a blasphemous parody.

Yet withal there remained the vast realm of men's material interests, whose existence, although deplored, could not be denied. What of them? Luther's answer reflected his whole pattern of thought. "There can be no better instructions in all transactions in temporal goods," he avowed, "than that every man who is to deal with his neighbor present to himself these commandments: 'What ye would that others should do unto you, do ye also unto them,' and 'Love thy neighbor as thyself.' If these were followed out, then everything would instruct and arrange itself."[21]

Everything would instruct and arrange itself. . . . Adam Smith would never state the issue more succinctly. The shadow of the "invisible hand" of the prophet of laissez-faire, endowing individual self-interest in economics with a mystical property of social good, was herewith performing a similar legerdemain in the more esoteric sphere of the spiritual. It has been said that one of the Western world's greatest tragedies was the coincidence of its most acute religious dissensions with the greatest economic crisis since the fall of the Roman Empire.[22] Yet men chose this, of all times, in which to demand, deliberately and insistently, that fellow men bury their institutional weapons and try to hammer dynamic economic forces into an ethical pattern with their bold, bare fists.

The tragic end was apparent from the start. History refused, as always, to instruct and arrange itself because men asked it to do so. Viewing the masses of the poor, Luther's conclusion was that "one of our greatest necessities is the abolition of all begging in Christendom." Urging that every city provide for its own poor and exclude all "foreign beggars," he admitted that under such a system "the poor would not be so well provided," but explains: "nor is it necessary. He who wishes to be poor should not be rich; and if he wishes to be rich, let him put his hand to the plow and seek his riches in the earth!"[23]

That cry—let them seek their riches in the earth—was to

be reechoed loudly in coming years in the life of the Liberal Society. The fruits of such a philosophy were no richer in the sixteenth than in later centuries. For, when faced with an immediate crisis in the form of the Peasants' Revolt, the substance of Luther's creed resolved itself into nothing more pretentious than invective. "They have forfeited body and soul," he cried, "as faithless, perjured, lying, disobedient knaves and scoundrels are wont to do. . . . I think there is not a devil left in hell; they have all gone into the peasants."[24] Faced with a problem of such satanic character, Luther apparently decided that the social expedient solving it must be commensurately satanic. "There is no time for sleeping," he warned, "no place for patience or mercy. It is the time for the sword, not the day of grace. The rulers, then, should go on unconcerned, and with a good conscience lay about them as long as their hearts shall beat. . . . One who is killed fighting on the ruler's side may be a true martyr in the eyes of God. . . . On the other hand, one who perishes on the peasant's side is an eternal brand of hell. . . . Strange times, these, when a prince can win heaven with bloodshed, better than other men with prayer! . . . Therefore, dear lords . . . stab, smite, slay, whoever can. If you die in doing it, well for you! A more blessed death can never be yours, for you die in obeying the divine Word and commandment in Romans xiii. . . ."[25] Strange times these, indeed—anointed with a not less strange sacred unction.

The miracle of all things instructing and arranging themselves was no more manifest in England. No more effective here than on the continent were fervent, scattered outbursts of eloquence assailing the new economic urges of the times. From their pulpits men like Becon, Crowley, Lever, and Latimer aimed telling shafts at the habitual business practices of the more opulent members of their religious communities. They were shocked by not only the material misery of the age, but, more basically, its announced intention of repudiating the principles "by which alone, as it seemed, human society is distinguished from a pack of wolves."[26] Their enemy was an idea: the idea that the individual is complete master of his own, that what he has he may exploit to the single end of personal gain, obligated to heed neither the need of his neighbor nor the precepts of any religious authority. What they attacked, in short, was the theory of property soon to be enthroned by all civilized communities of the West. All this they did—but they were trying to salvage the cargo of the ship they themselves had scuttled.

The English revolt from Rome itself had heated with new flame the economic crisis. As the Crown threw the confiscated monastery lands on the market, ambitious courtiers, shrewd middlemen, and large London syndicates engaged in a sudden, explosive frenzy of land speculation. Rack-renting, evictions of peasants, and conversion of arable land to pasture followed swiftly. The social results of sweeping away the monastic houses have been summarized by a French historian in these words: "the creation of a large class of poor to whose poverty was attached the stigma of crime; the division of class from class, the rich mounting up to place and power, the poor sinking to lower depths; destruction of custom as a check upon the exactions of landlords; the loss by the poor of their foundations of schools and monasteries; and the passing away of ecclesiastical riches into the hands of lay owners."[27] More than all this simply following in time the abolition of the monasteries, there was an intimate causal relationship: the eviction of monk constituted a sound precedent for the eviction of peasant. As one Sussex grantee inquired of his protesting peasants, "Doo ye not knowe that the Kinges grace hath putt down all the howses of mounkes, ffryers and Nunnes? thier for nowe is the tyme come that we gentilmen will pull downe the howses of such poore knaves as ye be."[28]

All this was a bitterly disillusioning experience. Men had set forth, moved by the passionate conviction that from the Reformation there would come not only a doctrinal purification, but also—and this was equally important to many—a sweeping reconstruction of society. In their attempt to realize a purpose so conceived, there was at hand but one instrument:

the temporal power. On their surface, the broad pattern of Elizabethan trade regulations seemed to signify the state's fulfillment, at least in part, of the hopes of Anglican divines. But it was to prove a brutally vicious circle: the more religious authority was predicated on the power of the state, the more the existence of the former became exclusively contingent on the support of the latter. The durability and effectiveness of Christianity's social ethics henceforth depended not on their own strength and vitality, but on the good will of the temporal power.

In this fashion did the Protestant Reformation cripple the effective control of economic appetites by ethical principles: "the ethical code of Christianity, which in the Middle Ages had possessed all the advantages of a system of law, sank to the position of a mere abstract philosophy of conduct."[29] By virtue of the organic character of the institution it attacked, the Reformation could never confine itself to a purely doctrinal reform. But by virtue of the institutional weapons it scornfully repudiated, it could never *equip* itself to inaugurate and sustain more than a formal reform of dogma.

The Reformation had heckled economic acquisitiveness, but it could not harness it. It tried vainly to use as lances the splinters of the social and religious framework it had destroyed.

Every genuinely revolutionary social movement demands, for substantial success, more than the removal of traditional institutional or intellectual obstacles in its line of march. It demands some form of ethical benediction which can convince men of both the worth and the finality of what they are seeking.

In the sixteenth century the Calvinist movement answered this need. Decisive influence exercised by Calvinism upon the rise of the bourgeoisie and the evolution of a capitalistic economy was to come from the forceful hands of England's Puritan leaders of the next century.* Yet, in its earliest form,

* See below, Part II, Chapter VI.

Calvinism conveyed an all-pervasive spirit, fortified by specific religious tenets, which was geared with striking precision to the aspirations of the middle class.

By the new faith, the economic ethics of the medieval era were either modified or inverted. As the impetus behind the new economics was to be production, so correspondingly did Calvinism exalt those virtues which were translatable into productivity. "Seest thou a man diligent in his business? He shall stand before kings" (Prov. xxii. 29): here was an appropriate Biblical text for the new economy. Thrift and industry, diligence and sobriety—these were qualities in men not to be throttled but to be applauded. More than being expedient they were Christian. Conversely, the indigent and slothful were not to be accorded public aid on any elaborate scale—as Luther, speaking in Christ's name, had proclaimed: "He will not have men running hither and yon with beggars' sacks, as men now run to St. James and to Rome."[30] Encouraging or patronizing these peripatetic rogues, more than being inexpedient, was un-Christian.

The medieval criterion of consumption was discarded; production and the qualities that induced industry were what men now sought. "What matters it," Calvin inquired, "if a man is able to make more money from business than from land-owning? Whence comes the wealth of the merchant? From his own unrest, diligence and industry."[31] Moreover, whatever a man's vocation, if he followed it with application and sobriety, it would assume virtually a spiritual character. For all men in all walks of life were, as truly as clerics, members of the spiritual estate. Work was sacred.

And if new virtues were to be socially and religiously sanctioned, then new economic instruments became acceptable. Usury was conceived as a vice in no absolute sense. If governed by but a modicum of charity, its practice was thoroughly legitimate. In any event, decision upon its legitimacy was to rest conveniently with the individual conscience. The time and labor which a medieval archdeacon spent in uncovering and suppressing the practice of usury was, in Calvin's theocracy, to be devoted to the prosecution of indigence: an economically fruitful substitution.

What in past ages were condemned as human vices were herewith canonized as economic virtues. The *appetitus divitiarum infinitus,* long chained as a menace to the integrity of human society, was now liberated as the energizing principle which could make that society rich. "Baptized in the bracing, if icy, waters of Calvinist theology," says Tawney, "the life of business, once regarded as perilous to the soul . . . acquires new sanctity. Labor is not merely an economic means: it is a spiritual end. Covetousness, if a danger to the soul, is a less formidable menace than sloth. So far from poverty being meritorious, it is a duty to choose the more profitable occupation. . . . Thus the pursuit of riches, which once had been feared as the enemy of religion, was now welcomed as its ally."[32]

To translate a sweeping religious movement into terms exclusively economic would be doctrinaire perversion of the facts, but to fail to observe—especially in the case of Calvinism—the intimate relationship between its theology and the economic aspirations of the men who subscribed to it would qualify as blindness to facts. In this latter manner of viewing Calvinism in its relation to and reflection of an emergent social philosophy, it has been said, with considerable accuracy, that Calvin did for the bourgeoisie of the sixteenth century what Marx was to do for the proletariat of the nineteenth.[33] He placed their virtues at their best in sharp antithesis to the vices of the inherited social order, sketched with a flourishing pen. He dignified their motives, incorporated their keenest desires in a creed which made them seem, to the receptive mind, like necessary parts of a divinely ordained plan. And the doctrine of predestination, like the Marxian theory of historical materialism, extended to the elect—in one case bourgeois, in the other proletarian—the solemn, immutable assurance that the great and compelling forces of the universe were their allies. Conceived in these terms, Calvinism came to perform its historical function largely as the religion of the bourgeoisie.

In this manner, the final social result of Calvinism was virtually predestined. "The classes whose backing was needed to make the Reformation a political success had sold their support on terms which made it inevitable that it should be a social disaster."[34] Those who most conspicuously supported the Reformation were the men who formed the new financial-mercantile class: the speculators who bought from the Crown thousands of acres of confiscated monastery lands and evicted peasants with the same lack of ceremony which had been accorded monks; the frightened German nobility who slaughtered fifty thousand peasants, under the solemn benediction of Luther; the Huguenot men of property who fashioned new theories of social organization not only to win religious toleration, but also to tighten their grasp on commercial holdings. These were the astute men who understood more vividly than their religious leaders that the first battle for the empire of free enterprise called for the annihilation of restrictive ethical precepts imposed by a Church which stubbornly refused to subscribe to the doctrine that the unfettered exercise of each individual's acquisitive instincts would either fabricate or purchase the good society.

From the subdued rumblings heard in the faubourgs of late medieval Europe had come the thunder of a new day. "The attack upon Rome is above all an attack upon a way of life which stood as a barrier across the new path."[35] And that new path cut no narrow trail. It moved into every sphere of society. By 1600 men were living in a new world, morally and intellectually, economically and politically.

The greatest single change in the institutional structure of society was realized in the substitution of state for Church as the preeminent guarantor of social welfare. As Machiavelli had anticipated, the state had been emancipated from its subordinate attachment to a religious hierarchy of ethical values, and religion itself was fast becoming an instrument in the hands of the state. In these events the Reformation had participated by both its direct assault on the authority of the Church, and its positive endorsement of the secular powers, endowing them with the social functions previously constituting the province of the Church. In coming centuries those functions still left to the Church were to be challenged by an ever more assertive temporal power.

There was, however, a change which had deeper roots than this institutional transposition. What the sixteenth century most clearly achieved was the sabotage of religious authority in the sphere of economics—the exile of religious precepts from the market place. Some men never anticipated this revolution. Some precipitated it.

The method to be pursued was logical. The key implement was to be the state, divorced from its previous religious associations and endowed with the fullest power to wield the temporal sword as it saw fit. There had to be some such agency as the state to meet the rapidly multiplying problems thrown to the surface by the new economic forces. From the chaotic political scene of the sixteenth century the state had emerged to restore order; to the same source men now looked to secure prosperity. Industrial expansion, commercial enterprise on a scale demanding government support, currency problems and price fluctuations, bitter struggles between master and employee as guild rule decayed—all these issues called for a single and strong authority, and one that viewed these problems from the standpoint of the businessman.

The mercantilism of the secular state thus registered the first step on the road to the Liberal Society.[36] Its habits inherited from the age past, it continued to pronounce rules of economic conduct as the Church had done. But its objectives were distinctly of the new order: "the motive of state action is no longer the good life, but the attainment of wealth, the enactment, by legislation, of the conditions that will make for wealth."[37]

As it was to evolve in the two succeeding centuries, mercantilism was a constant search for the means that would achieve that end: it was not a carefully patterned economic philosophy, but a trend of economic activity. A two-edged sword, it first of all represented the efforts of rulers of states to attain an economic solidarity consonant with political unification. But it also signified the commercial class's use of the state for its own economic gain; it might be summarized as the collective, sustained effort of businessmen to make the state responsive to the needs and the wishes of businessmen. Consumer and worker were to follow priest and monk to the fringes of society, the middle class to occupy the central citadel.

The second of these forces behind mercantilism came to be the dominant, energizing one. The secular-mercantilist state was thus, in reality, never the autonomous and omnicompetent institution suggested by its political facade. In all its coercive glory it remained sensitively responsive to the ambitions and demands of the most articulate members of its economy—merchants, middlemen and financiers. It had come into being largely as an institutional barricade from behind which men could successfully challenge the superior dominion of the Church. And it never came to assume an existence genuinely independent of the middle class sustaining it. This national economy, in short, was but one stage on the road to individual economy.[38]

While in the political sphere the state had successfully assailed the Church and in the economic realm a class had used the state as a weapon against the spiritual power, it was with the intellectual revolution that the individual rebelled. This shifting of the spiritual center of gravity from the Church to the individual engendered that climate of thought and opinion in which alone the political and economic revolutions could have been consummated.

More than a few forces went into the initiation of the intellectual revolution, forces that ultimately were to inspire in Western man wholly new conceptions of his own nature and his relationship to his God, his universe and his society. The scientific renaissance, only now showing the first stirrings of life with the work of Copernicus, was on its way to shattering the medieval cosmology; man's entire universe, suddenly and literally, would assume new proportions and indicate unmistakably his new relationship to it. As a preface to this, the religious upheaval had already launched men's conception and understanding of their God upon a vast sea from which no shore was visible. With the discoveries of new and disparate religious faiths in other lands, and with the revival of classical learning with its pagan heritage, the intellectual validity of Christianity was questioned at the very time when its internal life had become discord. As Bacon observed tersely, "if there is one main division it addeth zeal to both sides, but many divisions introduce atheism."[39]

As thoughtful men turned cynical faces on the spectacle of militantly competing Christian sects, the scepticism of a Rabelais or a Montaigne became the fashionable intellectual posture. Montaigne's was a characteristic conclusion of men who looked, listened, and pondered what they saw and heard throughout the sixteenth century: "We receive our religion but according to fashion. . . . Another country, other testimonies, equal promises, like menaces, would imprint a contrary religion in us."[40] Or, as George Rust said dryly: "Truth is a various and uncertain thing and changes with the air and climate—'tis Mahomet at Constantinople, the Pope at Rome, Luther at Wittenberg, Calvin at Geneva, Arminius at Oldwater, Socinus at Cracow."[41] This rationalist temper was beginning to seep through the whole intellectual world. And in the ensuing spiritual reorientation, there could be no such half-way house as the state offered in the economic revolution. When man had finally denied the authority of the single institution which for so long had commanded his allegiance, he had, in the last analysis, but one place to turn—to himself.

Thus, already in the sixteenth century, were sown the seeds of the spirit of Diderot and Voltaire, Locke and Smith, Hume and Kant. It seems, indeed, that more than a century has passed between the time of an English chancellor like More at the beginning of the century, and one like Bacon at its conclusion.[42] The author of the *Utopia* did not ignore the material and cultural triumphs of the Renaissance and the commercial revolution; he simply regarded them as more refined means to an end which did not change with each new technical improvement men came to possess. But the author of the *New Atlantis* attaches new ends to the new means, or at least abrogates old ends. He sees a self-sustaining objective in "the restitution of man to the sovereignty of nature"—but he anticipates the need of no final moral principles to govern men's exercise of that sovereignty. He envisions the goal of "the service of human convenience"—but in what service is humanity itself to enlist?

A new world is in birth—a new world of ideas and facts. A new social discipline with purely secular sanctions. A self-sufficient state, tied no longer to an intricate hierarchy of religious values. A new, unexplored and apparently boundless realm of scientific adventure and discovery. A newly defined spiritual sphere—where all principles flow from but one source, the individual . . . where all religious precepts have but one true province, the individual soul. An entire new world-perspective for men: self-confident and self-assertive, utilitarian and acquisitive.

The ground is cleared for the building of the Liberal Society.

Part II · The Making of the Liberal Society

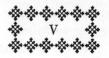

Philosophers in Arms: The New World of Ideas

THE bone and muscle of the Liberal Society were formed in that era of the history of the West marked off by the Protestant Reformation and the French Revolution. Two centuries of thought and deed administered last philosophic and social rites to that society which men had known, lived in, and believed in, since the passing of the Roman Empire. And the same two hundred years rang with a lusty, sustained summons for the mobilization of men's creative energies in the work of fashioning a new society.

Although many of its energies and inner compulsions had origins centuries old and still others did not reach fulfillment until centuries after, yet the Reformation period had been the great watershed. Up to and including that time, the constituent spheres of human society—religious and intellectual, economic and political—had been conceived as complementary, mutually-fulfilling parts of an integrated, Christian unity. Through the sixteenth, even into the seventeenth, century, intelligible synthesis of all human experience under the aegis of religion had continued to seem to most men sane, feasible, and necessary. But from this point in history, on through the eighteenth century, men advanced swiftly toward conception of society as a succession of autonomous spheres: some more worthy of exploration and exploitation, because their material fruits were more abundant, and all independent and bound only by definitions of truth and error, good and evil, justice and injustice.

As men conceive, so do they build. The now disengaged spheres of society are studied individually, each being pressed by philosophers to surrender to human inquiry the laws which govern its existence and operation. In this fashion, the swelling current of ideas and events pushing toward modern times comes to form divergent streams: sometimes rejoining to rush on in united force, sometimes maintaining an independent channel . . . but ever pressing on toward the great confluence which shall be the Liberal Society.

The narrative of these centuries is, then, a narrative of extension, development, and acceleration of the revolutionary forces at work in the Reformation era. It is the story of men's pilgrimage from the world of medieval man to the world of modern man—from the world of Spiritual Man to the world of Economic Man. It is the history of the rise of a faith—the Liberal faith: a faith which could bring vindication and purpose to action. For action, without a justifying creed, is naked and unavailing.

To build this faith men had to do yet one thing more. That one thing constituted the great intellectual *cause célèbre* of the age—the trial of the Christian God. Assurance of final Liberal victory was contingent upon success in this, and toward success were directed all the strength and power which the forces of Liberalism could command. The members of the prosecution and authors of the indictment were the Philosophes. The source of their evidence was the new science. Their judgment was pronounced in their literary and philosophical writings. And the factors impelling them to prefer charges were the basic social and economic energies of the Liberal Society.

Renaissance and Reformation had not signified total, categorical cleavage with the Middle Ages. For in all civilizations, no matter how profound be the intellectual or economic transformations experienced, there is a cultural persistence and fluidity by virtue of which the stream of inherited ways of thinking seems to discover almost imperceptible crevices in the new walls of thought. Through these last the stream passes into the fields beyond; sometimes to a degree that only serves to make more fertile and productive the newly-turned intellectual earth, sometimes to a degree that makes the new land philosophically uninhabitable—so that men must either surrender their new conquests and return to the old, or push ahead yet deeper into unexplored realms, to new heights across which the tide of the past cannot pass.

The intellectual soil of the Renaissance and Reformation periods had been inundated in this fashion. It is true that old authoritarian forms and institutions had been discarded, but the principle of authority itself, albeit cast in new molds, seemed to retain intellectual validity and still commanded men's respect. The man of the Renaissance looked to his classics, and his vision of the good life he saw realized in antiquity—to Petrarch, Europe's "mother, which invented every noble art."[1] The man of the Reformation looked to his Bible, and in primitive Christianity found a complete good that was beyond and above dispute or question. Neither denied all authoritarian precepts, or sought his intellectual weapons in the immediate present, or dedicated his struggle to creation of a new society in the immediate future.

Standing on ground thus washed by a legacy they had disavowed, the builders of the Liberal Society moved on. Of all great civilizations, only the West has produced a maturely developed science—and what the man of the Renaissance and the man of the Reformation did not venture, the men of the scientific revolution set out to achieve.* Not only was science instrumental in snapping the last vestigial bonds to the medieval world, but also it is science which is going to be the arsenal of the Liberal Society. Its weapons will be employed in pressing the retreat of religion, in supporting the social philosophy of the Liberal, and ultimately

---

* The Renaissance was in no substantial sense a precursor of the scientific revolution. From Petrarch to Erasmus, Renaissance humanists had spurned the study of nature for the study of man and had thus given to humanism a thoroughly anti-scientific basis. "Had it [humanism] not ventured the interests and the energies of the best intellects upon the essentially unscientific and even anti-scientific wisdom of the civic-minded and narrowly ethical classic Greeks and Romans, there is every possibility that a Galileo might have lived in the fourteenth century instead of the seventeenth, and that scientific investigation and discovery might have been three hundred years further advanced than they are." (Randall, J. H., *The Making of the Modern Mind* [New York: Houghton Mifflin, 1926], p. 212.)

[57]

in forging the vast industrial structure of the nineteenth century.

The substance of the scientific awakening of the seventeenth century was formed by the Copernican and Cartesian revolutions. It extended from the initial work of Copernicus to the climactic work of Newton: from the publication in 1543 of *De Revolutionibus Orbium Celestium*, to Newton's *Principia* in 1687. It embraced the work of Galileo, Leonardo da Vinci, Francis Bacon, Tycho Brahe, Kepler, Leibniz, Descartes.

For the seekers after nature's secrets, the new science established for itself both new methodology and new purpose. The first Leonardo summarized deftly. "Whosoever appeals to authority," he explained, "applies not his intellect but his memory. . . . While nature begins from cause, and ends in experience, we must follow a contrary procedure, that is, begin with experience and from that discover the causes."[2] At the same time, Galileo posited as the true object of scientific investigation "not the true and inner essence of substances, but a knowledge of some of their qualities."[3] Scientific learning, in the words of another of the prophets of science, must supplant both the "contentious learning" of the scholastics, and the "delicate learning" of the humanists.[4]

Great as was the substance of the labors of the new science—its assiduous application of reason operating through mathematical calculation, its ranging exploration of the heavens, its revelation of analytical geometry and the calculus, its measurement of world and universe by universal mathematical laws—great as was all this, yet two things were more important. One: the initial impulse inducing men's minds to enter upon this exploration of nature. The other: the broad impact on men's minds when the new world of science opened to their perception.

The impulse behind the scientific revolution was a *faith*, and that faith was: nature is simple, harmonious, and governed by knowable natural laws. Fortifying this belief, it is true, there was the semblance of a scientific tradition in the investigations of antiquity and the work of many students of the thirteenth century. But that tradition could never, of itself, validate and sustain a faith such as this. The faith sprang from within men—and they then sought evidence to confirm its authenticity by observation of the world of nature. In the words of a twentieth-century scientist, juxtaposing the Enlightenment and the age of the Scholastics, the latter was "an age of faith based upon reason," the former "an age of reason based upon faith."[5]

All the great mathematical physicists of the age partook of this faith—this immediate and compelling certainty that nature was simple, harmonious, knowable. Such was the classic dictum of Newton: "Nature does nothing in vain, and more is in vain when less will serve, for Nature is pleased with simplicity and affects not the pomp of superfluous causes."[6] Leonardo's *Notebooks* expressed the same confidence in natural simplicity and constancy: "Nature never breaks her own law. Nature is constrained by the order of her own law which lives and works within her."[7]

Descartes, because of his singularly profound influence, because of his intense and original genius, and because of his acceptance by many as uniquely personifying the transition to the new intellectual world, was, beyond doubt, one of the most distinguished apostles of the new faith. Born in an age which, in large measure, was immediately conscious of little more than the scepticism of a Montaigne, Descartes could understand and sympathize with Montaigne's resignation to ultimate ignorance—but it could never satisfy him. Instead, he sought a faith, and he found a faith by constructing one.

As Chanut's epitaph on the tomb of Descartes reads, "in his winter furlough, comparing the mysteries of nature with the laws of mathematics, he dared hope that the secrets of both could be unlocked with the same key."[8] On the night of November 10, 1619, it had come to him like a visitation of Reason—the intuitive perception that, not only geometry and algebra, but all sciences were *one*, whose properties and functions were deducible through the application of mathematical laws alone. "All things, to the knowledge of which man is competent"—such was the import of the revelation—"are mutually connected in the same way, and . . . there is nothing so far removed from us as to be beyond our reach."[9] Thus on this night for Descartes—and soon thereafter for much of the Western world—scepticism withered and died, while the faith of *mathematicism* rose to claim dominion over men's minds.[10]

With the fervent, unheeding zeal of a religious prophet, Descartes invoked mathematics to reveal and explain all reality. He had a jealous sense of personal mission, scorning collaboration with others in construction of his system and proclaiming that he had "never met with a single critic of my own opinions who did not appear to me either less rigorous or less equitable than myself."[11] Then, in his very philosophical structure, he took the foundation from the medieval era's most famous mystic. His proof of the soul's existence was his famous "I think, hence I am. . . . From the very circumstance that I thought to doubt of the truth of these things, it most clearly and certainly followed that I was."[12] Centuries before, in his dialogue with Reason, St. Augustine had been asked: "You, who wish to know yourself, do you know at least that you are?—I know it.—How do you know it?—I don't know. . . . But do you know that you think?—Yes, I know that.—Consequently, that you think at least is true.—It is true.—You know therefore that you are, that you live and that you think."[13] The cycles of Western thought, indeed, seemed perverse and unfathomable.*

In this spirit and with a basic philosophical premise of this origin, Descartes set himself to explaining the universe

* When the Augustinian origin of his thought was pointed out to him by Arnauld—whom he had personally urged to send him his objections—Descartes was bitter. "I shall not take up time here," he replied, "by thanking my distinguished critic, for bringing to my aid the authority of St. Augustine, and for expounding my arguments in a way which betokened a fear that others might not deem them strong enough." (Cited by Gilson, E., *The Unity of Philosophical Experience*, pp. 156-157.)

and constructing a faith, consciously and deliberately. In his eyes, the disquisitions of the ancient moralists were but "very towering and magnificent palaces with no better foundation than sand and mud."[14] At the same time, mathematics—"on account of the certitude and evidence of their reasonings"—deserved to have a "loftier structure reared on them."[15] And this Descartes proceeded to do—establishing, to his own satisfaction, the existence of his soul, God and the world of nature by mathematics and logic. Thus did the author of the great Cartesian revolution construct his mathematical scholasticism. That a later age dismissed this structure, too, as built on "sand and mud" does not alter this fact: for its founder, it was an autonomous faith, in the sense that its inception came with a sudden intuitive perception of the nature of creation; that its implications were elaborated and expounded with the uncompromising self-assurance of a religious zealot; and that its full and final exposition demanded acceptance as a self-sustaining explanation of the Almighty and all His works.

Less fraught with meaning for the future, perhaps, than Descartes' creed, but a simpler, more succinct representation of this whole trend of thought, was to be found in Kepler's *Mystery of the Universe*. Here a faith literally assumed cosmic proportions. For the vast universe was conceived by Kepler as a cosmic reflection of the Trinity. The central sun was the Father, the surrounding spheres the Son, and the geometrical relations between them the Holy Ghost!

Propelled by such impulses, the scientific revolution could not but meet men's minds with profound force and power: if the impulse was a new faith (or the seeking of it), the impact could not fail to jar old faiths. Simultaneously, the old was proved wrong, the new proved fruitful. The Ptolemaic cosmology was shattered, and religious authorities associated with its propagation were scientifically discredited. With the tight encircling limits of the medieval cosmology crossed, there loomed around and ahead only infinite spaces, infinite worlds. In such a universe, to insist on the dignity of man as God's special creature, made in His Own image, seemed as ludicrously out of proportion as it would have been to enthrone the cricket as king of the beasts. Man seemed lost in the limitless universe, a puny, imperfect and not very significant physical machine who could be cast in no major role on a cosmic stage that was boundless.

In the light of such an awakening, such a shattering of all known and understood physical horizons, the tumult that came in men's minds defied description. Perhaps the clearest suggestion of it was the frantic pantheism of a Bruno. Through all Europe he marched—England and Germany, Geneva and Rome—announcing his vision and proclaiming his gospel. . . . "Lo! here is one who has swept the air, pierced the heavens, sped by the stars and passed beyond the bounds of the world, who has annihilated the fantastic spheres with which foolish mathematicians and vulgar philosophers had closed us in. . . . We know that there is but one heaven, one immense ether, where magnificent fires maintain their proper distances by reason of the eternal life in which they have part. These flaming bodies are the ambassadors which announce the excellence of God's glory and majesty."[16]

Gone now for all time is the medieval conception of being, approaching perfection as it recedes from earth and moves toward heaven. Instead are substituted universal, inflexible natural laws, governing with equal compulsion the heavens as well as the earth. Gone is Aquinas's hierarchy of purposes in the universe, for the universe is convertible into a level, uniform mathematical system whose revelation to men Galileo commemorates by quoting the Scriptural passage, "God hath made all things in number, weight and measure." Reflecting upon the accomplishments of the men who propelled the scientific revolution, Diderot summarizes their achievement with precision. "Thanks to the toil of these great men," he exclaims, "the world is no longer a divine thing (*un dieu*); it is a machine which has its wheels, its ropes, its pulleys, its springs, and its weights."[17]

Perhaps intoxicated with the strong wine of intellectual

adventure, the men of science envision all nature revealed to the ever-widening scientific perspective of humanity. Devout in their belief that men would soon establish themselves as "the lords and possessors of nature,"[18] they venture to presage complete victory in less than a century. For in a century, Diderot informs the Enlightened, one will not be able to count three great geometers in Europe. Gone forever will be the Eulers, the Fontaines, the D'Alemberts. For the men of science already "will have erected the pillars of Hercules. Men will proceed no further. Their achievements will endure in the centuries to come, like the pyramids of Egypt, whose bulks, inscribed with hieroglyphics, inspire in us a startling conception of the power and resources of the men who have raised them."[19]

Believing themselves possessed of a scientific power so puissant, men are infatuated with the immutable, mechanical world of Descartes and Newton. It becomes one of those doctrines of an age which develops not as a subject for scrutiny, but as an object for faith. Nature, smooth and impervious in her symmetry; for men it is truly a majestic, consoling contrast to—and refuge from—the raucous, maddening uncertainty of Christian dialectics and forensics. To such a scientifically approved deity men can refer all their anguished strivings for order and balance, harmony and precision—a deity whose will has decreed that:

> All are but parts of one stupendous whole,
> Whose body nature is, and God the soul. . . .
> All Nature is but Art, unknown to thee;
> All chance, direction, which thou canst not see;
> All discord, harmony, not understood;
> All partial evil, universal good;
> And spite of pride, inerring reason's spite,
> One truth is clear, whatever is, is right.[20]

Enthralled with this omniscient vision, men turn to Nature—and worship her. They throw themselves upon the neck of the new divinity, and in one rapturous gesture they espouse the good, the true, and the beautiful. The symphony of ideas reaches its glowing crescendo as the voice of Nature (though the words are Holbach's) is heard crying out to man—"It is in my empire that liberty reigns. Tyranny and slavery from it are forever banished; equity guards the security of my subjects, maintains them in their just rights; charity and humanity link them by kind bonds; truth enlightens them, and never can imposture blind them with its dismal mists. Return then, wandering child, return to nature! She will bring consolation, she will drive from your heart those fears which crush you, those anxieties which torture you, those rages which shake you, those hates which cut you off from fellow man, whom you must love. Restored to nature, to humanity, to yourself, scatter flowers lavishly along the road of life; cease contemplating the future; look to yourself, look to fellow creatures; explore your own hidden depths, consider then the sensible beings who surround you, and leave behind those gods who can offer nothing for your happiness. . . . Be happy, then, O man!"[21] . . . . And to this not unwelcome exhortation, men respond in kind. . . . "O Nature! sovereign of all beings! and ye, her adorable daughters, Virtue, Reason, Truth! be for all time our only gods; it is to you that is due the incensed reverence of the earth. Show us, then, O Nature! what man must do to gain the happiness which thou makest him desire."[22]

And so the new faith grips men's imaginations, seizing them by heart and mind—and it is difficult to say upon which its grasp is firmer. Into that static world that has come from the mind of Newton, men have projected a goddess: a life-giving goddess into whose hands they commend themselves in their search for truth and virtue and freedom. From a dying world men's minds and spirits have been pried loose with a buoyant doubt—and a buoyant faith . . . a faith that inflames men's souls—

> Our souls whose faculties can comprehend the world,
> And measure every wandering planet's course,
> Still climbing after knowledge infinite
> And always moving as the restless spheres. . . .[23]

Men who could measure every wandering planet's course, men whose faculties could comprehend the world—these were they who summoned the Christian God to trial. Reading from the books of the new science, they presented their indictment at the bar of Reason. . . .

The universe with whose creation You are credited is governed by fixed, changeless natural laws. We have proven this. These universal laws dictate everything that comes to pass in nature; all that happens derives from them. Do You presume to claim that You could ever have decreed that there be more or less than three sides to a triangle, or that perfectly parallel lines cross each other? Therefore is it not manifest that You can never decree, nor ever could have decreed, anything but what is? You did not exist before Your decrees, and You could not exist without them.

Your self-appointed apostles on earth, they who call themselves Christians, have tried to attach spiritual purposes to the works of Nature. We now know that they are falsifiers. For Nature has no particular end in view; final causes are mere human figments.

These same men, in Your name, have tried to exalt that machine which is man and conceive it as a spiritual being with a soul, with an immanent dignity and worth that derives from its creation in Your image. This, too, is false. Human ideas and desires partake of the same properties and belong in the same category as lines, planes and solids.

In the affairs of this world, these Christians have told us, You intervene capriciously, through miracles and through revelation. This is a lie. Miracles, by definition, are impossible, because they signify suspension of natural laws—which laws we know to be immutable. Revelation is unjust and untrue. If there be such a thing as spiritual salvation, it must be an end which all men can achieve. It can therefore be attainable by only an instrument that is accessible to all. This cannot be revelation, for revelation is partial and particular: made manifest to a select group at a particular time and place. Whereas the instrument which is common to all mankind is Reason, and Reason alone.

All this being true—for our science has proved it so—then what the Christians advance as the one divine religion is revealed as nothing more than an over-elaborate tissue of superstition, an imaginative capitalization on men's ignorant fear of invisible power—power which our science renders no longer invisible but harnesses to the will of mankind. . . .*

This was the indictment of the Christian God: dictated by the new science, pronounced by the philosophic rationalists, aimed directly at the Catholic Church—its creed and its leaders. That the Western world listened to its enunciation attentively and receptively was due not only to soaring confidence in the boundless potentialities of science, but also to fretful distraction caused by the intellectual disorder into which the faith of past ages had fallen. Montaigne's scepticism had raised a sign foreboding enough for the future of Christianity, but what followed was worse. Men, as in the case of Descartes, dissatisfied with the philosophical foundation of the Christian structure of thought, had set out to support the ultimate truths of Christianity with the new doctrines of mathematical science. When mathematical scholasticism was discredited and it became obvious that Christian truths were not susceptible of geometrical or algebraic proof, then

* This indictment is a summary paraphrase of parts of the writings of the men who formulated it. The condemnation of miracles and revelation can be found in Hume's *Essay on Miracles*. It was Hobbes who disposed of Christianity in the fashion here indicated: ". . . And thence it is, that ignorant, and superstitious men make great Wonders of those works, which other men, knowing to proceed from Nature, . . . admire not at all. . . . And this Feare of things invisible, is the naturall Seed of that, which every one in himself calleth Religion; and in them that worship, or fear that Power otherwise than they do, Superstition." (*Leviathan*, Chapters XI and XXXVII.)

For the body of the indictment, Spinoza can be given credit: "Nothing, then, comes to pass in Nature in contravention to her universal laws, nay, everything agrees with them and follows from them. . . . God . . . neither can decree nor could have decreed anything else than that which he has decreed. . . . God has not existed before his decrees and can never exist without them. . . . Nature has set no end before herself, and . . . all final causes are nothing but human fictions. . . . I shall consider human actions and appetites just as if I were considering lines, planes or bodies." (*The Philosophy of Spinoza*, ed. by J. Ratner, First Part, Chapter VII; Chapter VIII; Second Part, Chapter XII.)

men—rather than question the validity of the method they had used to support them—looked upon the truths themselves as insupportable. In this manner all supernatural ingredients of Christianity were discarded.

Although multiplication of Christian sects made impossible a united defense, men who still adhered to their Christian allegiance fought back with vigor. More clearly than their adversaries they perceived that this was not a doctrinal or institutional issue which the age was debating; it was an issue of Christianity or no Christianity. Bossuet, for example, saw what was happening and described it clearly: "Some Christians deny the work of the Creation and of the Redemption of humanity, annul the conception of Hell, dispense with immortality of the soul, strip Christianity of all its mysteries, and convert it into a philosophical sect entirely accommodated to the senses: therewith is born religious indifference, and, as follows naturally, the very foundation of religion is attacked."[24] The Abbé Nonnotte, thinking in similar terms, exclaimed, "Religion, facts, events, proved geometrically! . . . . Can any but fanatics and madmen speak like the author of the *Pensées Philosophiques?*"[25] And Hayer's summary of the entire issue was calm and perceptive: "I am a body, and I think; I know no more, says a modern philosopher (Voltaire). I am a soul and have a body, says Plato with the wisest of antiquity. The question, then, is to examine whether my body is my whole being, or only a thing belonging to me, my possession; whether this body is Me or simply Mine."[26]

But the men who were indicting the Christian God were disposed to discuss matters in no such sober fashion as this. Neither calmly nor lucidly, but with passionate self-assurance and often iron-like intolerance, the rationalists presented their philosophical case. They talked much of reason, but their favorite weapons were ridicule and vilification: to mock a cleric was almost as gratifying a pastime as to have him exiled.* They spoke with moving eloquence of liberty of speech, but rarely extended such liberty to their opponents whenever they had the power to refuse it. Voltaire, Liberal titan of the Enlightenment, witnessed with evident relish the imprisonment of La Baumelle—the latter having been injudiciously critical of some of Voltaire's more injudicious writings. And to silence opposition two of the distinguished eighteenth century philosophic group appealed to the very censors whom truly enlightened thinkers were reputed to scorn.

The tactics and conduct of the Philosophes brought a stinging rebuke from even Herder, who certainly felt no attachment to French Catholicism. "How foolish," he exclaimed, "to brand them with the blackest devils of your century, with fraud and stupidity, superstition and slavery, to fabricate an army of priest-devils and tyrant-apparitions which exist only in your mind."[27] But the tyrant-apparitions remained and assumed ever more gross and terrifying stature. They inspired men to labor in the spirit of Vanini—the Italian atheist who went to the stake exultantly proclaiming that he would die like a brave man, and not like Jesus Christ, who had flinched from the Cross. Indeed, it is not surprising that Fréron should inquire pertinently, "Is not the fanaticism of your irreligion more absurd and more dangerous than the fanaticism of superstition?"[28]

While this fierce battle with the Church was still at its height, the Philosophes constructed a religious refuge of their own. And they called it Deism. Miracles, prophecy, revelation, ritual, dogma: all these were tossed aside as extraneous and misleading religious paraphernalia. With these was discarded the oppressing doctrine of original sin and man's moral bondage. Their positive creed the rationalists evolved from a quest for the common denominators to all

* In a single letter to Fréron, Voltaire called his correspondent a scribbler, scoundrel, toad, lizard, snake, spider, viper's tongue, crooked mind, heart of filth, doer of evil, rascal, impudent person, cowardly knave, spy, and hound. (Cited by Palmer, R. R., *Catholics and Unbelievers in Eighteenth Century France*, p. 7.)

organized religions; religious concepts, in other words, that would correspond to the universal natural laws which science was revealing to men. In that creed were incorporated but three discernible doctrines: existence of an omnipotent God, His will that men live virtuously, and reward for said virtue in a future life.

This much of the Christian tradition was endorsed by the Deists because science, for the time being, seemed to authenticate it. The Newtonian world-machine, that precisely articulated and complex mechanism of Nature, seemed too fine and elaborate a design to have come about by mere chance. Behind it all there must be a Master Technician—a magnified Boyle or Huygens or Harvey. This was "God." As Pascal had said of Descartes, the latter "would have been quite willing to dispense with God. But he had to make Him give a fillip to set the world in motion; beyond this, he has no further need of God."[29] Thus the Christian God yielded to the Deist God, a convenient appendage to the natural order whose explicit and exclusive function was to complement the discoveries of scientific logic.

It is just to say that, translated into action, the Deist creed possessed but two distinguishable qualities: militant antipathy to traditional Christianity, and an unfailing capacity to conceal its own doctrines behind an impenetrable veil of rhetoric. To meet a request for an intelligible statement of his doctrines, the Deist, more often than not, sought to stun his interrogator with some such vacuous platitude as:

> For modes of faith, let graceless zealots fight;
> His can't be wrong, whose life is in the right.[30]

It was characteristic of the age of Classicism that one of the things about religious zealots it found most irritating was the fact that they were "graceless."

This gracefully nebulous quality pervaded Deist thought. For Montesquieu the religion of benevolence was sufficient, consisting only "in fulfilling all the duties of charity and humanity, and in breaking none of the laws under which men live."[31] Voltaire was no more lucid. "What is a true Deist?" he asked rhetorically, and answered: "one who says to God I adore and love you, one who says to a Turk, a Chinaman, an Indian and a Russian, I love you."[32] In the opinion that there is a God, he confessed, there were difficulties; but he at once added triumphantly that in the contrary opinion there were absurdities. As a watch proved a watchmaker, so a good mechanical universe proved there was a master watchmaker, known to the initiated as "God." Beyond this, Voltaire's religious thinking and writing indicated little more than a facility for epigrams.

As for the matter of freeing shackled humanity from the bondage of superstition, it would seem that Voltaire's anxiety on this point arose most conspicuously from his concern for the welfare of the intellectual elite. Such, at least, was his outlook when he wrote to Frederick the Great in 1767. "As long as there are fools and knaves," he presaged, "there will be religion. Ours is the most ridiculous, the most absurd, and the most bloody that has ever infected the world. Your majesty will do the human race an eternal service in extirpating this infamous superstition, I do not say among the rabble, who were not worthy of being enlightened and who are apt for every yoke; I say among the well bred, among those who think, among those who wish to think. Their number is not very great."[33] If, as he himself once remarked, the superstitious in society were like the cowards in an army, Voltaire's generalship was not of the best, for he said, in effect: let the officers be well trained, let the rank and file desert if they so desire. In the final analysis his Deism was little more than a continuation of the utilitarian religious thought of the Politiques, in spirit essentially like Gibbon's: all religions were in the eyes of the people equally true, in the eyes of the philosopher equally false, and to the magistrate all equally useful.[34]

Fortunately, the Deist could forget the mist surrounding his own creed when he was engaged in his militant assault on the Catholic faith. For Montesquieu the Christian religion as a whole was suspect from the outset because it was "burdened with an immense number of tedious duties."[35] But the Catholic faith was doubly suspect, and Montesquieu, above the petty plane of theological disputation, disposed of it curtly. The Pope, he explained, was "an old idol, kept venerable by custom. Formerly he was feared even by princes. . . . He is, however, no longer dreaded. He declares himself to be the successor of one of the first Christians, called Saint Peter; and it is certainly a rich succession; for he possesses immense treasures, and a large territory owns his sway."[36] As for the Jesuits—who apparently remained willful and obdurate in the face of this succinct critique—they seemed to Montesquieu like people "struggling as in a battle, dismal, confused; they are fed upon subtleties, they live upon obscure arguments and false inferences."[37]

The irrepressible Voltaire rejoiced in the task of crushing the infamous Church whose legacy of superstition and ignorance threw a yoke over successive generations of men. With a self-conscious tone of assurance that more than suggested the sleekly supercilious, he proclaimed his boast and prophecy: "Like Cato, I always end my harangue by saying *Deleatur Carthago*. It is only necessary for five or six philosophes to understand in order to upset the colossus."[38]

The colossus, however, was destined to stand some considerable while longer than the structure of Deism. In such an age—with the Christian God standing judgment and men's most long-established religious allegiances torn asunder—it was impossible that the shallow humanitarianism of the Deist creed could rally or command men's newly liberated religious loyalties. Almost under an impulse of its own, Reason seemed to carry men, only half-knowingly, into the strange, unsought realm of atheism. Here men like Hume and Holbach took their stand, incisive and empirical in their criticisms of the whole Christian tradition—including the pallid reflection of Deism. At the most, they argued, from a finite and imperfect world, one could assume a finite and imperfect creator—who might be (or have been) wholly good, wholly evil, both, or neither. The scientific revelation, they observed, might be invoked to sustain belief in some initiating force called "God"—but it could not be called on to testify to the reality of an absolute moral code or a future life. "We cannot," Holbach affirmed, "go beyond this aphorism, 'Matter acts because it exists, and exists to act.' "[39] To these men, others who had built their frail religious structures on mathematical science had built on "sand and mud." Thus, as complete atheism and materialism is finally reached, all the diluted religious compromises of Voltaire and the Deists are swept away.

It is clear that through the whole indictment of the Christian God—Deist or atheist—ran one consistent thread: philosophic individualism, and a concomitant repudiation of religious authoritarianism. In this spirit shared men of as disparate character as Voltaire, Holbach, or Rousseau—*"le plus grand ennemi de la Révélation et de la Foi,"* as Nonnotte called him.[40] And against this spirit men of the Church tried in vain to fight: to argue that religion was not simply an esoteric emotional experience but, as Bergier expressed it, an alliance between God and man—with terms governing men's social order as well as their individual lives.[41]

To argue so was of no avail. To be philosophically insurgent, to be insistently inquisitive and critical, to be passionately individualistic—this was the common denominator to the variegated forms of religious thought in the eighteenth century. The human, individual passions themselves were exalted by the Enlightened. "Blunted passions," explained Diderot, "degrade men of genius. Constraint destroys the grandeur and energy of Nature. . . . It is only the passions, and the great passions, which can lift the soul to great things."[42] Or, as another of the Philosophes stated, the passions are to the moral world what motion is to the physical world.[43] To perceive clearly the intensely religious character of these new doctrines, one need only compare these words with those of the German Pietist, Hamann—"Passion alone gives to abstractions, as well as to hypotheses, hands, feet and wings;

to picture and drawings, spirit, life and tongue. . . . Nature works through the senses and the passions."[44]

All this signified much more than the erosion of institutional religious forms. It meant the categorical denial of the worth of discipline, the repudiation of all that men for centuries had understood as meaning moral order. It meant the subversion of the precepts of religion to the egoistic wills of men, the complete corruption of moral absolutes. What the Enlightened sought to do, in short, was to dignify their desires with the honorific title of virtue. *By the simple equation of virtue and desire in the realm of morals, these men anticipated—laid the necessary foundation for—the equation of social welfare and individual self-interest in the realm of political economy.*

The ethic of the Liberal Society is taking form.

The intellectual revolution propelled initially by the Protestant Reformation was running its swift course. From the Calvinist doctrine of predestination which made men puppets in the arbitrary hands of the Almighty, men had moved to the scientific creed of predestination, which made the Almighty Himself powerless against the fixed universal laws of Nature. From the day when Luther had arraigned a corrupt Church before the bar of an untarnished past, men had moved swiftly to the day when God Himself was summoned before the bar of Reason.

It was an age of dynamic transition, impossible to categorize by fixed stages of development. As Carl Becker has so clearly stated the issue,[45] most men dispensed with any deep fear of God, but maintained a respectful attitude toward an impersonal, mechanical Prime Mover. They disavowed Genesis, but held to a faith in a perfectly coordinated universe. They ridiculed the conception of a Garden of Eden, but exalted a similar, though less concrete, state of Nature. They repudiated the authority of both Church and Bible, but avowed a pure and abiding faith in Nature and Reason. They scorned theology and metaphysics, but revered the title of philosopher. They dismantled Heaven until it became something like a Christian Nirvana, but retained a misty faith in the immortality of the soul. They discussed atheism—but not before the servants; they pled for tolerance—but never tolerated priests. They challenged the right of others to derive the assumption of a perfect next-life from an imperfect this-life, but they indulged themselves the faith in a perfect society in the future of man's earthly existence. They scorned miracles, but they believed in the perfectibility of man.

The role of Deism in the realm of religious thought closely approximated that which mercantilism was to assume in the evolution of economic theory. The mercantilist economy was destined to be nothing more than a half-way house on the road to the individual economy of the fully-developed Liberal Society—a stage in that evolution which derived its importance from the attack it was able to launch against the economic order that came before it. So with Deism: its insubstantial pageant of ideas quickly faded; its service was its effectiveness as a weapon against the religious faith that preceded it; and the baseless fabric of its vision quickly became the completely individualized, atomistic ethical scheme of the Liberal Society.

Yet, beneath all this intellectual ferment, there came the rising consciousness that it did not suffice to condemn the Christian God—that to build was as imperative as to destroy. To forge a new faith, two instruments already had been uncovered. From the domain of science, men had learned of Nature: the word, the idea, the ideal. And having explored the realm of theology and metaphysics, men emerged with faith in but one thing, Reason: a clean, bright, new instrument which would scatter the hoary hosts of superstition, intolerance and injustice—and would clear the path for all mankind to the solid, true and good world that was to be the future.

Conscious that they were in a quest for a new faith that would govern a new society, men thought and acted with undisciplined fervor. When Diderot was corresponding with

Voltaire in the autumn of 1762, he was already aware of the all-consuming faith rising within him. A single letter, dated September 29 of that year, converted into the written word that spirit which ultimately was to produce Liberal victory. *"Très-cher et très-illustre frère,"* the letter began, and it read:

"Our standard reads: *sans quartier* to the superstitious, to the fanatical, to the ignorant, to the mad, to the malevolent, to the tyrannical. . . .

"It is not enough to know more than they [of the Church]. It is necessary to show them that we are better, and that philosophy makes more men of good will than sufficient or efficacious grace. . . .

"They are reduced to saying that God will not leave me to die in my unbelief, and that, in my last moments, an angel will descend without fail to convert me. And I, I promise them that I will return to their folly, if the angel comes. . . .

". . . Keep in good health, maintain your strength for your friends, for philosophy, for the arts, for the honor of the nation which has none comparable to you, and for the well being of humanity, for whom you are more essential than five hundred monarchs. . . . Ah! *grand frère*, you do not know how much those beggars [Christian prelates]—who, while incessantly provoking evil, persuaded themselves that it was their prerogative alone to do good—suffer when they see you the friend of mankind, the guardian of orphans, and the defender of the oppressed. Continue to do great labors and good works, and they will kill themselves in their vexation. Farewell, noble, loyal and dear Anti-Christ."[46]

In truth, the doctrines of the men who believed themselves Enlightened were much more than arid abstractions. They were the form and matter of a new faith. They were committed to condemning one world, building another. They were ideas born of mental anguish, torturing doubts, dangerous beliefs. If one seeks a lone, tragic figure to symbolize this rushing shock and clash of intellectual arms, there is Pascal —Pascal and his despairing cry. . . . "I look on all sides and

I find everywhere nothing but obscurity. Nature offers nothing which is not the subject of doubt and disquietude; if I saw nowhere any sign of a Deity I should decide it in the negative; if I saw everywhere the signs of a Creator, I should rest in peace in my faith; but, seeing too much to deny and too little confidently to affirm, I am in a pitiable state, and I have longed a hundred times that, if a God sustained nature, nature should show it without ambiguity, or that, if the signs of a God are fallacious, nature should suppress them altogether. Let her say the whole truth or nothing, so that I may see what side I ought to take."[47]

Thus men of the old faith came to doubt, while they who had doubted now found a new faith. Pascal spoke in words that were the last, tortured outburst of a world that was dying. And the future was to belong to those who inquired pragmatically—"When a man is completely initiated into all the mysteries of transubstantiation, consubstantiation, the Trinity, hypostatical union, predestination, the Incarnation, and all the rest, *will he then be a better citizen?*"[48]

This was the ultimate standard, the final test: good citizenship, social utility. And by this standard, this criterion of evidence, the Christian God stood condemned and the faith of the new world was measured.

And they who have denatured God shall now deify nature. For "Nature invites man to love himself, to preserve himself, to increase incessantly the sum of his happiness; Religion orders him to love only a formidable God, deserving of hatred—to despise himself, to sacrifice to his terrifying idol those pleasures of the heart which are most sweet and most lawful. Nature bids man consult his reason and take it as his guide; Religion teaches him that this reason is corrupted, that it is only a faithless guide, given by a deceiving God to mislead His creatures. Nature instructs man to seek light, to search for the truth, to study its products; Religion enjoins him to examine nothing, to remain in ignorance, to fear truth. . . . Nature says to man in society, 'Cherish glory, work to win esteem, be active, courageous, industrious'; Religion says

to him, 'Be humble, abject, pusillanimous, live in retreat, occupy yourself with prayers, meditations, pious observances;
be useless to yourself and to fellowmen.' . . . Nature proclaims to man: 'Thou art free, and no power on earth can
lawfully despoil thee of thy rights.' . . ."[49]

The foundations of the Liberal faith have been laid. To
men has come a new and revolutionary understanding of their
relationship to their God and to their universe. To complete
the creed, they have only to define their new relationship to
fellow men and to society.

The torch which has set to flames the City of God will
illumine the City of Man.

VI

The Liberal Faith: Civitas Hominis

M E N carry their past in their hearts and in their minds, as well
as upon their backs. History's greatest intellectual rebels are
understandable only in the context of the creeds and the conditions which they denied. And the rebels' faith itself always
is at least partly infused with ideas of ancient and majestic
origin—ideas which had carried hidden charges, exploding
only when ignited by the sudden flame of new and great
events, new and compelling human demands.

In tracing the emergence of the Liberal faith, therefore,
one must pause to observe, at least in broad perspective, the
frequently intimate interaction between the decay of one
creed and the rise of another. Violent as was the revolution
that created the Liberal Society, profound as was that society's
antagonism to the world of ideas it destroyed and supplanted,
yet—at certain critical points—the stone that went into the
new structure was taken from the old. . . .

England, in the seventeenth century, still lived within the fast-receding shadow of an age when men turned to their religion to discover the principles that were to guide them in the daily affairs of society. At the same time—with the Cromwellian era—she witnessed the first militant assertion of middle-class ascendancy, thereby outlining in broad pattern the course that the revolutionary growth of the new society was to pursue in other nations in the succeeding century. Logical it was, then, that England's national experience at this time should indicate close interaction between the legacy of ideas from the past and the Liberal faith of the future.

The Puritan movement it was which signified this interaction. The distinctive contribution made to the development of Liberalism by these English inheritors of the Calvinist tradition revolved around the Janus-like conception of the Economic Virtues. Reminiscent of an age when society's sanctions were essentially religious, these anointed canons of business enterprise were conceived to harmonize with the exigencies of the new economic forces: at one and the same time exalting the industrious pursuit of wealth, and stamping poverty as an ignoble mark of indigence and perversity.

Stated summarily, the issue of the Economic Virtues hinged on the Calvinist conception of the "Calling." As one of the time's most distinguished literary figures expressed it, "God doth call every man and woman . . . to serve Him in some peculiar employment in this world, both for their own and the common good. . . . The Great Governour of the world hath appointed to every man his proper post and province, and let him be never so active out of his sphere, he will be at a great loss, if he do not keep his own vineyard and mind his own business."[1] Diligently minding one's own business evolved in Puritan social thought as a divinely prescribed obligation binding on all men. Or, as Thomas Adams stated the matter, the true Christian "is blind to no man's cause, but best sighted in his own. He confines himself to the circle of his own affairs and thrusts not his fingers in needless fires."[2] One would have to search far, in the seventeenth century, to discover a more compact edition of bourgeois morality.

Men who thought in such terms as these could scarcely be expected to suffer the qualms of conscience that had plagued the medieval man of business whose religion furnished a less elastic code of economic ethics. The dictates of religion and the exigencies of business, for so long estranged, are now happily married—for better or for worse. In the mordant words of an historian of the period, "after all, it appears, a man can serve two masters, for—so happily is the world disposed—he may be paid by one, while he works for the other."[3]

The Puritan coin had yet another side. The same doctrine of the "Calling" which suggested to merchant or trader that his was a divinely sanctioned pursuit of business could be invoked with equal effect to convince the lowest classes of the realm that theirs, too, was a station dictated by Providence. Thus the poet Crowley put *The Beggars Lesson*:

> If God haue layede hys hande on the,
> And made the lowe in all mens syght,
> Content thiselfe with that defre,
> Ans se thou walke therin upryght.

Message of similar character was conveyed in *The Seruantes Lesson*, and *The Yeomans Lesson* concluded on this monitory note:

> Thus leaue I the, wyth threatenyng
> To the thy soulles damnation,
> If thou, mislykynge thy callynge,
> Wylt nedes change thy vocation.[4]

In prose, and with somewhat less presumption on the matter of the spiritual destiny of the poor, Arthur Young addressed a similar message to his age. His primary dictum was: "No society can, nor ever did exist, without the distinction of rich and poor. Equality is a romantic phantom of the imagination."[5] This much established, he continued: "If you talk of the interests of trade and manufactures, every one but an idiot knows, that the lower classes must be kept poor, or they will never be industrious; I do not mean, that the poor in England are to be kept like the poor of France, but the state of the country considered, they must be (like all mankind) in poverty or they will not work."[6] To render this social gospel palatable to the masses, Young's thoughts ran to religion—more particularly "that truly excellent religion which exhorts to content, and to submission to the higher powers." He urged that Christian churches multiply in the poor sections of England's cities, because "genuine Christianity is inconsistent with revolt, or with discontent in the midst of plenty. The true Christian will never be a leveler."[7] And thus did Arthur Young establish himself as one of the first in a long succession of leaders whose signal contribution to Liberalism would be conversion of Christianity into an instrument of economic discipline.

The statements of Arthur Young—and of innumerable Puritan divines who echoed his philosophy—should not be regarded as chance remarks of misanthropes but rather as commonplace pronouncements of what the age upheld as fact, not theory. They were, moreover, but threads in the texture of a social philosophy only beginning to take form. They were threads which could be followed back as far as the Reformation, when Luther—in his effort to assail monastic charity—had denounced the demands of beggars as blackmail; and when Calvin had branded almsgiving as provocation for slothfulness. In the final analysis, Puritan social thought was doing little more than echo Stockwood, who had stood up at Paul's Cross and cried out: "I conclude that all the large givings of the papists, of which at this day many make so great brags, because they be not done in the reverent regard of the commandment of the Lord . . . are indeed no alms, but pharisaical trumpets."[8] So Puritan England silenced the trumpets.*

* This discussion does not represent an ideological pattern read into the period by later historians. Men were *conscious* of the ideal affinity that was developing in Protestant thought for the new economy. One of the most striking passages in Montesquieu's *Persian Letters* illustrates this clearly. "The Protestant tradition," he explains, "grants the right of producing to everybody; it permits neither priests nor dervishes. . . . I dare say that in the present state

The second great instance of the recasting of religious thought pertains not to economic but to political developments. Here, too, the initial force stemmed from the sixteenth century; when the idea of a universal Christian society died, when the Church was removed as the guarantor of social order, and when the secular national state had emerged to fill the hiatus both in men's intellectual allegiances and in the institutional governance of their society. Now, in these seventeenth and eighteenth centuries, the Christian tradition began to bend before, if not support, these new political realities.

Perhaps the most succinct illustration of this change can be found in the writings of "the philosopher turned patriot," Lord Bolingbroke.[9] His view of the divine order of things political ran in this fashion: "As supreme Lord over all His works, His general Providence regards immediately the great commonwealth of mankind, but then, as supreme Lord likewise, His authority gives a sanction to the particular bodies of law which are made under it. . . . It follows, therefore, that he who breaks the law of his country resists the ordinance of God, that is, the law of his nature."[10] To ensure maintenance of these laws, Bolingbroke advanced what he considered the basic need: "There must be a religion; this religion must be national; and this national religion must be maintained in

of Europe, it is not possible for the Catholic religion to exist there for five hundred years. . . . The Protestants will become richer and more powerful, and the Catholics will grow weaker. . . . The Protestant countries ought to be, and are, more populous than the Catholic ones; from which it follows, firstly, that their revenue is greater . . . secondly that their lands are better cultivated; lastly, that commerce is more prosperous. . . . All this wealth [of Catholic monasteries] falls as it were into a palsy; it is not circulated, it is not employed in trade, in industry, or in manufactures. . . . Commerce puts life into all ranks among the Protestants, and celibacy lays its hand of death upon all interests among the Catholics." (Letter CXVIII.)

Pertinent to this discussion of Puritanism, one historian views French Jansenism as an analogous development: an essentially middle class creed that arose from within the Catholic framework of French thought because any other articulation of bourgeois ethics and religion had been impossible after the Calvinists (i.e. the Huguenots) were suppressed. "Savage persecution had stopped the growth of the Huguenot Church . . . but nothing could check the tendency of the middle class, at this stage of its ascent, toward some form of Puritanism." (Brailsford, H. N., *Voltaire*, p. 12.)

reputation and reverence."[11] The Viscount was an ardent Deist, and it has been aptly said of him that "whilst denying that 'traditional Christianity' was derived from a supernatural God, he affirmed that nationality came straight from the God of nature."[12]

The continent of Europe witnessed in this period two sweeping religious currents which reflected the same developments as the work of Bolingbroke. One was in France, the other in Germany; one in the seventeenth century, one in the eighteenth; one within Catholic ranks, the other within Protestant. One was Gallicanism, the other Pietism.

Seventeenth-century Gallicanism signified the spirit of national separatism, ever latent in France, which recurrently challenged the authority of the Papacy in its presumed dominion over the French clergy. It was inconceivable that the tide of national consciousness which had risen so precipitately in Reformation Germany would defer to the boundaries of states. A strong dynasty had been able to hold France to its traditional religious allegiance in the sixteenth century—but no dynasty could extirpate the political and economic forces that operated to make the Reformation a successful religious revolt. And the impact of those forces in France was registered in the surge of Gallicanism.

Summary manifestation of the spirit of Gallicanism came with the Gallican Articles of 1682, drawn up by the French clergy and stipulating the acceptable limits of Papal authority. In matters temporal, the king of France was to be regarded as in no sense subordinate to ecclesiastical power wielded by Rome. In matters spiritual, although the Pope was conceded "the principal part," the Articles insisted that "his judgment is not irreformable, unless it is backed by the approval of the church."[13] And in the eyes of the French clergy not the least significant and majestic segment of "the church" was the French clergy.

Almost constant in French religious thought of the time was this assertion of independence from Rome, and it became militantly manifest whenever a disputed religious issue came to the fore. Jansenism, the most critical heresy the Church faced after the sixteenth century, was in no small degree a new bottle for the old wine of Gallicanism. Not only intellectual movements but also political leaders—men like Mazarin and Richelieu—partook of the Gallican vintage. At least superficially, these Cardinal-statesmen tried to combine their allegiance to the Church and their compelling loyalty to the French nation. That their nationalist affiliations proved persistently dominant only stamped them as characteristic products of their era. That they succeeded in their dual roles, while Wolsey a century before had failed, testified eloquently to the progressive injection and insinuation of the new political forces into the framework of historic Christianity.

Like French Gallicanism, so German Pietism of the eighteenth century reflected and reinforced national self-consciousness. Still distracted and disunited by the awful effects of the Thirty Years War, the German people responded profoundly to the mystical message of Francke and his successors. In the course of a hundred years, Pietism made German soil fertile for the seeds of nationalism as few other movements could have done. It cut across class and provincial lines to give to a religious community representing all classes and provinces a corporate sense of sharing in the same ideas and emotions. Its exalted conception of individual *Wiedergeburt*, or regeneration, was easily translated into an ideal of national regeneration. Its tolerant belief that each religious sect was a noble reflection of some aspect of Christianity was converted into the analogous conception that each nationality was a divinely conceived embodiment of a given quality of the soul of humanity. The Pietist's sense of blind, utter dependence on God found logical political expression in the patriot's feeling of total and abject service and subservience to the nation. It is small wonder that Prussia's earliest patriots have been described as "enlightened Pietists."[14] For the tradition that went back to Luther's day bore its fruit in the dictum of the great Pietist-patriot, Friedrich Carl Moser: "We must believe in our fatherland just as we believe in one Christian Church. . . . "[15]

The third and perhaps most important bridge between religious and social currents of the seventeenth and eighteenth centuries was the growth of religious toleration. With enduring effect, the arguments of Bayle, Milton and Locke had registered on the conscience of the times. The foundations were laid by the first of these men, proclaiming that all religious "truths" were subject to suspicion; that the state was a purely secular institution; that morals and conduct were independent of religion; and that religious coercion impeded the free operation of God's gift to all mankind—intuitive apprehension of natural moral law. And it was the Puritan poet who made the tradition eloquent. "Give me the liberty," he cried, "to know, to utter, and to argue freely according to conscience above all liberties. . . . So Truth be in the field . . . let her and Falsehood grapple; who ever knew Truth put to the worse, in a free and open encounter?"[16]

But toleration was not an isolated social fact that came into being because of the eloquence of its advocates. However altruistic and humane may have been the motives of these thinkers, their ideals were translated into facts, in large measure, because those ideals harmonized with the demands of the new economy. For long, men like Petty, Pufendorf, and Sir William Temple had argued for the social and economic utility of religious toleration. They had observed the operation of a policy of toleration in the Netherlands. They had noted the commercial prosperity of the Netherlands. And they asked: is there no causal connection between these two facts? Their answer was a resounding affirmative.

Tolerance in religious affairs came, in short, because intolerance impeded the acquisition of national and individual wealth. Religious persecution was not only morally indefensible: it was expensive, and to a degree which men were not willing to pay. It destroyed national unity, thereby interfering with peaceful pursuit of business and distracting national attention from the more lucrative pursuit of commercial and colonial enterprise. It inspired emigration for conscience' sake, thereby banishing from the national economy some of its most productive groups—the Huguenots exiled from France, for example, or the religious refugees who went to the New World. And when the cost of religious intolerance became apparent, then its philosophical implications were examined and denounced. Once the man of commerce or finance concluded that national compulsion in matters religious meant appreciable loss of business, he was certain that it was contrary to the "true spirit" of Christianity. . . .[17]

Such were the ways of religious ideas and institutions while the Liberal Society was in the making: Calvinist endorsement of middle class business precepts: Gallican and Pietist mirroring of the spirit of nationalism: toleration signalizing and affirming the advent of the day when men ceased to consider their religion worth dying for. Thus was the old faith reshaped as the bourgeoisie bent to the task of creating a society in their own image.

The necessary preliminary labor had been performed. Religious ideas of the Western world had been recast. The Christian God had been indicted. The foundations of the faith of men who professed allegiance to Him had been shaken. Now the task becomes positive and constructive: the building of the City of Man. A City it shall be whose people will proclaim: "The special character of my religious faith is not to reap eternal happiness until I have secured my good fortune in this world."[18]

The Liberal faith, from the realms of science and metaphysics, had evolved two of its cardinal principles: Nature and Reason. In the construction of its social philosophy, both these precepts were applied and a third added: Humanity. These three—Nature, Reason, and Humanity—became the Trinity of the Liberal's world of ideas.

As in the case of religious thought, so with social philosophy men began to construct their creed equipped with concepts assimilated from the new science. Their fundamental belief was that the natural laws discovered and discoverable in the realm of natural science could be paralleled by similar laws in the field of humanity; as Spinoza had argued in the seventeenth century, men and human society were understandable (and, to the rationalist, hence governable) through the acquisition of laws comparable to those which governed physics. It was in fulfillment of this hopeful idea that men deduced from the new science the basic prerequisite for a new social philosophy: a new psychology of man.

Hobbes, Locke, Hartley, Condillac—these were the men who propounded the new psychology. In the eyes of discriminating intellectuals from the time of the Renaissance, the Christian conception of sin and of man's innately evil qualities had been suspect; but the capricious libertinism of the Renaissance period, while it might disparage the Christian idea, could never supplant it. Now—beginning with the *Leviathan* in 1651—a wholly new psychology of man was evolved. Sensationalist psychology, it came to be known as, and Hobbes summarized it simply: "There is no conception in a man's mind, which hath not at first, totally or by parts, been begotten upon the organs of sense."[19] With Locke the new psychology became popularized, and he described it in these memorable words: "Let us suppose the mind to be, as we say, white paper, void of all characters, without any ideas—how comes it to be furnished? . . . Whence has it all the materials of reason and knowledge? To this I answer in one word—*Experience*."[20]

This was the psychological gospel of the Enlightened and its import for the age was comparable only to that of Newtonian science. Implicitly and necessarily, it pulled the foundations from under the Christian conception of man. All doctrines, it announced, including those of the Christian religion, could never be accepted as being divinely inspired: they could never be regarded as more than fallible, if not accidental, intellectual results of each individual's necessarily limited experience. Spiritual grace had no place in such a depiction of man's mind. Man himself was born neither innately good nor innately bad; at birth, he was but an animate potentiality whose ultimate character would be dictated by experience. Man was neutral, a spiritual cipher.

But the new psychology said more than this. It proclaimed that since man was made by experience, the character of humanity could be dictated by control of that which alone provided the substance of man's mind and spirit—his intellectual and material environment. Wise education and wise legislation could achieve this end. The former, Helvetius announced, "is capable of effecting everything. . . . Education makes us what we are."[21] Complementing this, men must also learn of the puissant force that is legislation, for "the virtues and vices of a nation are always necessary effects of its legislation. . . . How can it be doubted, that virtue is not among all nations the effect of the greater or less degree of wisdom in the administration?"[22] With these instruments of education and of legislation ready for use, the capacity of humanity for change and improvement was infinite. Manipulate the environment, the new gospel proclaimed, and we shall have new men for old, good men for evil, wise men for fools. No wonder, then, that Fourier could anticipate a French nation of thirty million scientists as great as Newton and thirty million poets as great as Shakespeare.

In this fashion the whole Liberal faith, in the final analysis, came to rest its case upon its social philosophy. The old superstructure of religion was torn down—its objectives, its laws, its dogma, its graces. In man's own society of this world lay his future—a future whose character would be governed by his will if he were but instructed in its exercise. The Enlightened therefore believed they had found what Diderot had asserted was so necessary: a new instrument by which they might prove that their philosophy could make more good men than sufficient or efficacious grace.

Who were the men who set to realizing this new hope? From what intellectual and material environment did they themselves spring? What was their social creed? And to whose salvation was it directed—all men, or but a chosen few? . . . Locke and Burke, Voltaire and Montesquieu, Rousseau and Diderot, Adam Smith and Quesnay—these were but some of their names. Though their most glorious arena was France, yet they came from all parts of the world: there were Leibniz, Lessing and Herder in Germany; and in distant America there was Franklin, and there was Jefferson.

The social gospel of these men was a protest and a promise —a protest against a rigidified social organization built on dead religious and social premises, and constricting the naturally and, they believed, justly dynamic forces of the day; a promise that once those forces were released a new and better life for mankind would follow. These dynamic forces fighting for liberation were economic in origin, character and purpose. They constituted the economic upsurge of the new society: the economic aspirations of the ascendant bourgeoisie.

First great prophet to herald the advent of the new order was John Locke. He traced, in his social doctrines, the development of the political life of man from the original state of nature to the constitution of civil society. Rights men possessed in the former state, he explained, they sought to guarantee in the latter. Primary among these rights is the right to private property. "The great and chief end, therefore, of man's uniting into commonwealths, and putting themselves under government, is the preservation of their property."[23] The society so constructed was "nothing so much as a contract between a group of business men who form a limited liability company whose memorandum of association forbids to the directors all those practices of which the Stuarts had . . . been guilty."[24] It was an atomistic society, for rights were possessed by individuals before their association in a social organization: those rights being conceived as "natural" in origin, anterior to the development of civil society, and hence not contingent derivatives of the performance of social duties or fulfillment of social obligations. The state which Locke conceived thus was developed largely as an economic convenience, civil government serving as the sovereign guarantor of the rights of property. It was a political conception that was dignified and universalized somewhat by the theory of popular rights, which might make themselves articulate whenever civil government arrogated to itself more than its delegated functions. But the implicit right of revolution, with details undiscussed, was left by Locke as an academic issue. For what he was postulating, of course, was a retroactive vindication of the victory of the bourgeoisie in 1689—a political and economic settlement which he regarded as final, further modifications being conceivable but to be neither encouraged nor applauded. Pronouncement of such a sober blessing on middle class objectives was sufficient, in Addison's mind, to qualify Locke as "the glory of the English nation."[25]

Writing at the end of the seventeenth century, Locke had established himself among the earliest to solemnize as a social creed a new attitude of mind evoked by the political and economic aspirations of the bourgeoisie. Political thought of the eighteenth century perfected this art—the art of hallowing the efforts of the middle class to hurdle the contracting walls of state-mercantilism. This does not inspire a very exalted view of the men whose pens spilled forth such glowing phrases as the Rights of Man and the Dignity of Humanity. Neither does it vindicate the cynical historian in dismissing these men as enlightened pharisees or simple Mammon-worshipers. It demands that the historian remain constantly aware of this fact: that the intellectual ferment of the Age of the Enlightenment was inextricably interlaced with the evolution of capitalist economy, that then—as in almost all ages of history— men could not constrain the compelling impulse to project immediate objectives as natural universal principles, and that beneath every universal was a particular, a particular which pointed, directly or indirectly, to the demand of the middle class to be free to exploit on its own terms the vast new world of material things unfolding before its eyes.

It is so with Voltaire.

The bridge from English to French Enlightenment is formed by Voltaire's *Lettres sur les Anglais*; they may in fact be taken as the starting point for popularization of the Enlightenment. In them, as in almost all his works, Voltaire reflects the spirit of the bourgeois Liberal: the man who wants reform accommodating to immediate political objectives but is quick to fear too swift or deep-rooted a change. In terms of political organization, Voltaire—like the great majority of the Philosophes—yearns for an enlightened despotism, and what he criticizes in the Old Régime is its lack of enlightenment, not its despotic form of government. To him the English House of Commons (composed, of course, of the substantial men of property) is an idyllic social edifice—"in comparison with which the republic of Plato is merely a ridiculous reverie, and which might be thought to have been invented by Locke, or Newton, or Halley, or Archimedes."[26] To go beyond this—to allow the roots of social reform to reach lower than the middle classes—is to court chaos. It is, in the first place, futile. "It is impossible," Voltaire explains, "on our happy globe that men living in society should not be divided into two classes, the rich which commands, the poor which serves. . . . The laborer and the artisan must be cut down to necessaries, if they are to work: such is human nature."[27] In the second place, to try to elevate the status of laborer and artisan was not only futile but also unwise. For "the populace are oxen, which need a yoke, a goad and hay."[28]

It is so with Diderot.

Among the most radical of the Philosophes, yet Diderot propounded economic and political doctrines that integrated splendidly with bourgeois aspirations. The article on Representation in his great *Dictionnaire Encyclopédique* synthesizes European history, consciously and almost completely, along class lines; tracing the evolution of the modern state from the disorder of feudal times till the period when, as he so aptly puts it, "commerce and manufactures became state needs, and they demanded tranquillity."[29] In this historical context, he establishes his principles for political representation. Representative assemblies, he explains, "to be useful and just, must be composed of men whose possessions qualify them as citizens. . . . In a word, it is property which makes the citizen. Every man who is a property-owner in the State is concerned with the welfare of the State; and whatever be the rank which particular conventions designate him, it is always as a property-owner—it is by virtue of his possessions that he must speak and by which he gains the right of having himself represented."[30] The degree to which Diderot thus incorporates the bourgeois spirit was excelled only by the degree to which he disparages and scorns *"l'homme peuple"*—who are *"le plus sot et le plus méchant des hommes: se dépopularizer, ou se rendre meilleur, c'est la même chose. La voix du philosophe qui contrarie celle du peuple, est la voix de la raison."*[31]

It is so with Burke.

In three steps Burke constructs his outline of a simple system of natural liberty. Civil government, in a society being broken into autonomous spheres, is assigned that narrow zone of activity which Locke has already prescribed in classic form: "To provide for us in our necessities," Burke asserts, "is not in the power of government. . . . It is in the power of government to prevent much evil; it can do very little positive good in this, or perhaps in anything else."[32] Civil authority thus banished from the market place, Burke next defines the character and role of social classes. "Labor is a commodity like every other . . . an article of trade. . . . Labor must be subject to all the laws and principles of trade, and not to regulations foreign to them."[33] Charity toward the poor is urged by Christianity, Burke conceded, but its importance is "next in order after the payment of debts."[34] Now, as for the rich, they are "trustees for those who labor, and their hoards are the banking-houses of these latter. . . . I hear that middle men are accused of monopoly. Without question the monopoly of authority is, in every instance and in every degree, an evil; but the monopoly of capital is on the contrary. It is a great benefit, and a benefit particularly to the poor."[35] Finally, having thus defined the functions of government and social classes, Burke anoints his doctrines as humbly-spoken sentences of a divine social message. "The benign and wise Disposer of all things . . . obliges men, whether they will or not, in pursuing their own selfish interests, to connect the general good with their own individual success. . . . (We must pledge ourselves) manfully to resist the very first idea, speculative or practical, that it is within the competence of government, taken as government, or even of the rich, as rich, to supply to the poor, those necessaries which it has pleased Divine Providence to with-hold from them. We, the people [sic!], ought to be made sensible, that it is not in breaking the laws of commerce, which are the laws of nature, and consequently the laws of God, that we are to place our hope. . . ."[36]

What Locke and Burke, Voltaire and Diderot, were doing, in short, was the presentation of eloquent testimony to the fact that the synthetic framework of the mercantilist state was cracking. The omnicompetent state, completely emancipated from religious bonds, had emerged as a convenient, perhaps necessary, stage on the way to the individual economy of the Liberal Society. In the initial revolt from medieval economic organization, the state had been the logical refuge for men fleeing the old order, yet not self-confident enough to renounce all political authority over the economic sphere— whether in religious or secular forms. That confidence men at last derived from the fruitful results of commercial expansion and colonial exploitation, from the tangible achievements of the new science, from principles of the new science which seemed applicable to social philosophy, from the swift erosion of all institutionalized ethical authority. Men were at last ready to demand what Morellet so aptly called "freedom of conscience in trade."[37]

Translation, in classic form, of the exigencies of bourgeois economic ambitions into an integrated theory of political economy was made by the renowned Adam Smith. The economic creed of the great apostle of laissez-faire, moreover, was predicated on a specific conception of the nature and destiny of man. As expressed in *The Theory of Moral Sentiments*, this conception, probably more than any comparable philosophical statement of the age, was infused with the spirit, the world-perspective, which was inspiring the bourgeoisie in its victorious march to political dominion. "Man was made for action," Smith exclaimed, "and to promote by the exertion of his faculties such changes in the external circumstances both of himself and others, as may seem most favourable to the happiness of all. He must not be satisfied with indolent benevolence, nor fancy himself the friend of mankind, because in his heart he wishes well to the prosperity of the world." Man, Smith continued, must "call forth the whole vigor of his soul, and strain every nerve, in order to produce the ends which it is the purpose of his being to advance. . . . The man who has performed no single action of importance, but whose whole conversation and deportment express the justest, the noblest, and most generous sentiments, can be entitled to demand no very high reward, even though his inutility should be owing to nothing but the want of an opportunity to serve. We can still refuse it to him without blame. We can still ask him, What have you done? What actual service can you produce, to entitle you to so great a recompense? We esteem you, and love you; but we owe you nothing."[38] As surely as Machiavelli had embodied the individualism of the Renaissance, so did Smith embody the individualism of the Enlightenment, the immediate personal faith of the bourgeois: disdain for the contemplative life and regard only for action; depiction of man as created only to assert his sovereignty over his "external circumstances" and to bend them to his will; rigorous and demanding summons to man to "call forth the whole vigor of his soul" to reshape his material environment; almost unconscious association of adjective and noun in the derisive phrase "indolent benevolence"; reverent regard for nothing but the triumphant claims of success—and only a "we-esteem-you-and-love-you-but-we-owe-you-nothing" for those less swift and agile in the race for material acquisition.

The properly economic creed which articulated this spirit consisted, for Smith, of but two basic principles. The first was: "Every man, as the Stoics used to say, is first and principally recommended to his own care; and every man is certainly, in every respect, fitter and abler to take care of himself than of any other person."[39] And the second precept stated: every man, acting in and for his own interest, is "led by an invisible hand to promote an end which was no part of his intention"[40]

—that is, the well being of society. As in the realm of ethics, men had repudiated the claims of abstract virtue to govern individual desire, so now in the sphere of economics the philosophical technique of Liberalism declared null and void the exactions which, in an earlier faith, social welfare had imposed on pursuit of individual self-interest. As the previous century had established the equivalence of the industrious pursuit of business and Christian social duty, so now was posited—and this was obviously even more significant to men whose final goals were in human society of this world—the equation of the satisfaction of individual economic appetites and the sustained welfare of all humanity.

To such a wholly harmonious and singularly symmetrical society, civil government might be a crude and extraneous appendage—but for one fact. Civil government was needed to subdue those irresponsible members of society who might not be completely mollified by the we-owe-you-nothing dictum. This Smith perceived with characteristic clarity. "The affluence of the rich," he observed, "excites the indignation of the poor, who are often both driven by want and prompted by envy to invade their possessions. It is only under the shelter of the civil magistrate that the owner of that valuable property, acquired by the labor of many years, or perhaps many successive generations, can sleep a single night in security."[41] Conversion of government into a sedative for the propertied classes was, beyond doubt, one of the most astute and ingenious accomplishments of the Liberal economists.

Adam Smith was not alone in his triumph, for across the Channel the French Physiocrats had even anticipated him in their pronouncement, with almost equal skill and audacity, of the economic dogma of the new faith. They and their work have been appropriately compared with a religious sect. "They had their prophet in Quesnay, their creed in the *Table Oeconomique*, their inspired apostles in Mirabeau and Mercier de la Rivière, their *Summa* in the latter's *Ordre Essentiel*, their missionaries in men like Baudeau, their journal of faith in the *Ephémérides*, their organs of propaganda in the agricultural

societies and provincial academies, even their affiliated statesmen in men like Turgot."[42]

Pertinent basic principles of the Physiocrats did not mate-
rially differ from those of Smith. Their ideal social objective,
as Quesnay said, was "to obtain the greatest possible increase
of enjoyments by the greatest possible diminution of ex-
penses."[43] The guiding precept for social organization was
simple, according to Du Pont de Nemours: "The social laws
established by the Supreme Being prescribe only the preservation of the right of property, and of that liberty which is insep-
arable from it."[44] Civil government was expected to accept
gracefully the doctrine that its function "is not to make or
administer new laws but to maintain a condition in which the
laws of nature freely operate."[45] Men of the sympathies of
Burke and Smith could do little but applaud vigorously such
pronouncements.

Perhaps more eloquently and succinctly even than Smith,
Mercier summarized the whole of the new economic faith—
its secular base, its gospel of sensationalist psychology, its
trust in natural economic laws, its buoyant self-assurance. . . .
"Each of us, by favor of this full and entire liberty, and
pricked by desire of enjoyment, is occupied, according to his
state, in varying, multiplying, perfecting the objects of enjoyment which must be shared amongst us, and thus increases the
sum of the common happiness by increasing his private happiness. And so each in the sum total of the common happiness
would take a particular sum which ought to belong to him.
We must admire the way in which every man becomes an
instrument to the happiness of others, and the manner in
which this happiness seems to communicate itself to the
whole. Speaking literally, of course, I do not know if in this
state we shall see a few unhappy people, but if there are any,
they will be so few in number and the number of the happy
will be so great that we need not be much concerned about
helping them."[46]

The Liberal Society is not going to be much concerned.

From the fields of religious thought and scientific speculation had come the bone and muscle of the Liberal faith. Its
nerve was its economic creed. So, in effect, had one philosopher
taught: *Pecunia nervus rei publicae*, Bodin had asserted.
Nerve, bone and muscle—they were the substance from which
was fashioned the man of the new society, with his newly
defined relationship to his God, his universe, his neighbor.

Natural Man was the name given this creature of the intellectual revolution. He was to possess what Hume called "the
constant and universal principles of human nature."[47] He was
divested of those supernatural accretions which falsely had
been attributed to him by historic Christianity. The "constant
and universal" character of this man was to be ascertained by
no studious investigation of the Scriptures, no garnering of
dicta pontifically postulated by the Christian fathers, but by a
sober study of the "facts" of human existence—which would
yield data and laws as inflexibly true as the laws of physics.
Before engaging in such empirical search for truth, the investi-
gators admitted to one preconception—and it was an important one. This Natural Man is not natively depraved, burdened by any legacy of sin: he is "naturally good, and . . . by
institutions only is he debased."[48]

Since the wide vault of Heaven was a hoax, Natural Man's
destiny, his supreme goal, was in this life. Since only external
forms such as institutions debased him, only reform of such
institutions could elevate him. By such reform, scrupulously
following the dictates of Reason and Experience, he could
make perfect the good life on this earth. And in this great
adventure, his most immediate task was to claim his natural
freedom—freeing his mind from the shackles of ignorance,
his spirit from the yoke of religion, his senses and passions
from their bondage to abstract virtue, his body from the
slavery of arbitrary oppression.

Thus the creed took form. It had its heaven, its means of
salvation, its doctrines of faith. "For the love of God they substituted love of humanity; for the vicarious atonement the
perfectibility of man through his own efforts; and for the

hope of immortality in another world the hope of living in the memory of future generations."[49] It was the cry of the religious prophet, this cry of Diderot: "O blessed and sacred posterity! support the unfortunate one who is tyrannically ruled, you who are just, you who are never corrupted, who avenge the righteous, who unmask hypocrisy, who unseat the tyrant: sure idea, consoling idea, never desert me. Posterity for the Philosophe is what Heaven is for the religious."[50]

Reason, Nature, Humanity—these were the great, compelling dogmas of the faith: all, however, strangely subject to quiet qualifications, subtle modifications. Reason connoted both more and less than purely rational collation of empirically established truths. It meant, fundamentally, a non-authoritarian method of discovering truth—and this could and did embrace not only rationalism, but also immediate and intuitive apprehension of basic philosophic certainties. Unalloyed Reason was not followed, because it often pointed to facts or ideas which could not be integrated in any facile fashion with men's philosophical preconceptions. Thus, for example, when Reason designated atheism or agnosticism as the logical conclusion of the time's religious premises, the Philosophes retreated. They wanted no mere denial of Christianity or confession of ultimate ignorance. They wanted and they constructed a positive faith.

It was in like manner with Nature. Nature signified the profound belief that the affairs of men in society could be made subject to laws comparable to those governing physics, and the "natural" came to be a self-sustaining ideal. Yet here again the prophets of Liberalism retreated from the logical conclusion. If the "natural" was an ideal state, how was one to avoid the conclusion of Whatever is, is right? That would not be an inspiring doctrine for a revolutionary faith. Hence men qualified their categorical approval of the "natural," and they sought instead what they could define in their own terms, namely: those things which were "constant and universal" in Nature.

The idea of Humanity was no more than a still inexplicit

utilitarianism: the doctrine that the worldly happiness of humanity was the final absolute good. Although the writings of the men of the Enlightenment already suggested the answer, only the future would reveal clearly to what extent this third dogma of the Liberal faith would be qualified—to what extent the well being of "Humanity" would be limited and defined to signify the well being of a social class.

Aspiring to conversion of theory into fact, the Enlightened Liberals assumed a character and organizational technique reminiscent of the Jesuits. They did not seek to popularize their creed, to inspire the national masses with a new faith. Rather they sought to inject their ideas at the top stratum of society, to convert the political masters of the state to their cause, and in this way to conquer. They were flexibly organized into an international revolutionary society. Headquarters were near Geneva, where resided Voltaire—Loyola of the Philosophes. From all Europe, philosophic leaders came to consult with their acknowledged chief, to encourage him in his fight for ideals that were their ideals, to fortify their own courage by partaking of his. From England, from Germany, from the Netherlands, from France, they came—men whose characters and ambitions ranged from a Diderot to a Boswell. Almost all conceived themselves to be engaged in an international crusade against the forces of superstition, ignorance, injustice. In the *Encyclopedia* they had what approximated a Liberal Manifesto.

Exultant culmination of this insurgent rush of revolutionary ideas came in the dogma of Progress, which translated into an article of Liberal faith the zealous self-assurance which each of the Enlightened felt within himself. It was a logical, inevitable conclusion to the thought of the period. Were not men innately good? If they were not born so, as Rousseau believed, were they not, as Locke and Helvetius proved, capable of being made good through wise education and legislation? Were not men capable, guided solely by their own naked reason, of achieving the good society? Had not natural science already shown the path of the future, by its massed material advance, opening up vast and unexplored stores of wealth, and by its laws which were applicable to all fields of life and thought? Was not the good and the happy society a natural consequence, if men were but liberated, each to pursue his own path of self-interest?

These questions men answered with a categorical affirmative. They were convinced, with Voltaire, that

> . . . Monarchs by their grace
> Can shape the minds and morals of our race.[51]

From Bacon, through Fontanelle, Saint-Pierre, Diderot, Turgot, Rousseau—they all were possessed of the assurance that a humanity which for centuries had been enslaved and degraded by worship of false gods would now cut its way through the last crumbling ruins of a dying world into the clean, clear land of the future. For individuals, a fuller, finer life would reward those who were guided by the light of reason. For political states, a strong and productive land would be theirs if they but observed and respected the natural harmony of individual self-interest and social welfare. For the world of nations, peace and security would come to an age which could have no more wars; for all wars thus far had been either religious or dynastic, and peace would naturally follow when men dispensed with religion and overthrew dynasty. Rousseau, Saint-Pierre and Kant had specific programs which would ensure this imminent international harmony.

To set this faith in an historical context, men turned to contemplation and reassessment of their past. Far back in the age of antiquity they saw a light in the great eras of Pericles and of Augustus—a light which they hoped to rekindle and carry on, inextinguishable, into the future. The glories of the ancient world—men saw through the eyes of Gibbon—had been trampled upon when insurgent Christians "erected the triumphant banner of the Cross on the ruins of the Capitol."[52] After that had fallen the sullen darkness of the Middle Ages, the long night of humanity. . . . But now the light of knowledge and truth was burning again with new and stronger flame. Now had come science, the revelation of the world of nature, the awakening of man to a new sense of awareness and comprehension and power, the surging sense of inner strength that needed the nourishment of no false prayers, no false rituals, no false graces. Now . . . "human perfectibility is in reality indefinite. . . . The progress of this perfectibility, henceforth independent of any power that might wish to stop it, has no other limit than the duration of the globe upon which nature has placed us. . . . What a picture of the human race, freed from its chains, removed from the empire of chance as from that of the enemies of progress, and advancing with a firm and sure step on the pathway of truth, of virtue and of happiness!"[53]

Such was the dream of Condorcet. It was the dream of the Enlightenment.

In every age some men do not understand. When a social class fails to understand, it is lost. When a social order fails to understand, it too is lost. It was so with the Old Régime in the Age of the Enlightenment.

The middle class understood. It stated its demands. When its demands went unheeded, it ceased merely to demand. Fortified by material gain, sustained by a creed which dignified its ambitions, buoyed by vigorous sureness of its own strength and its own worth, goaded to fury by a social order which perpetuated a class structure and a political control geared to an economy that was dead . . . the bourgeoisie revolted.

The others did not understand. They talked of the right— and like all humanity, they could not help calling it a divine right—of one man to rule many, and the solemn obligation of the many to obey the one. They said that the men who were talking about freedom and the rights of the many were mad, traitorous, blasphemous. They believed that all such ideas could finally be driven behind the walls of the Bastille.

They built palaces at Marly and at Trianon. They built

yet another a short way from Paris, at a place called Versailles, and this was their best. They spent more than a million livres to build it. Thirty thousand men went to work to divert the waters of a nearby river. Many died of malaria. But they succeeded in bringing water to Versailles, so that the lawns would always look fresh and richly green, the fountains would always play, and the lake would always display clean, clear reflections—reflections never of the dirty *canaille*, but of men and women who strolled leisurely along its edge, fine men and women with fine clothes, with courtly airs, cultivated manners, witty speech.

They moved into their new house. They lived in a little world made in their own image. They were secluded from the rest of the people, from the Many they were to rule, the Many they did not understand.

Now they would never understand. . . . Many decades later Carl Sandburg wrote lines that seem to have been conceived to describe what happened here.

> Now the stone house on the lake front
>   is finished and the workmen are
>   beginning the fence.
>
> The palings are made of iron bars
>   with steel points that can stab the
>   life out of any man
>   who falls on them.
>
> As a fence it is a masterpiece,
>   and will shut off the rabble
>   and all the vagabonds and hungry
>   men and all wandering children
>   looking for a place to play.
>
> Passing through the bars and over
>   the steel points will go nothing
>   except Death and the Rain and Tomorrow.*

But tomorrow in France will be 1789.

* From "A Fence," by Carl Sandburg, in *Chicago Poems*, courtesy of Henry Holt and Co.

Men in Arms: The New World of Facts

In the sixteenth century, one of Martin Luther's most famous pamphlets had summoned men to rise and destroy the "walls" of the Catholic Church. The "walls" were those devices, doctrinal and institutional, by which the Church had maintained its dominion, spiritual and temporal. Those walls were breached.

Men forging the Liberal Society, however, had soon been confronted with new walls—those of the secular-mercantilist state. Although its ideals and institutions were fundamentally divorced from the faith and the society of the medieval era, yet the new state inherited from that period the habit of institutional regulation of the affairs of men, especially those affairs which were conducted in the market place. In time, the insurgent forces of the new economy found the walls of this state to be as constrictive as had been the walls of the Church.

Unwilling to be checked by a second line of institutional defense after the first had successfully been passed, the masters of the new economy resolved to seek peacefully to lower the walls of mercantilism or to reconstruct them according to their own design. Where and when this could not be done and the state remained stolidly entrenched in its authoritarian ways, there and then they stormed the walls in force. The bourgeoisie, determined to translate theory into fact, took up arms.

Experience of the Netherlands in the sixteenth and seventeenth centuries anticipated much of what was to come. As the center of the economic gravity of the Western world swung in its arc from the Mediterranean to the Atlantic, the Netherlands were in the front ranks of the advancing economy. With an industry rarely equalled, the Dutch converted their small homeland into a secure economic base for a far-flung colonial and commercial superstructure. Founding of the Dutch East India Company in the first years of the seventeenth century, the West India Company shortly after, the Bank of Amsterdam in 1609—these were the tangible evidences of the rise of the Netherlands. Commercially, she became the greatest trading nation of the world; industrially, Europe's greatest entrepot nation; and financially, the money market of Europe —all sustained by a commercial empire that reached from India to New York. In such a land, the bourgeoisie could not but come to guide the nation's political and economic destiny and dictate its cultural pattern. Accordingly the Netherlands became the strongest national seat of Calvinism on the continent; she became, in her civil government, religiously tolerant and at length completely secularized; and she became the cradle of middle-class republican ideals of government.

With such a national character and *weltanschauung*, the Netherlands' subordination to Spain became the major political incongruity of the Europe of the sixteenth century. When Philip II came to the throne of Spain, danger of revolt was almost at once evident. The Dutch middle class, Calvinistic and commercially ambitious, found intolerable Philip's policies of tight commercial regulation and religious oppression. Nationalistic fervor galvanized latent religious and economic grievances into open revolt.

While the men of the Netherlands were dying for national freedom, the Dutch bourgeoisie developed lucrative techniques in the art of converting war into an economic asset. Behind the lines of battle, the burghers of the Low Countries applied themselves to the task of building up "an oligarchy of the middle classes in the guise of democracy."[1] Towns and provinces came under the administrative dictation of merchants and financiers eager to insure a political environment conducive to the fullest exploitation of the economic possibilities of international warfare. To these men the rewards of trade were more compelling issues than the merits of a national cause. Dutch armies found themselves besieging towns that were being fed from behind their own lines. Similarly, in the bloody course of the Thirty Years War, the Dutch traders—anticipating a technique to be perfected in a later age—sold food and war materials to both belligerents, despite the fact that one side was nominally their own. When Frederick Henry, Dutch military leader, asked a Dutch merchant why he would betray his own country to sell supplies to the enemy, he was rewarded with an answer that spoke eloquently of the whole bourgeois spirit. "Trade must be free to all, and must not be interrupted by war," the merchant exclaimed. "We men of Amsterdam have a right to trade wherever we please. If I should have to sail into Hell in order to make a profit, I would do it even if I should risk burning my sails."[2]

The fight for independence that was finally won in 1648 signified more than a large-scale manifestation of bourgeois economic practices; it marked the advent of the day of anarchic nationalism in Europe. William the Silent of Holland had appealed to Europe against Philip II with the claim that he, too, had the right to be a sovereign ruler; that Holland, like Spain, had a national integrity which other, temporarily more puissant, European powers could not violate. Thus the Treaty of Westphalia, ending the Thirty Years War and proclaiming Dutch independence, virtually gave a legal sanction to international anarchy. Holland became an autonomous nation, with all privileges and immunities attaching thereto: she could now make alliances and declare wars, build colonial empires in her own name, conquer her own foreign peoples and oppress her own minorities. On the walls of Europe's political structure men already were learning to inscribe the rights of individuality, writ large in the letters of nationality.[3]

The success of the Low Countries, however, brought but brief prosperity, thanks to a consummately suicidal political policy pursued by the middle class. Fearful of too stringent economic regulation from the center, they kept the civil authority of the Netherlands scattered on provincial fringes. They engaged in a consistent overspeculation which made banks collapse like houses of sand. And eager to avoid too onerous taxes, they refused to consider seriously the military position and strength of their country, despite a consistent competition with commercial rivals which made imminent the prospect of war. Like some of their descendants in the third and fourth decades of the twentieth century, they garnered profits at the cost of their lives. War came—and brought the inevitable disasters. And the commercial leadership of Europe passed across the English Channel, where a more mature and circumspect bourgeoisie was proclaiming its destiny.

The Puritan Revolution, despite all its religious implications, was the first of the great attacks by the masters of the new economy upon the national citadels of political power. And here, as in Holland, religious and economic factors interlocked in bringing victory to the bourgeoisie. For the rising antagonism to the Stuarts, before the revolt of 1641, derived from resentment of controls as much economic as religious.[4]

While the religious authoritarianism of Stuart England was the consequence of the exclusive establishment of the Anglican Church, the social regulations were typical of a mercantilist state's exercise of control over its economy. Inherited in large measure from Elizabethan days, these controls supervised almost all business operations with fastidious thoroughness: labor contracts, terms of apprenticeship, poor-relief, wage regulations, price fixing. To extricate themselves from such a web of governmental controls, men of business came to believe and urge that regulation, as one of them expressed it, should be left to "the judicious merchant whose labor is to profit himself, yet in all his actions doth therewith benefit his king, country and fellow-subjects."[5]

When economic and religious oppression stemmed from a single source, as with the Stuarts, it was logical that the Puritans would be among the first propelled toward revolt, in their own theology having dignified, if not hallowed, industrious pursuit of business enterprise. In fact, both religious and economic issues were far from new. The religious problem of the Stuart era was nothing more than a legacy from the English Reformation period. Henry VIII's break with Rome had been largely political in character; under Elizabeth it had assumed some properly religious tone; but it was not till now, with the Puritan revolt, that the work of the English Reformation was truly consummated. At the same time, the economic regulations imposed by the Stuarts constituted, in reality, no more rigid or constricting employment of civil authority than had been exercised by the Tudors. What was lacking, however, was that deferential concern for middle class interests for which the Tudors had been so conspicuous. What made the issue crucial was the fusion, for the first time, of the economic and the religious problems.

Neither the course nor the causes of the Puritan Revolution qualified it as a popular uprising. Less than 3 per cent of the people of England ever participated actively in the struggle between monarchy and parliament. And as the war progressed, Cromwell and his New Model Army made it increasingly evident that they regarded themselves as competent to decide their country's destiny, with no guidance from men in Parliament. Victories at Marston Moor, at Naseby, and at Prescot confirmed the pretensions of the army and seemed to lend substance to their claims. They fought with a ferocity of attack seldom matched in the history of warfare— a ferocity that could rise only within men who conceived their cause as integral to a divine plan, a ferocity that was not to reveal its true proportions until Cromwell's men marched in Ireland, to engage in the butcheries of Drogheda and Wexford.

From Pride's Purge in 1648 and the creation of the "Rump" Parliament, the Puritan protest divested itself of any lingering qualities of a popular movement. Parliament, itself being far from representative of the people, was converted into a mere auxiliary to the army. When even the "Rump" became recalcitrant, Cromwell dissolved it and summoned "Barebone's" Parliament—a convention, almost exclusively composed of Puritan leaders, which succeeded remarkably in including in its ranks virtually all the ambitious and inept provincial leaders of England who aspired to the title of statesmen. When this proved a fiasco, the Instrument of Government was promulgated in 1653, establishing Cromwell as Lord Protector.* From that time until the temporary restoration of the Stuarts, Cromwell was master of England in as thorough a degree as any of his Stuart predecessors. Rebellious members of Parliament were excluded by force from participation in that assembly, arbitrary assessments on the property of Cavaliers were as capriciously imposed as any of the illegal tax measures of the Stuarts, and military rule was inflicted on twelve districts of England when popular revolts reflected mass unrest.

At this point the historian of the period is confronted with an interesting question: What had happened to the masses of the people, the army of apprentices and journeymen, artisans and peasants—those men who had, in the last analysis, made the Puritan protest articulate and militant, who had believed in that protest as firmly as their bourgeois allies? The answer is that both very much and very little had happened to them: they had experienced a great deal, and they had won next to nothing.

In this seventeenth century in England, there were, in effect, two revolutions.[6] The first was led by Cromwell and it was a resounding success. Its ultimate objective was to render the English state apt for the purposes of men of property. Its leaders were men who had no patience with Christian constriction of the naturally vigorous impulse to make and amass wealth; who maintained, on the contrary, that active and remunerative vocational endeavor yielded not only great economic rewards but also substantial spiritual profit; who denied that the poor had any distinctive claim on divine mercy and love; who proclaimed that, on the contrary, it was the rich who were society's benefactors and therefore most merited divine commendation and guarantee for the perpetual exer-

* One historian has dated the "Thermidorean reaction" in the Puritan Revolution from the establishment of the Protectorate: *cf.* Brinton, C., *The Anatomy of Revolution*, p. 245.

cise of their political and economic prerogatives. This first revolution brought to the men of property control of the army, freedom from the threat of arbitrary taxation and arbitrary imprisonment, and termination of social disciplines, be they religious or regal.

The other revolution failed. It was a social revolution engaged in by men who had suffered keenly from the emergent social order, who struck at authoritarian state and established church as what seemed the most evident and concrete causes of that suffering, who believed that the new economic forces and the increase in material wealth could and should yield benefits to all. When they had placed Cromwell in London, they had waited for the radiation of social decency and justice which all expected to shine forth from the center of their realm. They waited in vain. For no new day came, and the light which men had misunderstood was only the flashing, glancing flare that rose from the center of a battle fought in a long, unbroken night.

The men who led this vain social revolution called themselves Levellers and Diggers. In many respects their radical program of social reform anticipated demands of the proletariat of the nineteenth century. Vigorously they asserted that it was "an undeniable equity that the common people ought to dig, plow, plant, and dwell upon the Commons without hiring them or paying rent to any." Simply and directly, they turned to their government and said: "Open and present the state of community to the sons of men."[7]

But such words did not harmonize with the temper of the men who decided such issues. The more militant of these social rebels Cromwell answered with the sword—and the following invocation: "It is some satisfaction if a Commonwealth must perish, that it perish by men and not by the hands of persons differing little from beasts! That if it must needs suffer, it should rather suffer from rich men than from poor men, who, as Solomon says, 'when they oppress leave nothing behind them, but are a sweeping rain.' "[8]

Thus Cromwell's God anointed the revolution of the bourgeoisie, for which men of all classes had died. The Restoration period was but a brief diversion of the irresistible new forces, and the Glorious Revolution of 1688 secured for all time the victories of the Puritan revolt. The advent of William of Orange suggests in retrospect the days of Holland's commercial glory, that glory which now becomes the pride of the little scepter'd isle across the Channel. Thinking of the future, one sees now the English stage being prepared for the drama of the great commercial rivalries of the eighteenth century, the stupendous colonial wars which will lift England into the front-rank of national empire-builders. Only one ominous event seems foreshadowed: the revolt of the American colonies. For the English revolution of the middle class, while it buttressed the triumphant home economy, yet turned England's colonial policy onto that road which led to disaster in 1776.

For the moment, however, there was only the imperturbable joy of victory. A victory it was which brought that double delight of being both economically fruitful and religiously consecrated. First of the great succession of revolutions whose climax France was to bring a century later, this was the only one in which traditionally religious overtones of thought were conspicuous. Three centuries later, commemorating the victory of Naseby, one of England's most distinguished literary figures and one of the stalwarts in the ranks of the Victorian bourgeoisie was to recapture poetically the spirit that was the Puritan Revolution. . . .

Of evil was the root, and bitter was the fruit,
    And crimson was the juice of the vintage that we trod;
For we trampled on the throng of the haughty and the strong,
    Who sate in the high places, and slew the saints of God. . . .

Like a servant of the Lord, with his Bible and his sword,
    The General rode along us to form us to the fight. . . .

Their heads all stooping low, their points all in a row,
   Like a whirlwind on the trees, like a deluge on the dykes,
Our cuirassiers have burst on the ranks of the accurst,
   And at a shock have scattered the forest of his pikes. . . .

Down, down, for ever down with the miter and the crown,
   With the Belial of the Court, and the Mammon of the Pope;
There is woe in Oxford Halls; there is wail in Durham's Stalls:
   The Jesuit smites his bosom; the Bishop rends his cope.

And she of the seven hills shall mourn her children's ills,
   And tremble when she thinks of the edge of England's sword;
And the Kings of earth in fear shall shudder when they hear
   What the hand of God hath wrought for the Houses and the Word.[9]

While the victorious and sanguine bourgeois of England might envision with unbounded delight the quaking of Rome's hills, there were men who lived and labored by other mountains who did not tremble perceptibly when they thought of the edge of England's sword. By the Green Mountains, the Alleghenies, and the mountains of Virginia, these men lived.

On the rim of the expanding world of the new economy, the American colonists worked out their livelihood under the most constrictive aspect of the mercantilist system: its insistence on the right of the "mother" country to exploit all colonial possessions for her own gain. Until the 1760's England's supervision of her colonies' economic activity had been little more than academic. Then bonds that had been held so loosely were suddenly tightened by the victorious and assertive middle class of England. There followed swiftly that fateful succession of regulatory measures which were the immediate pretext for the revolt of the colonies: the Proclamation of 1763 reserving all western lands, prohibiting their exploitation by men from the seaboard and transferring their title to Canada; the trade restrictions—Sugar Act, Townshend Acts, Tea Act; and the tax laws—Stamp Act and the second wave of Townshend Acts. The policy of Britain, implicit in these acts, was simply an effort on the part of the Tory-merchant oligarchy to pass to the colonies a substantial share of the expense of the empire that had but recently been wrested from France. But to the colonists it seemed that the prospect was opened of converting America into a subsidiary adjunct to the economic machine of England. That prospect they were willing to fight.

Within the colonies, by the middle of the eighteenth century, a strong and competent merchant class had developed a highly rewarding trade and industry—which they felt quite capable of handling without the unsolicited advice or guidance of Britain. Along with this had been woven a pattern of social and economic ideas from the threads of the Liberal philosophy coming to maturity on the other side of the Atlantic. Men of the colonies, in fact, had given a sharp edge of reality to ideas which, in Europe, had as yet gone little further than the salons of Paris. The conception of the social contract, for example, became understandable and concrete to men who had in actuality formed such compacts when they had come to a new world to fight nature and natives. In such a world, too, the state of nature was no Rousseauvian political abstraction, but the environment of men's daily lives, the immediate and intensely real environment in which they had to earn their livelihood. And on the frontier, severed from the comforts and urbanities and complacencies of a developed community, men had come to know what the "individual" meant. Then, pervading much of this environment, had come the strong strain of religious freedom—and, in New England particularly, the Puritan tradition, with its concomitant benediction for individual enterprise.* A bourgeoisie in com-

* Strikingly reflective of this tradition was the New England clergyman who addressed this sermon to his congregation:

"It were better for the most of the people to be poor than to be born Rich. For such have, in general, really a more comfortable Life here and far less dangerous as to the next Life. . . . A Rich man has a *miserable* life: for he is always full of Fear and Care. . . . Whereas a man that has but Food and Raiment with honest labour, is free from these Fears and Cares. . . . We *need* to *pity* and *love* Rich Men. . . .

"But what am I doing? If this discourage People from seeking after Riches,

mand of a strong economic machine and fortified in such a manner by tradition and environment was, indeed, a dangerous group to endeavor to harness with unprecedented and unexpected mercantilistic regulation.

But in addition to the ascendant American bourgeoisie's resentment of efforts to control them by their British counterpart, there was, in the colonies, another wave in the tide carrying men toward the events of 1776. For here, as there had been in seventeenth century England, there were effectively two revolutions. In addition to the sectional revolt of thirteen colonies against an imperial centralization jeopardizing the prosperity of the bourgeoisie, there came a class upheaval from the bottom of the colonial social structure—a revolt against local vested interests and propertied classes.[10]

In almost every colony class issues were sharply drawn and had roots in every sphere of social organization. The economic problem hinged largely on the efforts of the lower classes to escape a mounting burden of debt and taxation—a debt owed to, and a tax system imposed by, the wealthy merchant and landowning class on the seaboards. Paper money, stay and moratorium laws were the commonest legislative weapons of the masses along the western frontiers, fighting desperately to escape complete subjection to their creditors. In the political realm, these same western masses challenged repeatedly the iniquitous franchise and representation system by which merchant and landowner held with firm hands all state legislative assemblies. Finally, these men protested against what seemed to them marks of social stratification and symbols of discrimination: the establishment of the Anglican church in the southern colonies, and the maintenance of slavery, which seemed to be the badge of privilege.

In all parts of the colonial settlement these issues were

it would be a great Detriment to the Publick, if not the undoing of the world. ... A rich Man is a great friend to the Publick, while he aims at nothing but serving himself. ... Each man coveting to make himself rich, carries on the Publick Good: Thus God in His Wisdom and Mercy turns our Wickedness to Publick Benefit." (Cited by Corey, L., *The Crisis of the Middle Class*, pp. 72-73.)

more than debated; they were fought. In the South, the rising of the Regulators signified the outburst of western resentment in North Carolina. In Pennsylvania, where the frontiersmen were exceptionally bellicose and well organized, the rebellion led by the Paxton Boys in '64 had reflected the same underlying issue. And in New York—where, Governor Bellomont said, the "whole province" had been "given away to thirty persons"[11]—there recurred furious popular riots against rents, debts and prices, ten years before the outbreak of the Revolution.

It was from this tremendous current that there came the most vital force making for the Revolution. Popular resentment against the local ruling groups was ingeniously canalized into resentment against British hegemony. Middle class discourses convinced the masses that all grievances were provoked by London's Board of Trade, an interpretation which, for the bourgeoisie, was correct. Thus bourgeois resentment against England actually was reinforced by popular resentment against the bourgeoisie.

The war itself was, in some substantial senses, a civil war. Middle class and laboring masses joined hands against the old landed aristocracy, the Loyalists, who joined forces with His Majesty's armies. The home country conducted the war with an air of calm condescension, complacent in the presumption that Lord North was a statesman and Howe and Cornwallis were generals. Yorktown was a shock.

With peace, it was apparent that one revolution had succeeded. The thirteen colonies were free from foreign political rule. But the social revolution came to a vastly different conclusion—the revolution to which the masses of the people had surrendered their hopeful allegiance. This revolution failed.

For a time, in the period of the Articles of Confederation, it seemed that success might possibly be achieved. The Articles provided that loose framework of government which the mass of the people wanted. The radical leaders of the Revolution had smashed British instruments of coercion with no intention that domestic agencies of the same character be established by a centralized system of executive, legislative and judicial control.[12] At the same time, the several new state constitutions incorporated at many points the demands of these radical leaders; widened franchise was established, and liberal monetary policies induced an inflation which often came close to cancelling the obligations of the debtor class. All this, superimposed on a currency issue during the war which itself had come close to half a billion dollars, marked this period as the day of the debtor.

But the day of victory was short. In Massachusetts, commercial interests had captured the constitutional convention and had rigged the state constitution against the western farmers. Taxes were thrown almost entirely onto land, currency was frozen, debtors were evicted from their homes by force. Daniel Shays and a handful of men rose in bitter protest and marched on the Springfield arsenal. But they were quickly broken by the state militia, aided by a cavalry force recruited from the more exuberant of Harvard College's undergraduate body, who pursued their retreating foe westward with the relish that a good foxhunt always inspires.

Shays' uprising was sufficient to frighten the propertied classes throughout the land. Affairs were clearly getting out of control. The President of Congress entered into negotiations with Prince Henry of Prussia, to ascertain the latter's interest in the prospect of an American throne. But events moved quickly and satisfactorily along another line, equally acceptable to the forces of business enterprise. The Congress of the Confederation, on February 21, 1787, invited the several states to send delegates to a convention in Philadelphia "for the sole and express purpose of revising the Articles of Confederation," as the call stated. That "revision" was to become the Federal Constitution.

Along with the understandable urge for a government stronger than that provided by the Articles, what was the driving impulse behind this swift move? It stemmed from the groups associated with large property rights, security investments, the fur trade, manufactures, and foreign commerce.[13]

And what did they seek? They desired a government that would insure that political stability which was necessary for national economic expansion; a government that would pacify and organize the West for speculative penetration, pay interest and principal on government securities, enter fruitful commercial treaties with the nations of Europe, institute a single tariff system, organize a navy to hunt down piracy, guarantee the validity of contracts, establish a fixed currency, project the horizon of business on a national scale—and recapture the state and national citadels of political power which had fallen into the hands of the radical leaders. The day of the debtor was over.

To attend the Constitutional Convention, through the notes made and preserved by Madison, is to hear succinct and frank expression of the political conceptions that will come to dictate the character of the new government. Gerry of Massachusetts sounds the keynote: "The evils we experience flow from an excess of democracy. The people do not want virtue, but are the dupes of pretended patriots."[14] Sherman of Connecticut echoes these sentiments and urges that the people "should have as little to do as may be about the government." Madison declares himself in favor of the policy of "refining the popular appointments by successive filtrations." And he adds, reading the lessons of history into his political conceptions: "Democracies have ever been spectacles of turbulence and contention; have ever been found incompatible with personal security or the rights of property; and have in general been as short in their lives as they have been violent in their deaths."

Injection into the political debate of the theme of "the rights of property" makes the unseen gallery of future generations wonder if the men on the floor of the Convention are going to voice openly the economic conceptions on which their political doctrine is predicated. They graciously do so. Gerry rises and strikes a profound response in the minds of fellow delegates with this proclamation: "The people have two great interests, the landed interest, and the commercial, including the stockholders. To draw both branches from the people will leave no security to the latter interest; the people being chiefly composed of the landed interest, and erroneously supposing that other interests were adverse to it." Butler of South Carolina applauds verbally, believing in, as he says, a government "instituted principally for the protection of property, . . . itself to be supported by property." The delegates have obviously studied their Locke to good advantage.

The words of the *Federalist* seem to be finding echoes in the hall of the Convention. "From the protection (by government) of different and unequal faculties of acquiring property, the possession of different degrees of property immediately results," Madison had written in famous Article X; "and from the influence of these on the sentiments and views of the respective proprietors, ensues a division of the society into different interests and parties." To perpetuate this natural and just division, "our government ought to secure the permanent interests of the country against innovation." The function of government, in short, is, among other obvious civil functions, this: "to protect the minority of the opulent against the majority."

And so, knowing his *Federalist* intimately, Hamilton speaks from the floor of the Convention and pronounces his economic creed to his fellow delegates. "All communities divide themselves into a few and the many. The first are the rich and well born, the other the mass of the people. The voice of the people has been said to be the voice of God; and however generally this maxim has been quoted and believed, it is not true in fact. The people are turbulent and changing; they seldom judge or determine right. Give therefore to the first class a distinct, permanent share in the government. They will check the unsteadiness of the second, and as they can not receive any advantage by a change, they therefore will ever maintain good government. . . . Nothing but a permanent body can check the imprudence of democracy." Such was Hamilton's unwritten economic preamble to the Constitution.

The political document inspired by these beliefs, the Federal Constitution, substantially succeeded in imbedding in the basic law of the land the will of the men who feared "an excess of democracy." In the way of financial safeguards, it forbade any of the states either to undermine the stability of the national currency or to impair in any way the obligations of contracts. In the way of political safeguards, it harnessed popular will with an elaborate system of check, balance, and qualification: sovereign powers were divided between the several states and the federal government; national power was divided into three compartments, sealed as tightly as possible; and all laws, state or federal, were to be subject to review by a court removed as far as possible from the people. In addition to and reinforcement of all these prescriptions, the President was to be elected by a system twice-removed from the people; the Senate, elected by the state legislatures, was to serve as a conservative check on the popular lower house; and the amendment process was made tortuous in the extreme. What was achieved, in short, was establishment of a central government strong enough to affirm and safeguard the economic ascendancy of the bourgeoisie—yet a government far enough from the reaches of the people and sufficiently confined to specified functions to ensure against its capture and use by men not wholly convinced of the finality of middle class dominion. What the whole political framework signified was the reestablishment of what had been the centralized rule of Britain—but now the civil power was exercised by the native propertied class.

It has been said—with considerable justice, in reference to the achievement of political order—that "seldom has a class acted more wisely for the good of the whole."[15] But it should be added that seldom has a class spoken with more audacious presumption that its was the voice of the people. This was a fact perceived clearly by men of that time—by none more clearly, perhaps, than by Patrick Henry, eloquent representative of the Piedmont masses and militant protagonist of that social revolution which now seemed lost. In his fight against ratification of the Constitution, he rose on the floor of the Virginia state convention and exclaimed: "Is this a monarchy, like England—a compact between prince and people, with checks on the former to secure the liberty of the latter? Is this a confederacy, like Holland—an association of a number of independent states, each of which retains its individual sovereignty? It is not a democracy, wherein the people retain all their rights securely."* He continued, stating with accuracy that "here is a revolution as radical as that which separated us from Great Britain." And he concluded with an admonition whose implications went to the roots of the great debate. "You are not to inquire," he warned, "how your trade may be increased, nor how you are to become a great and powerful people, but how your liberties can be secured."[16]

Thus was drawn from the outset the issue which was to dominate the struggles of coming years. The Revolution was, indeed, but one dramatic phase of a social process of change whose beginning was long before the founding of Jamestown, whose sweeping scope was confined to no one nation nor even continent, whose full course would not yet have been run even a century and more later. The nation founded on these terms was to be, in the nineteenth century, the theater of the great Liberal adventure, the crucible of the Liberal economy. But now, for at least a moment, midst the strident noise and clash of competing creeds and greeds, men paused—and thrilled to the exultant cry of Thomas Paine. . . . "O! ye that love mankind! Ye that dare oppose not only the tyranny but the tyrant, stand forth! Every spot of the old world is overrun with oppression. Freedom hath been hunted round the globe. Asia and Africa have long expelled her. Europe regards her as a stranger and England hath given her warning to depart. O! receive the fugitive and prepare in time an asylum for mankind."[17]

An electric current shot from America to the Old World. Charged with the voltage of the example of the colonies

---

* The Constitution which Henry was attacking, it must be recalled, as yet contained no Bill of Rights.

across the ocean, theories moved swiftly toward conversion into facts. The field of battle ceased to be the gorgeous salons of the Age of Classicism, its most terrifying weapon the definitive epigram: instead—the streets of Paris, marched by angered, hungry men.

In the early and middle decades of the eighteenth century, intellectual and political leaders had believed in the reality of "enlightened despotism"—the political compromise of the Philosophes by which the noun of the old order would be qualified by the adjective of the new. When such a compromise was proved a manifest impossibility; when men lost all patience with *lits de justice* and *lettres de cachet*, grafting tax-farmers, parasitical nobles, indolent clerics, and extremely unenlightened kings; when the masters of the emergent economy saw that the political order was too inelastic to be made to bend to their will and would have to be broken; and when the work of the colonies in America revealed that old and long-established political orders could be broken . . . then men took to arms. In Sorel's phrase, events had reached a point at which there had to be either a great king or a great revolution. The former being nowhere in evidence, the latter was the only alternative.

Immediate occasion for summoning of the Estates General in 1789 was furnished by the bankruptcy of the French state, an eventuality which had seemed imminent for almost a century. Class backbone of the Estates General was the bourgeoisie, which stood in an indeed enviable relation to the government. For the political machinery of France—by virtue of the state's chronic habit of borrowing money—had become, in effect, "the property of the middle class." The Estates General was less a revolutionary assembly than a meeting of the government's creditors, convening to liquidate the estate of a client whose financial reputability was gone—who was, in fact, bankrupt.[18]

When the Estates General convened, it was not looked upon as a parliamentary body with legislative powers, much less an instrument of revolution. It met to effect—as the *quid pro quo* for allowing assessment of taxes—specific reforms demanded by the *cahiers*, which were petitions for redress of grievances addressed to a king whose dethronement was seriously contemplated by no substantial group of the people. But, like the Constitutional Convention which had met in the American colonies but a few years before, the Estates General rushed beyond the bounds of delegated authority, constituted itself the National Assembly, and proceeded to remake the state and society of France.

The Revolution now inaugurated admits of summary characterization. Whether the historian considers the composition of this National Assembly and of future conventions, the most consistent demands of the petitioning *cahiers*, the voiced objectives of the great revolutionary leaders, or the mass of exhorting pamphlets and journals distributed throughout the period—at all points he is witnessing the insurgent affirmation of the bourgeois social ideal. The truth was clearly perceived by the Chevalier de Moret, writing in 1789. "We are wrong," he said, "in thinking of the Third Estate as a single class; it is composed of two classes whose interests are different, and even opposed."[19]

Reading quickly from right to left, one can know the essential character of the Revolution from the pronouncements of its leaders. In one of the Western world's most famous pamphlets, *Qu' est-ce que le Tiers Etat?* the Abbé Sieyès summarized at the outset of the Revolution the bourgeois pretensions to political dominion. Fervently and audaciously, he publicized the Third Estate as the whole of the nation. "Who will dare assert the Third Estate lacks any requisite for forming a complete nation?" he exclaimed. "It is the strong, robust man, one of whose arms is still chained. . . . So what is the Third Estate?—All, but an all that is trapped and oppressed. What would it be without the privileged order?—All, but an all free and flourishing. . . . The Third Estate embraces all that belong to the nation; and any not of the Third Estate cannot be regarded as being of the nation."[20] And Mirabeau—the man who, with Sieyès, was the

Revolution's most outstanding early leader—reaffirmed these ideas explicitly. "Le souverain et les propriétaires . . . ," he avowed, "voilà ce qui compose l'Etat": the political sovereign and the propertied classes—they alone constitute the state. And would it not be a rewarding day when these two could be made to coincide?

The Revolution did indeed, at times, race in a bloody course toward a more radical social reconstruction, and solid men of property were often terrified by what seemed an uncontrollable monster of their own making. But ever present were leaders to reassert the necessary economic principles which were to be so zealously guarded. Danton, in 1792, anxiously denied any rumor "that friends of liberty may do harm to the social order by exaggerating their principles. Well, let us now eschew all exaggeration, let us declare that all territorial, individual and industrial property shall be for ever maintained."[21] And Robespierre, radical father of the Cult of Reason and chieftain of the Committee of Public Safety in its most terroristic period, was equally categorical about such economic issues. "Equality of wealth is a chimera," he announced. "For myself, I think it even less necessary for private good than for public happiness. It is much more important to make poverty honorable than to proscribe riches. The cottage of Fabricus need not envy the palace of Crassus. . . . Let us therefore honestly declare the principle of the right of property."[22]

It was thus honestly declared in the great constitutional documents embodying the principles of the Revolution. The Declaration of the Rights of Man, although it was thoroughly secular in all its affirmations but this last, concludes on the beatific note struck in famous Article XVII: "Property, being an inviolable and sacred right, can in no case be taken away except where public necessity, legally determined, clearly demands it, and always on condition of a preceding indemnity." Even clearer exposition of the bourgeois political settlement was made in the Constitution of 1791. This document was predicated on one of the most expedient double-standards by which a single class ever incorporated its ambitions into general law. To all Frenchmen were granted certain fundamental rights of opinion, speech, justice and opportunity. These were *passive* rights, and their beneficiaries were known as *passive* citizens. In addition, however, there were *active* rights, logically the political prerogatives of only *active* citizens; these alone had the right to vote. And was there not but one intelligent way to establish oneself as an *active* citizen—qualifying oneself as a member of the propertied class by virtue of payment of taxes not less than the equivalent of three days' labor? It is doubtful if men yet understood how great would be the number of "passive" citizens in the Liberal state of the coming century.

When the Constitution of the Year III was presented to the Convention, it was Boissy d'Anglas who introduced it. His speech was a judicious summary of the middle class political outlook. "We ought to be governed by the best men," he averred, "and these are they who are most instructed and most interested in the maintenance of the law. Now, with very few exceptions, such men will only be found among the owners of property who thereby are attached to their country, to the laws which protect their property, and the social peace which preserves it. . . . A country governed by property-owners is a true civil society; one where men without property govern is in a state of nature."[23]

Such, then, were the energizing principles behind the French Revolution. Whatever, in thought or in deed, was projected beyond these prescribed limits of bourgeois objectives was committed to failure. Ideals that transcended these, conceptions of society that struck deeper social roots than these, men who died for purposes other than these: those ideals were conceived and those men died in vain. From this came that terrifying sense of aimless, fruitless bloodletting which was so much a part of the tortuous course of the Revolution: the risings of the Jacquerie and the razing of the hated manors . . . the tumultuous night of August 4, 1789, when feudal privilege pronounced its own sentence of death

. . . the almost convulsive radical turn in the course of the Revolution that reached its climax when twelve men ruled a nation through a Committee of Public Safety . . . the stupendous clash of men in arms along the western line of France, where armies of successive coalitions of frightened dynasties tried to plunge their swords deep into this monster of republicanism astalk in western Europe . . . the feverish surge of patriotism that rose in the French nation in repelling these attacks, identifying the cause of the Revolution and the national integrity of France . . . all this—revolving madly around the constant focal objective that France might become "a country governed by property-owners."

Whether deliberately or not, the advent of Napoleon secured the victory of the French middle class; for behind all the grandiose patriotic flourishes of his hegemony, there prevailed all the political accommodation to bourgeois economic objectives which the businessmen of France could desire. Financial reform embraced a refined tax system, strict economy in government, and the founding in 1801 of the Bank of France. Public works—roads, canals, bridges, and fortifications —lubricated the fast-developing machinery of the national economy. The Concordat with the Papacy—established in the same year as the founding of the Bank of France—secured the triumph of Gallicanism, an insurance against papal interference in the national life of France. Finally, the Civil Code, legal depository of the work of the Revolution, affirmed the victory of bourgeois economics. "Its most precious maxim," wrote Judge Lahary, "is that which consecrates the right of property; everything else is but the logical consequence of this fact." As the French historian, Glasson, wrote: "To tell the truth, the worker was pretty completely forgotten in the Code."[24] But to tell the whole truth, he was not; he was forbidden to organize and he was forbidden to strike.

Before the French Revolution had come to this conclusion —perhaps in order that it might so do—it had assumed the proportions of a religious crusade. For the men who saw themselves as architects of a new and good society, the faith in

Nature and Reason took on a quasi-religious form. What the Calvinist's God of might had been for the Calvinist, and what dialectical materialism was to be for the Marxist, Nature and Reason were for the revolutionary Liberal.

As with Calvinism and Marxism, old religious faiths had to be broken, and the Liberal of the French Revolution set himself to the task of destroying traditional Christianity. The whole Christian structure was to be razed. Substantial beginning was made with the Civil Constitution of the Clergy and surrender of the tithes, which reacted most heavily on the impoverished country priest and was greeted with most enthusiasm by the rural landowner who had borne the burden of the priest's salary. In effect, the clergy of the Church was now rendered completely dependent on the national state for their livelihood. Few disputed that the action of the National Assembly was anything but dictatorial; but, as one historian of the Revolution says of the Assembly, "it would not recognize of itself that it was less representative of France in the matter of religion than in any other; for it was the intellectual and professional class only, to which nearly all the deputies belonged, that was Voltairean or anti-Catholic; the mass of the people were still attached to their ancient faith."[25] The Assembly's was a policy completely in accord with the spirit and letter of the principle Voltaire had communicated to Frederick the Great: extirpate the nation's religion in the avowed interest of the intellectual elite.

Initial impetus behind the assault on the Church, however, was not the National Assembly's preoccupation with Voltaire's religious thinking: that impetus came from the financial crisis of the French realm. That crisis could not be met by a policy of confiscation of wealth; for by such an act the Assembly would outrage the bourgeoisie's reverence for private property, so recently made explicit in the Declaration of the Rights of Man. There emerged—in the collective mind of the Assembly—one type of property which was not sacred: the property of the Church. Confiscation of this property was vindicated, as Thouret explained, by the fact that the Church was a corporate, fictitious person, whereas the guarantee in the Declaration extended only to individuals. How strangely different was to be the definition of legal individuality but a few years later!

The militant campaign to destroy Christianity reached its crescendo in the years 1793 and 1794. It was inaugurated in the provinces, under the astute guidance of revolutionary missionaries known as representatives *en mission*. The practice of the Catholic faith was hunted underground with an insistency and competence which, in most particulars, anticipated the technique to be invoked in most finished form against the Jews by the German Gestapo in twentieth century Nazi Germany. In the rising heat of national feeling inflamed by the invasion of foreign armies, the Alfred Rosenbergs of the French Revolution summoned men to abandon all old allegiances and, in the words of Fouché, "to substitute the religion of the Republic and natural morality for the superstitious and hypocritical cults to which people are still so unfortunately devoted."[26]

Actions followed exhortations. The provincial town of Ris-Orangia, in the center of the Ile-de-France, set a useful example in deposing the traditional local patron saint of Christianity and instead inserting the figure of Brutus. Mennecy partook of the same inspiration, the villagers removing busts of Peter and Paul from their homes, supplanting them with Lepeletier and Marat, and finally setting up a statue of Liberty on the altar of their parish church.

Quickly the central government in Paris absorbed and directed the infectious new cult. In the fall of 1793, the Assembly witnessed approvingly a parade by the "Section of Unity," grotesquely attired in the robes of priests and presenting, with manifest relish, a jovial parody of Catholic worship; and the spokesmen of the delegation pledged themselves to no religion other than that of Reason, Liberty, Equality, and the Republic. Then the substitution of the Republican for the Gregorian calendar was at once a religious and a political action, creating new festivals for old, substituting the tenth day for Sunday, and replacing the names of saints with those "of objects which constitute true national wealth."[27] In October of 1793, Marie-Joseph Chénier, speaking for the Committee of Public Safety, summoned his cheering audience in the National Convention to emancipate itself from the Christian tradition and to kneel at the altar of the fatherland. "Wrench the sons of the Republic from the yoke of theocracy which now weighs upon them," he cried. "Then, freed from prejudice and worthy to represent the French nation, you will be able, on the ruins of fallen superstitions, to found the one universal religion, which has neither secrets nor mysteries, whose one dogma is equality, whose orators are the laws, whose pontiffs are the magistrates, which asks no incense from the great human family to burn save before the altar of our country, our mother and our deity."[28] Thus men of the Liberal faith openly urged and applauded that eventuality which Bossuet had warned would follow from the upheaval of the Reformation: consecration of the nation-state as the pontifical institutional organ of the Liberal Society.

The will for concrete manifestation of the new faith was satisfied by Robespierre and his Worship of the Supreme Being. Inspired by Rousseau—who had urged use of religious forms to cultivate the "social sentiments"—Robespierre, in atmosphere clouded with the incense of patriotism, spoke his gospel clearly: "To the legislator anything that is of practical utility to the world is true. The idea of the Supreme Being and the immortality of the soul is a continual reminder of justice: therefore, it is social and republican."[29] And so, too, the Religion of Expediency found a Messiah.

On the 17th Brumaire 1793, the Commune and Department of Paris ordered that on the next tenth-day there should be held at the cathedral of Notre Dame the "Festival of Liberty and Reason." Then and in that place a statue of Liberty should be erected "instead and in place of the former image of the Blessed Virgin."[30]

On the 20th Brumaire, it is done as it has been ordained. "To Philosophy," reads the new inscription in the great

cathedral. The busts of four philosophers are enshrined—
Voltaire, Rousseau, Montesquieu, and Franklin. Upon the
altar flames the Torch of Truth. Now, in procession up the
wide aisle, file young girls dressed all in white. On their heads
are wreaths, and in their hands are lighted torches. Around
their waist flashes the bright tricolor sash. Suddenly, upon the
altar there emerges a beautiful woman, her gown of blue, her
cap of red. She is Liberty. She is also a famous actress, and
this is her greatest dramatic role. She receives the homage of
the Republicans, who stretch their hands toward the altar
where she stands, as they sing Marie-Joseph Chénier's hymn:

> Come, Holy Liberty, inhabit this temple,
> Become the goddess of the French people.

No more shall Notre Dame be a cathedral of the Christian.
It shall be the cathedral of the Liberal.

VIII

The Mountains Made Level

For more than three centuries men and ideas had been on
the march. Protesting and promising, vilifying and vindicating, indicting and inciting: they had fashioned the Liberal
Society. The revolution of the times had made level the mountains of the past.

The building of the Liberal Society can be conceived and
summarized as forming two titanic revolutions: each pro-
gressing through three stages, each producing a fundamental
change in the institutional structure of society. The first was
the Revolution of the Church. Achieving triumph in three
distinguishable phases of its evolution, it had derived its economic initiative from the signal commercial developments
which breathed life into the still bodies of medieval cities. Its
philosophical affirmation came with the work of those who

broke the medieval synthesis, the Renaissance humanists, and the intellectual precursors and leaders of the Reformation. Finally, its conversion into triumphant institutional fact was achieved in the actual Protestant revolt from the Church and the splintering of the unity of Christendom.

The second Revolution was that of the State. Its economic base was laid in the sixteenth-century commercial revolution; its intellectual ferment reached climactic proportions in the age of the Enlightenment; and its victory was assured by the great political revolutions which brought political forms into correspondence with economic realities.

Of the two great institutional changes, the first followed, from the Revolution of the Church: the substitution of the unity of money for the unity of faith.[1] International bonds had formerly sprung from an intellectual and religious harmony which found its concrete representation in the Vatican. In a world freed from the dominion of the Church and swept by new economic forces, not popes but the international financiers became the men whose wills and deeds commanded the respect, if not the total allegiance, of nations. Bardi and Peruzzi, Medici and Fugger: it was they who took up the stations, once filled by popes, behind the thrones of nations. It was they who were able to determine, to large degree, the fates of men and governments: to sustain economic activity— or to throttle it; to command wars for national economic interests, as ecclesiastic leaders had once urged them for religious causes, and to provide financial sinews for their prosecution; to maintain rulers or, in effect, to issue financial interdicts against their rule. In the new world this was the international bond of decisive force: the bond of money.

It was within the frameworks of states that there came the second signal institutional change. Even after the emancipation of the secular power from the dominion of the Church, the Church remained in a role equivalent to a state within a state: it raised its own taxes, it paid its own agents, it had its own legal code and its own ecclesiastical courts, it exercised control over education and public opinion. The vital institutional change implicit in the creation of the Liberal Society was not only the destruction of this semi-independent power, but also the displacement of this by another state within a state: the realm of private business and private proprietorship.

The basic character of the Liberal Society dictated this change. As the religious basis for political authority slipped away, the economic took its place; men came to test and to measure the validity of political action, not by its translation of a prior moral purpose, but by its acceleration of the economic progress of the community. And of this shift in foundations, the rise of the autonomous realm of business enterprise, as a state within a state, was the tangible evidence. At the end of the eighteenth century its prerogatives were far from completely defined, but in a short time it was to claim and exercise more than a few of the privileges which had formerly attached to the Church. It levied, in effect, its own taxes in the form of prices adjusted by the consuming community no more than government taxes were—less so, in fact. Within limits fixed by the exigencies of business and the size of the labor supply, it paid to its workers a dictated wage. It claimed for itself exemptions from many forms of state taxes. It exalted its right to free economic enterprise as solemnly as the Church had avowed its right to free religious endeavor, unencumbered by state supervision. And it claimed for its gospel of material acquisition and accumulation the power of bringing to all society happiness and virtue. This was the institutional essence of the Liberal Society.

In retrospect, one can see to what degree the Reformation era had signalized the first militant movement of the forces that were to make the new order. Total assault on a Church which had been the stone and cement of a whole social structure meant, logically and inevitably, the wreckage of that structure. The elaborate medieval synthesis of ideas and values was shattered. Totally and irreparably it was broken by the detachment and isolation of man's conception of his relationship to his God from his conception of his relationship to fellow men. A man's religion became a personalized experience in which there were but two participants, God and man himself: God distant and omnipotent, man weak and depraved. In this conception of religion, man's role in society could find little or no place: religion became an "internal" matter, the affairs of the world were "external" issues, and between the two was no spiritual bond. In the final analysis, everything in society would instruct and arrange itself, as Luther had said; and if it did not, the poor could still follow Luther's prescription to go and seek their riches in the earth. Thus the Reformation achieved the *sine qua non* of the Liberal Society: emancipation of the problem of man's relationship to man in society from the effective dominion of religion.*

In a yet more positive and specific sense, the Reformation era had anticipated and propelled the vital political, economic and intellectual forces behind the Liberal creed. In the political realm, the necessary substitution of state for Church as guarantor of social order had been propelled by the Lutheran gospel of the satanic character of the massed ranks of common people who must be governed by the princes, those gods of this world. Equally effective, especially cast in the Puritan mold, had been the Calvinist benediction of the basic bourgeois economic urges. Finally—mystical and medieval in tone as had been much of the Reformation—yet it opened the way for the great intellectual ferment to follow and to culminate in the rationalists' trial of the Christian God. For that indictment derived ultimately from two facts: one, Luther's conception of God as unapproachably distant in His arbitrary omnipotence; second, science's erection of an autonomous natural world, material and self-sustaining. The picture of a natural world governed by natural laws and a Divinity

* This vital disintegrative process is approached in a similar, though distinct, manner by Gerhart Niemeyer. He summarizes the issue thus: "The idea of the state gradually conquered the entire theory and practice of European politics. The characteristic feature of the new phenomenon was that it drew a line between political matters and the rest of life, that it separated public affairs, or the 'State,' from private relationships, or 'Society.' The feudal system knew of only one comprehensive social order, comprising authority, law and morality in one undifferentiated cosmos of norms." (*Law without Force*, p. 29.)

whose decrees and very existence stood beyond the reaches of reason—such a combined picture left only a central void, and the traditional religious allegiances of men were not of tough enough fiber to bridge that gulf. In this fashion, these two ideas united in forcing the exile of the Christian God from the realm of the known, rational world. If He existed, at best he was *Deus Emeritus.*

In the centuries following the Reformation, the centuries in which men built the Liberal Society, the forces of religion, of science, and of social thought—all seemed to synchronize and to interlock. Politics and religion were like mirrors, one to the other. As the Renaissance despot had been a political facsimile of the Calvinist God, so the enlightened despot of the Philosophes was a political translation of the god of the Deists. Both the Almighty and the king were expected to obey consistently the natural order of reason. God became something like a constitutional monarch whose throne was in the Heavens, rather than in Versailles.*

In analogous fashion, science and social philosophy reflected and reinforced each other. The conditions which science demanded for its success were the same as those the new economy demanded.† The psychology and temper of science were perfectly geared to the spirit of bourgeois business enterprise: precision, experiment, daring, realism—these were virtues of the merchant as well as of the chemist and physicist. Science's triumphs affirmed men's power over nature, and this lent substance to the Liberal dogma of progress. Science denied arbitrariness and caprice in the cosmos: Liberal political thought was directed to the task of removing arbitrariness within the state.

Philosophic individualism and economic individualism

* Lord Bolingbroke, in his *The Idea of a Patriot King*, expressly stated this thought: "God is a monarch, yet not an arbitrary but a limited monarch, limited by the rule which infinite wisdom prescribes to infinite power." (*Works*, Vol. II, p. 382.)

† Almost all the Philosophes studied some branch of science: Voltaire studied chemistry, D'Alembert was a physicist, Diderot did minor work in almost all the sciences, and even Rousseau wrote a botanical dictionary.

were currents that flowed from the same central stream. Both the philosopher and the man of business sought to exploit his own realm on his own terms, and both were supremely confident that the harvest would be almost boundless. Once men had accepted the axiom that the individual was capable of realizing his own spiritual salvation, the next step was already half-taken: the individual was equally competent to attain his own *economic* salvation. Neither religious dogmas nor state regulations, neither Church councils nor state boards of trade, could inhibit the individual in the cultivation of his own garden. As it had been stated so succinctly, let there be "freedom of conscience in trade." Hence, in a sense Adam Smith completes an evolution that was continuous from the Reformation: the latter substituted prince for Church as governor of social behavior; Locke and his school substituted Parliament for prince; and Adam Smith concluded that, with few exceptions, no agent of social discipline need interfere with the individual in his pursuit of happiness and wealth.

Viewing a revolution from the summit of the society which it created, men are easily led to the assumption that the success of that revolution was somehow inevitable, that it was— as some of the Enlightened might have believed—in the "nature" of things. But while philosophers and rationalizing intellectuals might conclude that mighty forces of the universe made their own destiny triumphant, the actual leaders of the Liberal revolution—men of courage and consummate daring—rested secure in no such assurance that a kind fate would secure final victory. For at almost every stage of the struggle, they met militant opposition. To large extent, though not exclusively, this protest and criticism emanated from the Church. Insistently and incisively, men of the Church denied the basic premises of the Liberal faith.

Most frequent target of Catholic attack in the Age of the Enlightened was the Liberal's conception of the "Natural." As one thinker inquired, "Where then is it established, this natural religion that we hear of endlessly? Nowhere on earth.

It is in the heads of our philosophers, and different in each head. We defy them to form a fixed symbol that may serve as a rule of faith."[2] Extravagant indeed was the confusion surrounding this whole Liberal conception. Revering empiricism, the Liberal had first conceived the Natural as the actual: the concrete, existent facts revealed by the new science. But finding it impossible to remain purely and perfectly empirical in thought, the Liberal quickly had come to regarding the Natural as also the good and the just—that is, the ideal. The logical consequence was that, when he spoke in reverent or exultant tones about the "Natural," the Liberal was rarely certain in his own mind whether he meant the what-is or the what-should-be. Pope's identification of the two was the most facile resolution of the dilemma, but it would be at best unconventional for rebels from a social order to accept the dictum that whatever was, was right. Essentially the same problem evolved from Christian theology, in seeking to explain how God, who willed all things, yet willed only the good and the just; but here at least the inner logic of Christianity had been maintained by the doctrine of sin and of man bringing evil through his free and corrupted will. In the Liberal creed no such resolution was to be found, and in the mind of the Liberal of the Enlightenment the actual and the ideal connotations of the "Natural" never became disentangled.

Another object of repeated Church assault was the Liberal dogma of the essential goodness of man and the consequent inevitability of progress. To the Catholic thinker, the doctrine of man's innate goodness seemed little more than a philosophic veil behind which men were seeking to vindicate their abrogation of all moral authority. That man was a perfectible creature, and that his destiny was one of unrelenting progress —that this doctrine should be propounded by the Enlightened, who scorned Christian mysteries as baseless appeals to the credulous seemed to men of the Church more than a little ironic.

A third point in the Liberal faith at which the Church

injected a sharp wedge of criticism was the atomistic view of society which seemed implicit in Liberal individualism. By virtue of their conception of a state of nature antedating civil society, the Liberal had endowed men with rights that had no roots in civil society itself but derived from this anterior natural state. There was to these rights, then, no contingent basis in the fulfillment of social obligations: the way was open for men to view them as unconditional prerogatives. To men speaking in the name of Catholic social philosophy there seemed nothing firm that stood between this doctrine and the chronically atomistic society.

The entire Church criticism followed from the traditional conception of three kinds of Christian duties: duties of men to God, to their neighbor, and to themselves. Duties to God had been qualified and diluted by the Liberal faith until they became, at best, passive and tacit recognition of the existence of a mechanical Prime Mover. Duties to one's neighbor, as conceived in Christian thought, Liberal doctrine had discarded as superfluous: the simple, undisguised pursuit of self-interest was decreed the true manner of serving one's fellow man. There existed for the Liberal no moral obligation to work, immediately and directly, for the welfare of society; as Frederick the Great had said, virtue was only "a happy disposition of the mind, which has many faculties, one of which impels us to fulfill duties to society for our own satisfaction."[3] Finally, man's duty to himself—construed by Christianity to mean recognition by man of his spiritual destiny and performance of all that worked toward its fulfillment —came to be conceived by the Liberal as nothing more complex than the individual's obligation to work for his own happiness and welfare.

It was, then, when Liberalism seemed to emerge as little more than philosophic apologetics in the interest of economic acquisitiveness, that Church criticism became most vehement. One of the most eloquent expressions of this came from Bossuet, who, even at Versailles, plagued his audience with his sermon on poverty. "Oh, ye poor, how rich you are!" he exclaimed. "But oh, ye rich, how poor you are! . . . If you do not carry the burdens of the poor, yours will crush you, the weight of your ill-spent wealth will carry you into the pit; but if you share with the poor the burden of their poverty, taking part in their misery, you will deserve altogether to share in their privileges. . . . [It is not enough] to open the eyes of the flesh upon the poor, it is necessary to consider them with the eyes of the intellect. Blessed is he who understands. The man who truly understands the mystery of charity is the one who considers the poor as the first children of the Church, who, honoring their position, thinks himself obliged to serve them; who only hopes to share in the blessings of the Church by means of charity and brotherly intercourse."[4] In these words were no construction of abject poverty as a disguised blessing and state to be endured in perpetuity; no hallowing of the most degraded occupation as a divinely appointed vocation; no benediction for acquisitiveness as a magic sword which, in one and the same motion, stabbed for individual profit and struck for social well being.

Meanwhile, although cultural values were fast accommodating themselves to the new order, men of letters joined men of the Church in competent and eloquent challenges to the ascendant creed. A lone, raging critic, Jonathan Swift, attacked the complacent optimism of his age, persistently and brutally. His *Argument to prove that the Abolishing of Christianity in England, may, as things now stand, be attended with some Inconvenience* was a brilliant exercise in the art of irony, scornfully illumining with flashes of biting wit and sarcasm the pit into which diluted religion had fallen. But it was a fact eloquently indicative of the character of the age that Swift's most devastating satire should be construed as a tale of fantasy for children in the nursery.

In his great religious poems, John Dryden drew succinct poetic pictures of the main religious faiths of his time. He had only contempt for those who enshrined their own reason in that place once held by the Christian God.

> Dar'st thou, poor worm, offend Infinity?
> And must the Terms of Peace be given by Thee?
> Then Thou art Justice in the last Appeal;
> Thy easie God instructs Thee to rebell:
> And like a King remote, and weak, must take
> What Satisfaction Thou art pleased to make.[5]

And when the vicissitudes of his own religious experience were past, his allegiance to the Church was complete.

> What weight of ancient witness can prevail,
> If private reason hold the publick scale?
> But, gratious God, how well dost Thou provide
> For erring judgments an unerring Guide!
> Thy throne is darkness in the'abyss of light,
> A blaze of glory that forbids the sight;
> O teach me to believe Thee thus conceal'd,
> And search no farther than Thy self reveal'd;
> But her alone for my Directour take
> Whom Thou hast promis'd never to forsake![6]

Of all minds sensitive to the awful dangers ahead, of all poets who lashed the sublimation of avarice, probably the most eloquent indictment came from Goldsmith. From one to the other of the three great nations of Europe where the forces of the emergent society had become victoriously evident, *The Traveller* went—to find only sanctified sham. First France "displays her bright domain":

> . . . Ostentation here, with tawdry art,
> Pants for the vulgar praise that fools impart . . .
> Here beggar pride defrauds her daily cheer,
> To boast one splendid banquet once a year:
> The mind still turns where shifting fashion draws,
> Nor weighs the solid worth of self-applause. . . .

To Holland, next, "where the broad ocean leans against the land." . . . Here convenience, plenty, elegance, and arts. . . .

> But view them closer, craft and fraud appear,
> E'en liberty itself is barter'd here.

> At gold's superior charms all freedom flies,
> The needy sell it, and the rich man buys;
> A land of tyrants, and a den of slaves,
> Here wretches seek dishonorable graves,
> And, calmly bent, to servitude conform,
> Dull as the lakes that slumber in the storm.

To England, finally, where "stern o'er each bosom reason holds her state." All has become but "one sink of level avarice." . . .

> Ferments arise, imprison'd factions roar,
> Repress'd ambition struggles round her shore;
> Till, overwrought, the general system feels
> Its motions stop, or frenzy fire the wheels.

It is everywhere the same, everywhere only:

> . . . the long pomp, the midnight masquerade,
> With all the freaks of wanton wealth array'd.[7]

Before the citadels of society be surrendered to them, let but one thing be asked of philosophers and statesmen who believe themselves to be the Enlightened: that they judge how wide the limits stand between a splendid and a happy land. . . .

> . . . Verging to decline, its splendors rise,
> Its vistas strike, its palaces surprise;
> While, scourged by famine, from the smiling land
> The mournful peasant leads his humble band;
> And while he sinks, without one arm to save,
> The country blooms—a garden and a grave.[8]

But, voluminous and vehement as were the protests of ecclesiastic and poet, they did not suffice. The pace of Liberal victory they retarded, and they suggested lines to be taken by future and more effective critiques of the Liberal creed—to be addressed to an age less hypnotized by the Liberal promise. For the present, however, all the nostalgic poetic refrains of a century of bards could not breathe life into sweet Auburn.

In the story of the rise of the Liberal faith was the narrative of a whole world in birth. As with the chart of any great social evolution, the historical pattern of the revolution that created the Liberal Society did not admit of graphic, precise and uncompromising delineation. Lines of battle were not always clearly drawn, issues not always categorically conceived. Statesmen like Richelieu and Mazarin, for example, helped to form the new world while working under the insignia of the old; and thinkers and poets like Pope, whose nominal allegiance was to the old faith, made articulate a spirit that essentially partook of the new. No more than individuals could nations maintain unqualified allegiance to one combatant or the other. The truth of this was in the history of Spain—she who was as much a tragic national symbol of the Liberal revolution as Pascal was a tragic individual symbol. Geographically located to capitalize most quickly on the expanding world of commerce, Spain of the sixteenth century had clambered to the top of the European heap of nations. But unable to inject herself with the spirit of the new age, incapable of reorienting her national ideals to harmonize with the pursuit of commercial enterprise on a world scale, possessed of a national heritage not flexible enough to embrace the new economic virtues of ordered business, diligence, thrift—with her cultural allegiance thus committed to the old order, Spain gave way before the economically insurgent North.

Like individuals and like nations, so ideas and beliefs often assumed strange new forms, undergoing an unseen and often uncomprehended metamorphosis. So it was that much of the Liberal faith—particularly what it pleased to call its humanitarianism—was coin taken from the treasury of Christian thought, melted into new forms in the heat of the intellectual upheaval, and made to bear the stamp of a new King and the inscription of a new legend.

Most striking and significant example of this transmutation of ideas was to be found in relation to the conception of natural law and derivative natural rights. Imbedded deep in

Part III · Liberal Society and Church Militant

The Rationale of the New Order

THE nineteenth century is the century of the Liberal. His creed dominates the epoch, his faith gives it guidance, his works give it substance. It is his world, made in his own image.

Virtually the entire narrative of this time can be depicted as the Liberal pageant: a pageant of a faith's development, articulation, and translation into institutional forms—a pageant that is constantly unfolding from the Congress of Vienna to the Congress of Versailles. It brings the triumphant establishment of an industrial civilization. It casts Great Britain in the major role of commercial titan and empire-builder extraordinary. It tells of the growth of the United States, the continental frontier of the Liberal Society, which has within itself in turn yet another frontier which men push ever Westward: this is the land where the Liberal faith has its grandest opportunity to fulfill its gospel of freedom. It testifies to the victory of the political principles of representative government and universal suffrage. It witnesses the march of the insurgent forces of national consciousness, the triumph of the ideal of the coincidence of lines of nationality and national states, the victorious proclamation of self-determined nationality by the peoples of Germany, Italy and the Balkans.

But as the victors approached the task of writing their doctrines in the institutional letters of social organization, the exigencies of the latter demanded revision of the former. In the intellectual struggle of the centuries just past, men had learned and understood vividly that ideas were weapons. But it was only now, when they had to employ these ideas in the urgent and immediate problems faced in making their victory secure, that men came to realize that these weapons were graced with a quality of mutability to which instruments of steel or iron could never aspire.

The volatile character of any pattern of ideas sufficiently unified to be regarded as a social philosophy was rendered doubly manifest by the fact that the intellectual legacy of the Age of the Enlightened was neither compact nor cogent. For all its incisive critical review of an anterior faith, the Liberal philosophy of the eighteenth century was, in great measure, a confused combination of immediate political and economic demands, specific condemnations of state and church abuses, and broad principles of social philosophy assumed to have universal validity—many of these latter being mutually contradictory. The nature of this disharmony of thought merits attention not only of itself, to qualify any conception of the development of the Liberal faith as a precise and consistent evolution, but also because this is the philosophical context and background for the emergence of what finally is to be the dominant and compelling strain of Liberal thought.

More than anyone else, Jean Jacques Rousseau reflects the character of the eighteenth century's legacy of ideas—its chronic and dramatic confusion, its germination of divergent and ultimately hostile philosophical forces. Not only did Rousseau's thought stand widely separated from that of either a Voltaire or a Helvetius, but also his own doctrines, at distinct stages of development, sprang from profoundly disparate premises and worked toward far from identical or even harmonious conclusions. In his exultant breaking of the chains with which he thought men everywhere were fastened, in his rousing faith in the innate goodness of man, in his proclamation of the inner virtue of man which, unencumbered with the onerous accretions of civilized life, would bravely uproot and destroy social evil—in all this Rousseau assumed almost messianic proportions. The consequence was that like most prophets—religious or political—his work came to assume almost as many significations as it had disciples. Society's economic foundation, its desired political institutions, and its ultimate social ideals and objectives—all three of these aspects of Rousseau's gospel contained, within themselves, germs of competing, contradictory doctrines.

The economic basis of social order, revolving on the critical issue of property, is conceived by Rousseau, at two different points in his career, in two contradictory fashions. The early *Discourse on Inequality* would have seemed to have disposed of the issue quite categorically, for it proclaimed the common ownership of the fruits of the earth, denounced as an impostor the man who had first seduced his fellows into the social sin of private ownership, and deduced all human inequality and most human misery from this original transgression. Rousseau, in short, came close to viewing the invention of private property as the Christian regarded original sin. . . . But the *Social Contract* tells a vastly different story. The social pact, Rousseau explains, is entered into by men when they reach "a point at which the obstacles that endanger their preservation in the state of nature overcome by their resistance the forces which each individual can exert with a view to maintaining himself in that state."[1] The terms of this contract are then divulged by Rousseau: "What man loses by the social contract is his natural liberty and an unlimited right to anything which tempts him and which he is able to attain; what he gains is civil liberty and property in all that he possesses."[2] In the Roussellian terminology, possession is supplanted by property; titular right is established where before the pact there was but forceful occupancy. Therefore, in contradiction to his first diagnosis of the economic base to social order, Rousseau now finds that property is one of the basic individual assets which constitute man's reward for the institution of civil society.

The political operations and objectives of the society thus constituted are no more logically or cohesively developed. The very conceptions of Liberty and of Equality, so exalted by Rousseau, are lacking in consistency or logical foundation. The Equality of Roussellian theory is associated with the social contract in this way: "Instead of destroying natural equality, the fundamental pact, on the contrary, substitutes a moral and lawful equality for the physical inequality which nature imposed upon men, so that, although unequal in strength or intellect, they will become equal by convention and legal right."[3] In this issue Rousseau had apparently first sought some foundation for the doctrine of Equality other than social sanction. Having rejected the political content of the Christian tradition, however, the only alternative roots to Equality which he could unearth were in "nature"—but he found none there: instead, only the obvious physical disequalities of men. This forced the inevitable conclusion that Equality then derived from nothing more pretentious or innate in man than "convention and legal right"—which therewith became the precarious foundation for the most central Roussellian doctrine.

In the instance of Liberty, the issue is not so much one of a tenuous philosophical basis as of manifestly inherent and menacing inconsistency of emphasis. If one looks to Rousseau's earlier works, or particularly to the *Confessions*, one will find the thoughts impregnated with a spirit of atomistic individualism difficult to match. The all-sufficient guide for man is simple and natural morality, unobscured by the accretions of custom or the hollow rituals of organized religion. The individual is conceived as the sacred tablet on which Virtue, sublime science of simple minds, engraves her clear and indelible principles.

But these initial individualistic conceptions—which can certainly be viewed in large measure as abstractions and projections of Rousseau's own personality—are disregarded and contradicted in the precepts of the *Social Contract*. The condition of Liberty obtains in society when men obey the law which they have prescribed for themselves. It is neither animal freedom nor freedom found in obedience to a God-given law, but that freedom which is implicit in men's obeisance to their own wills incorporated into law. But what is to be done when some in society do not choose to defer to what the majority deems best and have imbedded in the law of the land? The answer Rousseau finds in the terms of the social contract governing the creation of civil society. "As nature gives to every man an absolute power over all his limbs," Rousseau explained in terms of the organic analogy, "the social pact gives the body politic an absolute power over all its members."[4] This entails what Rousseau bluntly describes as "the total alienation to the whole community of each associate with all his rights."[5] Complete dominion exercised over the individual by a civil order whose sanction and origin was secular and man-made might seem to jeopardize any intelligible idea of Liberty, but Rousseau, in his most famous paradox, succeeded to his own satisfaction in equating what to most men appeared antithetical. "Whoever refuses to obey the general will," he announced, "shall be constrained to do so by the whole body; which means nothing else than that he shall be forced to be free."[6] Here, then, was a doctrine vastly different from the insurgent emotional force of individualism. The vintage from these grapes was to be trampled out by the wrathful, puissant force of national consciousness, until in the twentieth century men would drink deeply of the strong wine of totalitarianism.*

What was thus true of the most dramatic participant in Liberalism's legacy from the eighteenth century was characteristic of the whole of that inheritance, lacking inner consistency, generally accepted premises, or universally espoused conclusions. To cite again an important example previously mentioned, the whole of the theory of natural rights had been a fabric carelessly cut from the cloth of Christian social thought, and its loosely-bound threads unravelled swiftly with changing years. By the men of the Enlightenment natural rights—the *inalienable* rights of the individual—had been regarded as a conception virtually antithetical to the idea of popular sovereignty—the *absolute* sovereignty of the majority. To secure the latter seemed to mean placing the former in serious jeopardy, and, unless he was to accept Rousseau's doc-

* Rousseau revealed explicitly the essential nature of this subordination of the individual to the corporate will in his outline of government for the Corsican republic. Every citizen, in this program, is to take an oath "in the name of Almighty God" to join himself, "body, goods, will and powers," to the Corsican nation, "granting to her full ownership of myself and all that depends upon me." (Cited by Martin, K., *French Liberal Thought in the Eighteenth Century*, p. 209.)

trine that an individual could be forced to be free, the Enlightened thinker upheld one dictum to the exclusion of the other. But the average nineteenth century thinker perceived no such distinction, or at least tried to compromise with both by predicating that system of government which he called democracy upon both absolute popular sovereignty and individual or minority rights. That political tension, confusion and contradiction should ensue was logical and inevitable.

Translation of these ideas into governmental forms was achieved with no greater lucidity or consistency of thought. The republicanism of Montesquieu, predicated on his famed separation of powers, had been insistently denounced by Rousseau as a denial of the principles of true popular rule. For Rousseau representative government was as serious a political distortion as absolute monarchy. It was evolved from the fallacious premise that will—the general will of the people—was susceptible to delegation; power, Rousseau had maintained, could be delegated, but never will. Again, however, this dichotomy was ignored by the nineteenth century Liberal. He invoked Montesquieu's conception and elaboration of the system of representative government, at the same time proclaiming it as a political fulfillment of the Roussellian ideal of popular rule—what Rousseau had called "democratic" rule. Future implications of this conjunction of disparate doctrines were to be at least as far-reaching as the consequences of failing successfully to reconcile the principles of natural individual rights and absolute popular sovereignty.

In these ways the vast current of the Liberal faith rushed over the cataract of the Napoleonic era: its many blended streams surged roughly against the hidden rocks of unforeseen historic events, broke into many channels, and finally were reformed and redirected into the course of newly framed doctrines. The character of this redirection was not new. As mercantilism had been but a half-way house on the road to individual economy, as Deism had been a half-way house on the road to atheism, so too, was the dominant Enlightened belief in natural rights but a half-way house for the Liberal on the road of social philosophy. From a doctrine of natural rights conceived as deriving from God's will and man's character as His creature, men had passed to a faith in natural rights which had no supernatural sanctions and were derived exclusively from the experience and evidence of this world. Now the thinkers moved on again. Reacting emotionally and instinctively against the passionately exultant spirit of the days of the Revolution and of Napoleon, intellectually fatigued by the expenditure of frenzied energy which those days had demanded, they sought a simpler, less emotionally charged and more prosaically conceived foundation for their faith. Thus the roaring torrent of the Liberal creed poured itself into the calm and level waters of Utilitarianism. And men were confident that upon these waters they could forever walk.

"Nonsense on stilts": that was how Jeremy Bentham disposed of the doctrine of natural rights. It seemed mystical, nebulous, lacking in the tough substance of logic. He regarded it in much the same manner as the sound materialist of the Enlightenment viewed the humanized religion of the Deist: he saw clearly that the doctrine of natural rights, like Deist religious doctrines, had no substantial philosophical foundations when dissociated from the Christian tradition in which they had been born. He understood that natural rights was an empty phrase when it was derived from nothing more enduring than a nature which science was revealing to be without inner purpose or organic virtue. He concluded, logically and in harmony with the spirit of his age, that utility could be the only basis for human rights or civil society.

Born before the middle of the eighteenth century and living until 1832, the year of the first great English Reform Bill, Bentham personified the transition from the intellectual pattern of the Liberal faith in the Enlightened era to the dominant form which the creed was to assume in the nineteenth century. The principles upon which Bentham worked were succinctly summarized in a simple note made for his own studies: "*Association Principle*. Hartley. The bond of connection between ideas and language; and between ideas and ideas. *Greatest Happiness Principle*. Priestley. Applied to every branch of morals in detail, by Bentham; a part of the way previously by Helvetius."[7]

A more lucid thinker than many of the Enlightened, Bentham initially took care to make his use of terms explicit and understandable. As a confessed "believer in the principle of 'utility,'" he explained what this principle signified in operation. The terms "just" and "unjust," "moral" and "immoral," "good" and "bad," he explained, he would use as "collective terms standing for the concepts of certain pains and certain pleasures, without attaching any other sense to them." He elaborated further that he wanted the terms "pleasure" and "pain" to be accepted in "their ordinary sense." His was the spirit of the humanist of the Renaissance when he proclaimed enthusiastically: "There is no subtlety in my use of the words and no metaphysics! There is no need of consulting either Plato or Aristotle. 'Pain' and 'pleasure' stand for what each person feels as such, the peasant as well as the prince, the plain man as well as the philosopher."[8] Truly Bentham sounded like a nineteenth century Petrarch protesting against the scholasticism of the Enlightenment—echoing Petrarch's assurance that the fisherman knew more of happiness than the great Aristotle.*

Having defined his terms, Bentham posited his moral philosophy. This he resolved into three basic axioms. First: "Every act whereby pleasure is reaped is, all consequences apart, good." Second: "Every act by which pleasure is reaped,

* It was in this definition of pleasure and pain that Bentham was most manifestly anticipated in his thought by Helvetius. Thus Helvetius had summarized the issue: "By annihilating the desires, you annihilate the mind; every man without passions has within him no principle of action, no motive to act. . . . The springs of action in man are corporeal pains and pleasures. Pleasure and pain are, and always will be, the only principles of action in man. . . . Corporeal pleasure and pain are the real and only springs of all government. We do not properly desire glory, riches and honors, but the pleasures only of which glory, riches, and honors are the representatives. . . . In man all is sensation. . . . All our desires, and all our passions . . . are nothing more in us than the application of self-love to particular objects. . . . Self-love makes us totally what we are." (Helvetius, *A Treatise on Man*, Chs. IV, IX and X.)

without any result of pain, is pure gain to happiness; every act whose results of pain are less than the results of pleasure, is good, to the extent of the balance in favor of happiness." Third: "Every person is not only the best, but the only proper judge of what, with reference to himself is pleasure, and what pain."[9] Thus happiness is equated with virtue (as the Enlightened had equated the latter with desire), pleasure and pain established as the only criteria of happiness, and the individual exalted as the only proper judge of pleasure and pain, hence also of virtue.

Having advanced thus far, it next becomes essential for Bentham to construct some nexus between the purely egoistic pursuit of individual happiness and the welfare of society. As he had conceived individual happiness in quantitative terms, he invokes the same standard to define social welfare: "the greatest happiness of the greatest number." As the individual should strive to amass quantities of pleasure in excess of quantities of pain, so society must seek to multiply the number of single individuals whose state is one of happiness—and thereby the welfare of society will be achieved. To the sceptical it might seem that myriad individuals in the quest for nothing but a net personal surplus of pleasure over pain would not be profoundly inspired to contribute to social well being. But this, Bentham explains, is a superficial view, because the individual can win happiness for himself only when his actions are socially beneficial or at least not socially harmful. To illustrate this, Bentham tells the fable of Timothy Thoughtless and Walter Wise: Timothy, a habitual inebriate, because of his vicious conduct suffers physical discomfort, loss of friends, professional disgrace, confinement in jail, and loss of almost all chances for his soul's salvation; while wise Walter, by prescient abstinence, wins health, friends, business success, elevation to the judiciary, and bright prospects for eternal spiritual bliss.

Since there exists, then, this remarkable identity of acts which bring individual gratification and acts which generate universal social health, all artificially created or externally imposed social disciplines are needless: social sanctions, Bentham is certain, will spring from the individual's own perception of his best interests. Therefore, when he outlines the just political ordering of society, Bentham proclaims that "the general rule is that nothing ought to be done or attempted by government. The motto, or watchword of government on these occasions, ought to be—*Be Quiet*." Reason for this quietism is that interference in the economic affairs of society by the government is both needless and often pernicious. It becomes pernicious government interference because constraint comes to be imposed on "the free agency of the individual." This limitation of individual freedom is "bad," Bentham explains, not because it violates any moral conception of liberty, but because "pain is the general concomitant of the sense of such restraint." In other words, liberty emerges as a political good because liberty is expedient. And the reason why political liberty seems expedient to Bentham is finally made clear in his unqualified endorsement of bourgeois economics. "With a view of causing an increase to take place in the mass of national wealth," Bentham concludes, ". . . *security* and *freedom* are all that industry requires. The request which agriculture, manufacturers, and commerce present to governments, is modest and reasonable as that which Diogenes made to Alexander: 'Stand out of my sunshine.' We have no need of favor—we require only a secure and open path."[10]

To sceptics who still questioned the Liberal's fervent exaltation of rights to the exclusion of all talk of social duties, who still wondered if the destruction of all social disciplines was the only necessary prerequisite for the creation of the good society—to critics such as these Bentham has a forthright answer. It is, he explains, "very idle to talk about duties; the word itself has in it something disagreeable and repulsive." This was a truth enthusiastically affirmed by the masters of the new economy. And Bentham continued: "A man, a moralist, goes into an elbow chair, and pours forth pompous dogmatisms about *duty*—and *duties*. Why is he not listened to? Because every man is thinking about interests . . . and with these the well-judging moralist will find it for *his* interest to begin. Let him say what he pleases,—to interest, duty must and will be made subservient."[11]

To the devout adherent of Utilitarianism, such a doctrine as this was not mere sublimation of the ego, for belief in the creative and civilized character of the impulse of rational and calculating self-interest was the essence of the Liberal rationale. "Self-regarding prudence is not only a virtue," Bentham explains, "—it is a virtue on which the very existence of the race depends. If I thought more about you than I thought about myself, I should be the blind leading the blind, and we should fall into the ditch together."[12] Everything in human society, in short, revolves around the equivalence of individual self-seeking and social well being, acquisitiveness and beneficence. Hence "in the moral field it cannot be a man's duty to do that which it is his interest not to do. Morality will teach him rightly to estimate his interests and his duties; and examination will show their coincidence. . . . When interest and duty are considered in their broadest sense, it will be seen that in the general tenor of life the sacrifice of interest to duty is neither practicable nor so much as desirable; that it cannot, in fact, have place; and that if it could, the happiness of mankind would not be prompted by it."[13] Thus, with duty and interest harmoniously integrated if not identified, that happy social order was anointed in which the bourgeoisie could freely and justly consult the latter to ascertain the former. How the Liberal could do thusly and still have his remain a brave new world was clearly set forth in

DEONTOLOGY

or,

The Science of Morality:

in which the Harmony and Co-Incidence of

Duty and Self-Interest,
Virtue and Felicity,
Prudence and Benevolence,

[155]

The task facing the Liberal of the nineteenth century was not an easy one: to convert those intellectual weapons which had been employed in the destruction of an old faith into instruments which could fortify a concrete institutional structure and a victorious social class. The bourgeois Liberal had no longer to frame his philosophical arguments as a hopeful aspirant; he had to pronounce them as the victor in tones of righteousness and forbidding solemnity which would make anyone intemperate enough to question his claims to dominion seem like a blasphemous violator of the eternally good, true, and beautiful. In the early part of the century, it was the new economics which thus blessed the claims and premises of the Liberal gospel. And the men who most significantly contributed to construction of bourgeois economic necessities as part of historical necessity were three: Malthus, Ricardo, and Spencer.

The work of Malthus was one of the most significant examples of the manner in which the form and substance of ideas were modified to fit a changing context of social fact without, however, impairing the support which those ideas lent to the economic premises of the Liberal Society. Malthus shared little of the easy social optimism of the Philosophes. But the Enlightenment's proclamation of the inevitability of progress, once the new economic forces were unfettered, was herewith converted into a doctrine more immediately appropriate: the doctrine that widespread poverty and misery were inevitable among the lower classes. His law of population postulated, Malthus's conclusions were grimly fatalistic. "I see no way which man can escape from the weight of this law which pervades all animated nature," Malthus proclaimed. "No fancied equality, no agrarian regulations, in their utmost extent, could remove the pressure of it even for a single century. . . . To remove the wants of the lower classes is indeed an arduous task. The truth is, that the pressure of distress on this part of a community is an evil so deeply seated, that no human ingenuity can reach it. Were I to propose a palliative, and palliatives are all that the nature of the case will admit, it should be the total abolition of all the present [forms of public charity and relief]. To prevent the recurrence of misery, is, alas! beyond the power of man. In the vain endeavor to obtain what in the nature of things is impossible, we now sacrifice not only possible but certain benefits."[15]

The fact that Malthus was not writing a conscious apology for bourgeois economic practices in no way limited the utility of his work in that regard. To exploit to the fullest the immediate economic possibilities with their "certain benefits," to dispense with consideration of social reform which would limit such exploitation, to devolve responsibility for the state of the laboring masses upon the impersonal and relentless laws of economics—to do all this was to make meritorious contribution to the rationale of the Liberal Society.

Not less noteworthy a contribution was that of David Ricardo, at whose hands another pillar of Liberal economic doctrine underwent revision but remained as substantial a support for the superstructure as its predecessor. It was evident to Ricardo that the idea of the natural harmony of class interests was sophistic and that unharnessed economic competition could not disperse equal benefits to all. For the harmony of classes he substituted the hierarchy of classes, their interests conflicting and contradictory but the respective validity of those class claims and interests firmly fixed in a rigid economic pattern. The essential character of that pattern was dictated by the Iron Law of Wages, which read: "The natural price of labor is that price which is necessary to enable the laborers one with another to subsist and perpetuate their race without either increase or diminution."[16]

The premises for this conception of a "natural" price of labor were clearly expounded by Ricardo. There exists a fixed amount of funds and goods. If labor's wages are raised, there will follow an increase in population, an increase in the supply of labor—and hence an eventual decline in wages. The only expedient was to impress on the collective mind of labor the necessity for harnessing the function of reproduction. As a witty anthropologist of a later age would state the matter: "Only illiterates have litters."[17]

As with Malthus, the significance and value of Ricardo's theory was that it defined the function of government and affirmed the stratification of society in words which brought understandable delight to the economic masters of the age. The wondrous discovery was made that, in effect, bourgeois dominion was secured for all perpetuity by the rigorous and inflexible laws of economics. "There is no means of improving the lot of the worker," Ricardo informed his age, "except by limiting the number of his children. His destiny is in his own hands. Every suggestion which does not tend to the reduction in number of the working people is useless, to say the least of it. All legislative interference must be pernicious."[18] These words were a bracing tonic to the enlightened mill owner whose workers, aged six to fourteen, worked sixteen hours a day until their spines bent. The cause of all the mischief was, in truth, too many children of the poor.

Herbert Spencer perceived all this. Eloquent propagator of the Liberal economic gospel, he saw in his mind's eye the eternal verities which underlay the isolated social phenomena of strapped backs, stunted figures, wrists snapped in machine-belts. . . . "The poverty of the incapable, the distresses that come upon the imprudent, the starvation of the idle are the decrees of a large, far-seeing benevolence." There are, by frank admission, some slight incongruities to be faced in the operation of this large, far-seeing benevolence. . . . "It seems hard that a laborer incapacitated by sickness from competing with his stronger fellows, should have to bear the resulting privations. It seems hard that widows and orphans should be left to struggle for life or death." This, indeed, does seem hard, even for those who are no more than the incapable, the imprudent, the idle. . . . "Nevertheless, when regarded not separately, but in connection with the interests of universal humanity, these harsh fatalities are seen to be full of the highest beneficence—the same beneficence which brings to early graves the children of diseased parents, and singles out the low-spirited, the intemperate, and the debilitated as the victims of an epidemic."

In these words of Spencer, the Liberal faith in the application of natural laws to the sphere of political economy comes to fruition; for here is the politico-economic translation of the scientific law of natural selection. It is an iron-like law which cannot, Spencer explains, be contravened by the wishes of those who call themselves friends of the poor—those "spurious philanthropists" who ignore the tough facts of social reality. Worse, these latter men seek to subvert the poor's natural and only incentives to work. "That rigorous necessity which, when allowed to act on them, becomes so sharp a spur to the lazy, and so strong a bridle to the random, these paupers' friends would repeal, because of the wailings it here and there produces." These ignoble social radicals, irrational sentimentalists and would-be perverters of nature's laws, are all "blind to the fact, that under the natural order of things society is constantly excreting its unhealthy, imbecile, slow, vacillating, faithless members."[19] There were, no doubt, sanguine Liberals who read the pages of Spencer and who were disappointed by his apparent satisfaction with a natural process of excretion and his dismal failure to conceive a social purgative for the body politic.

The Liberal faith has now entered its final stage of development. No longer the insurgent appeal and challenge of a class which views itself as denied its just station in society, it has become the rationale of that class, now triumphant and eager to perpetuate its estate.

In its final form the Liberal faith becomes the rationale of industrial capitalism. It has divested itself of the disorder and contradiction of much of the intellectual legacy of the Enlightenment. It is basically a simple faith. Pragmatism is its hope; fatalism is its apology. On the one hand, through the self-interested and unfettered pursuit of material gain, the good society is promised to come to pass. On the other hand, there is nothing society can do for those who fall and cry out as the human herd rushes over them. They are but the unfortunates who have been caught in the whirling wheels of a machine which no one can control, which no one should control, and whose only sure end is to maintain the dominion of the bourgeoisie. They are, moreover, abnormalities—exceptions proving the rule of the basic harmony of self-interest and social welfare.

Now, as always, the decisive fact of the age is men's conception of their own nature and of their relationship to their God and their neighbor. Spiritual values, religious truths, moral absolutes find no place in this world; they are left for investigation by men in the monasteries, as one leaves toys for idle children in the nursery and then goes about the day's arduous business. Human character is resolved into the primary ingredients of self-love and acquisitiveness, and the welfare of society admits of no criterion beyond its massed material wealth. Men—strengthened by no supernatural graces, impelled to govern their activities by no uncontingent and fixed body of social ethics, but by the simple and direct articulation of their own reasoned desires—can and will fashion the good society from the tough, durable fiber of material progress. The Economic Man is come to life.

Outward sign of the birth of this social savior is the ascendant star of the science of economics. No hierarchical scale of values integrates its precepts with those derived from other studies of man's life and nature; no transcendent ethical criterion assesses its judgments in the light of a more universal definition of men's needs. The aims of economics are isolated and consecrated as the only valid objects of human endeavor; the criteria of economics are accepted as the only authoritative evaluations which can be made of the facts of man's social existence. Its station is supreme because it alone can measure what men wish measured: pleasure and pain, profit and loss.

From Christian Man to Natural Man to Economic Man:

it is a logical and direct succession. The second repudiates the first and anticipates the third. Natural Man conceived of human salvation on this earth; Economic Man promised to realize that salvation.

The Liberal Society is here.

The Titan of Industrialism

THE days of revolution are over.

In the days of the not distant past whose heritage of hates is yet alive, the militant Liberal has had to fight with all intellectual and physical power at his command. He has had to storm the walls of a whole world of ideas and facts to which many men had remained loyal, either because they believed in their integrity or because they were habituated to them. Perhaps because too many of the defenders of the strongholds of the old faith were no more than habituated to their beliefs, they lost. And the Liberal triumphed.

The victorious faith is largely an articulation of the buoyant hope of the Liberal that the vast material resources at hand can be exploited to create a better world than men have ever known. It will be a world in which the material conquest will be so complete that men can dispense with concern for almost all else, a world in which they will not have to experience the rigorous and exacting governance of social or moral disciplines, a world in which they will not have to believe, a world in which they can become simply habituated.

The labor is undertaken. Not revelry but prudence, not waste but thrift, not indulgence but economic asceticism; exalting these virtues the Liberal bends to his task. Not with prayer and fasting, not with piety and good works; but with coal and steam and gas, with oil and iron and steel—with these can man's salvation be won. The faith which has won dominion in men's minds now demands their sustained allegiance, mobilizes their energies, and summons their hands to the great work of making the ideal the fact—the triumphant fact . . .

When the centuries behind me like a peaceful land reposed;
When I clung to all the present for the promise that it closed;
When I dipped into the future far as human eye could see,—
Saw the vision of the world, and all the wonder that would be . . .
Men, my brothers, men the workers, ever reaping something new:
That which they have done but earnest of the things that they
  shall do:
. . . Saw the heavens fill with commerce, argosies of magic sails,
Pilots of the purple twilight, dropping down with costly bales;
Heard the heavens fill with shouting, and there rained a ghastly dew
From the nations' airy navies grappling in the central blue;
With the standards of the peoples plunging through the thunderstorm;
Till the war-drum throbbed no longer, and the battle-flags were furled
In the parliament of men, the federation of the world.
There the common sense of most shall hold a fretful realm in awe,
And the kindly earth shall slumber, lapt in universal law. . . .
Not in vain the distance beacons. Forward, forward let us range;
Let the great world spin forever down the ringing grooves of
  change. . . .[1]

Like monumental products of every epoch, the titan of industrialism had his feet upon the ground of past ages. Its material substance, its economic foundations, its political milieu, its philosophical implications, its social and psychological overtones—all these ingredients of what men were to call the Industrial Revolution were germinated in decades long dead.

Economic fiber from which industrial triumphs could be fashioned had been furnished, in large measure, by Europe's commercial expansion in the seventeenth and eighteenth centuries. For a short while the rewards of exploration and colonization actually militated against intensive economic development in the home countries, because profits thus amassed from trading were so lucrative that men dared not desert this for the industrial field and hope to achieve comparable success. But soon commercial expansion itself demanded productive expansion at home, and the great impetus to industrial development began to make itself felt. And from the fortunes built up through commercial and colonial endeavors, men found at last the financial resources with which to propel the revolution of machines.

In philosophic rather than economic terms, the scientific cult of nature had formed the intellectual basis for the mechanization of life in the nineteenth century. The discounting of qualities and the standardizing of quantities; the emphasis on the neutral, objective observer; the isolation and categorization of facts for scientific study and analysis, more or less untouched by any normative scheme of values—these rituals of the scientific faith were the all-important prologues to the pageant of industrial life: satisfaction with mass for its own sake, demand for unreasoning automatons to keep turning the wheels of industry, and the isolation and specialization of not only facts for analysis, but also occupations for life— the specialization of labor as well as thought. In fact, the total conception of reality nurtured by the scientist pointed directly to the society of the machines. A world stripped of moral values, a world of no spiritual dimensions, as Lewis Mumford has stated the issue, had to be filled at least with representations of the new values—had to be given at least material dimensions. There developed from the scientific faith the ancillary doctrine of the duty to invent—the duty to translate scientific abstractions into mechanical realities. As Mr. Mumford has written, "machines—and machines alone— completely met the requirements of the new scientific method and point of view; they fulfilled the definition of 'reality' far more perfectly than living organisms. . . . Were machines not conceived in terms of primary qualities alone, without regard to appearance, sound, or any other sort of sensory stimulation? . . . Indeed in this empty, denuded world . . . by renouncing a large part of his humanity, a man could achieve godhood: he dawned on this second chaos and created the machine in his own image: the image of power, but power stripped loose from his flesh and isolated from his humanity."[2]

The great and specific precursor of industrial life and organization was to be found in the army.[3] In the most concrete terms the art of warfare stimulated the art of mechanical invention: it demanded for the first time large-scale use of iron; the gun—mechanically a one-cylinder combustion engine—was the prototype of the power machine; fortifications demanded refinement in all the construction techniques; the relentless military demand for goods en masse propelled the development of factory organization; and military equipment necessarily presented the first large demand for completely standardized goods. More vital, however, than these specific productive connections between military and industrial forces were the social and psychological implications of military life which were inherited by men of the industrial order. The life of both master and slave in the new economy was foreshadowed, as Lewis Mumford has pointed out, by that of commander and soldier. Long before the intricacies of corporate economic organization were explored and exploited, the military general staff had evolved a blueprint of the art of organizing masses of men: topographic surveys, plans of campaign, charts and graphs of action completed and action projected, coordination of specialized army units, division of military labor. All such matters had become refined arts in the hands of the leaders whose power was the cannon, before they were adopted by the leaders whose authority and strength was the limited liability corporation.

At the same time and in a similar manner, parallel habits of life and thought were inherited by the common soldier and the common laborer; the military proletariat and the private of the industrial system were virtually interchangeable types of humanity. With the barracks as a model, the factory system was a logically evolved method of organization. Military regimentation served as an admirable model for industrial regimentation. In both, men had to be harnessed to a purpose and method of action which found no inspiration in individual minds and wills. It was a strange fact that the sense of duty and discipline which the Utilitarians had scorned—the sacrifice of individual interest to communal purpose—should be made articulate, in the Liberal Society, only in the army, and here on a scale unprecedented in history. It was a strange—and foreboding—fact that this society should pattern its system of production after its system of destruction.

Out of this range of development the machine age sprang, fortified by economic sinews and philosophical impetus of an earlier age, and building on this variety of past patterns of human organization. As the gospel of the mechanical societies of the eighteenth century had argued, men now fervently believed that the sanctifying grace of the machine would assure mankind's redemption. The Egypt of intellectual slavery had been left far behind. From the Jacobin "Mountain" had come the Tablet of the precepts to govern the Liberal Society —graven not in stone, but in the hearts of men. By the great revolutions the Exodus had been victoriously achieved. And now the gates of the Promised Land were to be pried open with tools of steel and iron. . . .

England was the first province won. The reasons why this was so are clear. There had been here no internal disruptions to impede economic development since 1689: the Napoleonic wars, with all their threats to national integrity, yet had furnished festive opportunities for commercial expansion. This expansion had been inflated to world-wide proportions by the great colonial triumphs of the eighteenth century. Natural resources abounding in the soil of the country—coal, iron, tin—provided the necessary sinews for the new industry. The supply of labor was bountiful: population was increasing in absolute terms, and the labor market was overrun with immigrants from the continent and with tenant-farmers who were hurled, by the enclosures, from the rural areas into the industrial vortex. And finally, what was basic to all considerations, the masters of the new economy by the middle of the seventeenth century had effectively broken the harness of social disciplines of either religious or regal origin. Equipped with all these advantages, the island of Britain took swiftly to the vanguard of the new economy.

For all the peoples just becoming industrially civilized, the immediate triumphs seemed as startling as had been the military victories of Napoleon, and none presumed to affix limits to the conquest that could be made. Each victory seemed to presage greater ones to come. Inventions produced machines. Machines demanded resources. Resources demanded markets and colonies. These entailed renewed demands for machine-made products and for transportation advances which would bind the origin of natural resources to the processing centers of the national economy, which would extend to the colonial peripheries of the national economy radii of communication with the industrial centers. Each progressive step in transportation, in turn, drew new markets into the orbit of economic activity or tapped new and greater natural sources of power—and all reacted back to press for ever more elaborate and productive mechanical and industrial devices. What could break such a necessary cycle of economic triumph?

Population soared past calculated expectations of the statisticians' most recent graphs: Britain's total population was more than doubled in the course of the century, and the new realm of the United States expanded from five to over seventy-five millions of people. From rural to urban areas men moved by the millions, as cities became the nerve centers of the new economy. Without a single city of over a million inhabitants in 1800, the Western world had more than a score of such man-heaps in the early decades of the next century.[4]

In a great wave, humanity and its machines surged over and past old geographical lines. In the great countries of the West, new cities meant the conquest of new lands, the reclamation of areas long dormant, which had moved only in the quiet, even tenor of agrarian economy. And in the wider range of his conquest, from San Francisco to Singapore, from Hamburg to Valparaiso, from Glasgow to Bombay, Economic Man subdued and brought under his dominion the great areas of

America, Asia, Africa. These lands too he summoned to the sterner, swifter pace of the new life; to the peculiar exigencies of his way of living and producing; to the special gospel and promise of his faith.

The great gates at last were opening wide. Within the gates was the City in all its splendor: *Civitas Hominis*.

There were four people who, in the simple eloquence of plain language and with no self-conscious appeal to the refined dialectic of social theory, revealed the essentially true character of the world in which they lived. Their names could not be found in the hagiography of the Liberal Society. They themselves but spoke words which might have come from the taut lips of millions of their fellows. They were: Mathew Crabtree, Elizabeth Bentley, Patience Kershaw, Sarah Gooder. To make their acquaintance was to know the City of Man. . . .

In London, in 1832, the Sadler Committee is investigating life in the textile factories . . .

MR. MATHEW CRABTREE, CALLED IN AND EXAMINED:[5]

What age are you?—Twenty-two.

What is your occupation?—A blanket manufacturer.

Have you ever been employed in a factory?—Yes.

At what age did you first go to work in one?—Eight.

How long did you continue in that occupation?—Four years.

Will you state the hours of labor at the period when you first went to work in the factory, in ordinary times?—From six in the morning to eight at night. . . .

When trade was brisk what were your hours?—From five in the morning to nine in the evening. . . .

How far did you live from the mill?—About two miles. . . .

During those long hours of labor could you be punctual; how did you awake?—I seldom did awake spontaneously: I was most generally awoke or lifted out of bed, sometimes asleep, by my parents. . . .

What was the consequence if you had been too late?—I was most commonly beaten.

Severely?—Very severely, I thought.

In those mills is chastisement towards the latter part of the day going on perpetually?—Perpetually.

So that you can hardly be in a mill without hearing constant crying? —Never an hour, I believe.

Do you think that if the overlooker were naturally a humane person it would be still found necessary for him to beat the children, in order to keep their attention and vigilance at the termination of those extraordinary days of labor?—Yes; the machine turns off a regular quantity of cardings, and of course they must keep as regularly to their work the whole of the day; they must keep up with the machine, and therefore however humane the slubber may be, as he must keep up with the machine or be found fault with, he spurs the children to keep up also by various means but that which he commonly resorts to is to strap them when they became drowsy. . . .

When you got home at night after this labor, did you feel much fatigued?—Very much so.

Had you any time to be with your parents, and to receive instruction from them?—No.

What did you do?—All that we did when we got home was to get the little bit of supper that was provided for us and go to bed immediately. If the supper had not been ready directly, we should have gone to sleep while it was preparing. . . .

Were the rest of the children similarly circumstanced?—Yes, all of them; but they were not all of them so far from the work as I was.

And if you had been too late you were under the apprehension of being cruelly beaten?—I generally was beaten when I happened to be too late; and when I got up in the morning the apprehension of that was so great, that I used to run, and cry all the way as I went to the mill. . . .

ELIZABETH BENTLEY, CALLED IN AND EXAMINED:

. . . Suppose you flagged a little, or were too late, what would they do?—Strap us. . . .

Constantly?—Yes.

Girls as well as boys?—Yes. . . .

Could you eat your food well in that factory?—No, indeed I had not much to eat, and the little I had I could not eat it, my appetite was so poor, and being covered with dust; and it was no use to take it home, I could not eat it, and the overlooker took it, and gave it to the pigs.

[168]

It is London, ten years later. The Ashley Commission is conducting an investigation of life in the mines. . . .

No. 26.—Patience Kershaw, aged 17.

. . . All my sisters have been hurriers, but three went to the mill. Alice went because her legs swelled from hurrying in cold water when she was hot. I never went to day-school; I go to Sunday school, but I cannot read or write; I go to pit at five o'clock in the morning and come out at five in the evening; I get my breakfast of porridge and milk first; I take my dinner with me, a cake, and eat it as I go; I do not stop or rest any time for the purpose; I get nothing else till I get home, and then have potatoes and meat, not every day meat. I hurry in the clothes I have now got on, trousers and ragged jacket; the bald place upon my head is made by thrusting the corves; my legs never swelled, but sisters' did when they went to the mill; I hurry the corves a mile and more underground and back; they weigh 300 cwt.; I hurry eleven a-day; I wear a belt and chain at the workings to get the corves out; the getters that I work for are naked except their caps; they pull off all their clothes; I see them at work when I go up; sometimes they beat me, if I am not quick enough, with their hands; they strike me upon my back; the boys take liberties with me sometimes and pull me about; I am the only girl in the pit; there are about twenty boys and fifteen men; all the men are naked; I would rather work in mill than in coal pit.

No. 116.—Sarah Gooder, aged 8 years.

I'm a trapper in the Gawber pit. It does not tire me, but I have to trap without a light and I'm scared. I go at four and sometimes half-past three in the morning, and come out at five and half-past. I never go to sleep. Sometimes I sing when I've light, but not in the dark; I dare not sing then. I don't like being in the pit. I am very sleepy when I go sometimes in the morning. I go to Sunday schools and read Reading made Easy. . . . They teach me to pray. . . . "God bless my father and mother, and sister and brother, and everybody else, and God bless me and make me a good servant. Amen." I have heard tell of Jesus many a time. I don't know why he came on earth, I'm sure, and I don't know why he died, but he had stones for his head to rest on. . . .

There were many Crabtrees, Bentleys, Kershaws and Gooders. There had to be, to spin the wheels of industry carrying men forward with Tennyson, ever forward, down the ringing grooves of change. They built the City of Man. Their hands worked in its industrial barracks, fashioned its great buildings, laid its binding roads, dug into the earth for its resources.

But perhaps even more than men, the cities spoke for the age, for men were either its masters or its victims, while cities were its products and its symbols. They were the logical, necessary results of the creed that ordained their existence and defined their functions. Production and profit were the only ends and criteria governing their erection. And hence their two great institutions were factory and slum.[6]

Focus of the urban center was the factory, and its needs took precedence over all else in dictating the character and pattern of the municipal environment in which men were to live. It claimed the best available site in the urban area, that is, wherever natural power was readily accessible; it prescribed that railroad cuttings run through the town to its gates; in effect it designated in what part of the city its workers must reside. Its select situation was established and its attendant demands met, even before government buildings or the most basic municipal utilities and public services. It was at once the pivot and symbol of the city of the new society, as surely as the cathedral of the middle ages contained within itself the character of the medieval city. Each, in a certain sense, claimed dominion over the city of its age. In each was the age's conception of beauty—or the necessity which took precedence over beauty. Each affirmed its prerogative to define for men the manner in which they must earn their bread. Each absorbed and commanded the energies of the men of its age. And each was the structure which spoke in mute stone of the faith of men.

The houses in which lived the Crabtrees and Bentleys, Kershaws and Gooders were noticeably less commodious than the buildings which protected machines from deterioration or depreciation in value. This was logically so, because so long as the birth rate maintained itself men could be replaced in the labor ranks at no cost. Sometimes they lived on the surface of the ground, in shacks thrown up against the walls of the city's gas works, against an iron mill, or a railroad cutting. Often they moved underground: one-sixth of Liverpool's men lived in cellars. Water was frequently an absent necessity and, when this was so, the poor could be seen going from door to door in the more respected sections of towns begging water, as men in a famine beg for bread. Infant mortality in appalling numbers became an accepted condition in the life cycles of the poor, for all aspects of the environment which multiplied the hazards and tortures of childbirth combined to form an ideal breeding-ground for bacteria.[7]

For many this could not be a happy or creative life—for those who were, as Spencer had explained, the incapable, the imprudent, and the idle. But for others, the wheels of industry seemed to be moving resolutely toward the good society: that is, the wheels were turning at a profit. . . . "The towns had their profitable dirt, their profitable smoke, their profitable slums, their profitable disorder, their profitable ignorance, their profitable despair. . . . The new factories and the new furnaces were like the pyramids, telling of man's enslavement, rather than of his power, casting their long shadows over the society that took such pride in them."[8] . . . Were these, then, the pyramids of which Diderot had spoken, those monuments to science which would "inspire in us a startling conception of the power and resources of the men who have raised them"—monuments beyond which "men will proceed no further"?

Incapable, imprudent, idle or not, men were broken by the towns they made. Bodies bent under the labor of the factory, limbs were twisted or severed by machines, lungs polluted by dirt and smoke, nerves shredded by the insistent machine-gun rhythm of the factory's turning wheels and driving pistons. Minds ceased to grasp any rationalizing purpose for the mechanics of existence; specialization of labor destroyed any comprehensively creative impulse within men; the dumb brute necessity of staying alive alone claimed men's strength and energy. And senses were blunted: in the sultry, charcoaled factory areas and industrial towns, men lost for life the sight of rich green hills or warm, fertile plains; the smell of great pasture-lands, sun-baked piles of hay, or dark, newly-turned earth; the sound of spring on wings in the open country, the clean rush of waves on an open shore. All this was gone.

A great cycle was almost closed. From the first stirrings of renewed economic life in the Italian cities and the Flanders of the late middle ages, cities had been the mark, symbol and focus of the insurgent commercial and industrial forces. From the small faubourg and portus had come much—from the time when the ambitious merchant had been compelled to settle outside urban walls because he was essentially a suspect social figure. In the mordant words of Patrick Geddes: "Slum, semi-slum, and super-slum—to this has come the evolution of cities."[9]

The greatest triumph achieved within the walls of the City of Man was neither the efficiency of its industrial organization nor the productivity of its massed machines—but the fact that its laboring masses survived its way of life. That they continued to live and work, to raise families, to affirm a dignity and morality in their lives which no industrial order could destroy—that they did this was a timeless tribute to their inner integrity and courage. Economic subjects though they might be, they stubbornly refused to permit their own surrender to the motives and scale of values which were their masters': so that even as they rose above their material environment, so also did they rise above the faith of their rulers. Conscious of fighting for an end no more pretentious than the earning of a decent livelihood and the maintenance of self-respect, they effectually labored that their sons—or their sons' sons—might live to attest the day when men would reach for a faith of more strength and integrity than that of the Pharisee.

No longer merely a subject for intellectual discourse among the Enlightened, the Liberal Society had taken clear form from the tough tissue of fact. It was constituted, moreover, of fact animated by action, by a considered social policy which imprinted a distinct and visible pattern upon the multiform political and economic operations of the Liberal Society. This considered and deliberate method of social action dictated the rations of the Liberal Society prescribed for its working masses.

It would be historical fantasy to imply that men of the nineteenth century who governed the affairs of state did so in the light and guidance of a carefully conceived and universally accepted plan for perpetuation of bourgeois social dominion. But as the economic needs and appetites of the triumphant middle class were the primary forces to which political leaders paid unstinted deference, it was logical and inevitable that the pattern of political action would assume a specialized character. And this character was preconceived and predetermined in the sense that, in the consciousness of the age, there was firmly rooted the profound belief that the bourgeoisie merited and should claim the bounteous bulk of the rewards of social organization.

These were not abstract considerations far removed from the open arena of political debate: they were in the forefront of the Liberal's mind and he spoke frankly of them. In 1832, for example, pleading for the Reform Bill of 1832, Lord Chancellor Brougham addressed these words to the House of Lords. . . . "If there is a mob, there is the people also. I speak now of the middle classes—of those hundreds of thousands of respectable persons—the most numerous and by far the most wealthy order in the community; for if all your lordship's castles, manors, rights of warren and rights of chase, with all your broad acres, were brought to the hammer and sold at fifty years' purchase, the price would fly up and kick the beam when counterpoised by the vast and solid riches of those middle classes, who are also the genuine depositaries of sober, rational, intelligent, and honest English feeling."[10] The distinction thus drawn between the "mob" and the "people" was implicit in almost all the effective utterances of the day; and the "people," as Lord Chancellor Brougham explicitly stated, were those who constituted "by far the most wealthy order in the community."

Forty years later the same political creed was expounded in almost identical political circumstances, this time by scholarly Walter Bagehot, the great English constitutionalist. When he spoke the Second Reform Bill, further enlarging the enfranchised electorate, had just been passed by Parliament. His concern was the concern shared by all men of the bourgeoisie: fear that statesmen might try to rise to power on the shoulders of "the lower orders"—the incapable, the imprudent, the idle. He spoke anxiously of the possible intentions of new political leaders who might represent a "people" which was not defined in terms of the middle class. . . . "If they raise questions which will excite the lower orders of mankind; if they raise questions on which those orders are likely to be wrong; if they raise questions on which the interest of those orders is not identical with, or is antagonistic to, the whole interest of the state, they will have done the greatest harm they can do. . . . They will have suggested topics that will bind the poor as a class together; topics which will excite them against the rich; topics the discussion of which in the only form in which that discussion reaches their ears will be to make them think that some new law can make them comfortable—that it is the present law which makes them uncomfortable. . . . If the first work of the new voters is to try and create a 'poor man's paradise,' the great political trial now beginning will simply fail."[11]

The "great political trial" to which Bagehot referred meant effectively one thing: the experiment to see how far political liberty could be extended to the masses without their being allowed to reach a position from which they might successfully challenge the economic premises of the Liberal Society. In deprecating efforts of the laboring class to effect a change in their estate through legislation, Bagehot was reflecting one of the most dexterous changes in the development of Liberal social thought. In an age when the men of commerce and industry had aspired to political control, they had postulated the dogma that all things could be realized through legislative action, if only that action were governed by "true" principles. But when these men had won their victory, and a class below them claimed the right to invoke the legislative process for their own just ends, they were suddenly informed that legislative fiat, so recently depicted as omnicompetent, could do nothing to serve those ends; and men who rose up and demanded that the governments of men take concrete action to relieve the poor were denounced as demagogues and bidden to realize that legislation could not help a condition generated by natural economic laws!

Perhaps most eloquent and representative of all prophets and apologists of the benevolent bourgeoisie was the Right Honorable Thomas Babington Macaulay—the same who, in his poetic endeavors, had been so profoundly impressed with the triumph of the Puritan Revolution. His parliamentary speeches, in the rich, sonorous prose that made him justly famous, were winning summations of the age's guiding beliefs. "The end of government," he explained, "is not directly to make the people rich, but to protect them in making themselves rich."[12] To achieve this end the class upon which the state must place full reliance was that class which was the great hope of England's future—"the middle class of England, with the flower of the aristocracy at its head, and the flower of the working-classes bringing up its rear."[13] Carrying his argument one step further, Macaulay explains that this class is the heart of England because "civilization rests on the security of property," and hence the following is an axiom upon which all sound political systems must be built: "that we never can, without absolute danger, intrust the supreme government of the country to any class which would, to a moral certainty, be induced to commit great and systematic inroads against the security of property."[14]

The pattern of political action woven from these premises

was simple: to extend the franchise to the widest reaches of the middle class, and to unite the middle class with the aristocracy to secure property, prosperity, and progress, against the malevolent threats of the working masses. In his speech pleading for the same Reform Bill which Brougham had advanced, Macaulay illumined the whole conception of the right social order of things which dominated the Liberal Society of his day. The object of the Reform Bill was "plain, rational, and consistent"—almost the same adjectives Brougham had used to describe the middle class: sober, rational, intelligent, and honest. And he continued: "It is this—to admit the middle class to a large and direct share in the representation, without any violent shock to the institutions of our country."[15] To go beyond this would be to solicit social disaster, because "universal suffrage would be fatal to all purposes for which government exists, and for which aristocracies and all other things exist."[16] To admit the laboring class to the political community "would produce a destructive revolution," while the enfranchisement of the bourgeoisie "is our best security against a revolution."[17] In the same academic way in which Locke had discussed the right of revolution Macaulay conceded that government must take account of the welfare of those below the bourgeois level; but, he adds swiftly, "that they may be governed for their happiness, they must not be governed according to the doctrines which they have learned from their illiterate, incapable, low-minded flatterers."[18]

Macaulay's conclusion from all this is logical and ineludible: the aristocracies of birth and of wealth must unite to quell the demands of the poor's "illiterate, incapable, low-minded flatterers" and secure for all time that property which is the common economic base for their welfare. Finishing his address to the Lords of the realm, Macaulay concludes in a magnificent peroration: "The end of government is the happiness of the people; and I do not conceive that, in a country like this, the happiness of the people can be promoted by a form of government in which the middle classes place no confidence. . . . Pronounce in a manner worthy of the expectations with which this great debate has been anticipated, and of the long remembrance it shall leave behind. Renew the youth of the state. Save property divided against itself. Save the multitude, endangered by their own ungovernable passions. Save the aristocracy, endangered by its own unpopular power. Save the greatest, and fairest, and most highly civilized community that ever existed, from calamities which may in a few days sweep away all the rich heritage of so many ages of wisdom and glory."[19]

Thus, behind all the resounding verbiage and beatific platitudes of the new social thought; behind all the supple generalities that veiled the particulars of economic acquisitiveness; behind all the pontifical economic laws which essayed to prove the inevitability of human poverty and degradation —behind all this stood the calculated compendium of bourgeois economic appetites and political ambitions.

There were, it is true, protests and revolts. There was the succession of poets and thinkers who could not view maimed bodies and maimed minds with the accomplished complacency of the Victorian Liberal: Byron, Southey, Coleridge, Carlyle, Ruskin, Arnold, Morris, among them. There was the succession of uprisings from the masses of labor which condemned as false the Liberal belief in the innate harmony of clashing self-interests, the serene identity of wills of all individuals and all classes. The years 1830, 1848 and 1870 were ominous times on the Continent, while Luddite riots and the march of the Chartists revealed that the same rebellious forces were but relatively more subdued in the island where Victoria reigned. Outbursts like these—ultimately vain and costly in blood and human hopes though they were—at least for a fleeting moment ripped the seams of the Liberal Society long enough for some men to see what lay at its center.

Such, then, was this Liberal Society: the culmination of the sweeping evolution of cities, the final conquest brought by the victories of the new science, the triumphant conclusion to the century-spanning revolt of ideas. At the center of the social order stood the citadel of economic power, occupied and vigilantly guarded by the masters of the new economy. Surrounding this there stood the vast rings of out-works, the myriad lesser political, social and religious institutions. Of these last, many, if it were necessary, might be surrendered slowly and circumspectly—so long as the central citadel remained unassailed.

The pattern of social action which governed the rations of the Liberal Society was indeed skillfully knit. By modest compromises, by properly publicized concessions, by elaborately staged gestures of self-effacement, the bourgeoisie would perpetuate its dominion: by ransom the rebels would be bought off. . . . Let there be more popular education: for, as Macaulay noted, "can it be denied that the education of the common people is the most effectual means of protecting persons and property?"[20] Let there be wider political enfranchisement: for economic discontent can thereby be channeled into easily governable streams. Let there be modest moderation of factory and wage conditions: for then "the ignorant, the imprudent, and the idle" will not become victims of "illiterate, incapable, low-minded flatterers" attacking the very sanctity of free competition and private property. Let benevolent humanitarian impulses spend their energies on the non-essential issues; let the English fight against Negro slavery assume noble and grandiose proportions, because factory conditions then will pall beside the plight of the men of the dark race. Let candidates for Parliament, Chamber, Reichstag and Congress enrich their campaign speeches with daring denunciations of social injustice; for it matters little which party be the titular victor, so long as both agree on the fundamental economic precepts. . . . This was the institutional technique of the Liberal Society, at least as important as its more refined rationale, and much more intimate with reality.

Now the history of the Liberal Society becomes almost exclusively the history of this collective effort to sustain illusion in the presence of fact: to maintain the inherited fiction of freedom and equality in a text of economic and social conditions which denied to the masses the means of reaching that ideal. This was the task to which the rulers of the City of Man dedicated themselves: to subdue the tension, to moderate the strain, to lessen the friction which sprang logically from the inner conflict of their creed—the conflict between the gospel of freedom and the ambitions of its prophets.

The Liberal Society thus had been constructed from a philosophical technique which entailed the precarious, if somewhat ingenious, equation of antagonistic ideals, rather than the elaboration of a system of social thought with positive content and inner consistency; and it was perpetuated by an institutional technique composed of little more than dynamic, amoral expediency. Such an essentially tenuous structure would probably have survived but a short while the days when men were first brought to see clearly the reality in which they had believed—but for two factors: two factors which eased inner tension and fortified falling hopes. The first was the rich field of imperial expansion to which the bourgeoisie of Europe set their plow. The fruits of colonial exploitation were to be great: great enough to reinvigorate the Liberal dream with the prospect of still new and wider worlds to claim, great enough to propel even further the advances of the new science and its material rewards, great enough to increase the ransom which the economic masters could pay their workers.

The second factor which steadied the structure of Liberalism was America: an America which at once furnished a release for Europe's oppressed and a reaffirmed hope that surely, in this vast land of natural wealth, economic progress could realize freedom and equality for all: an America to which the masses of Europe could attach their dream of deliverance, as they came to despair of the fulfillment of their ideals in their native lands: an America where the Liberal faith might yet bring to pass the good society. The building of America became the great Liberal adventure.

The Great Liberal Adventure

Bow down, dear land, for thou hast found release!
　Thy God, in these distempered days,
　Hath taught thee the sure wisdom of His ways
And through thine enemies hath wrought thy peace!
　Bow down in prayer and praise!
No poorest in thy borders but may now
Lift to the juster skies a man's enfranchised brow;
O Beautiful! My country! Ours once more![1]

IN THESE words did James Russell Lowell herald the victory
of the cause of liberty in the American Civil War. The aristocracy of the South had been broken and scattered, and the
slaves of the South had been declared free men. From the
throats of men who had led the crusade for emancipation came
now exultant cries of victory, unstinted faith in the future
suffusing a nation like the clear early light of morning. And
from gutted plantations of the South came the freedmen's
echoing chorus.

Every nigger's gwine to own a mule,
　Jubili, Jubilo!
Every nigger's gwine to own a mule,
An' live like Adam in de Golden Rule,
An' send his chillun to de white folks' school!
　In de year of Jubilo![2]

A yet larger chorus proclaimed an equally strong faith
in the promise of American life: they who came from the Old
World—from the hills of Ireland, from the valley of the
Danube, from the banks of the Rhine and the Arno and the
Vistula, from the plains of Campania and the steppes of the
Ukraine. In forty years their throng was fourteen million
strong. Unparalleled since the surge of the barbarians into the

Roman Empire, theirs formed the greatest folk movement of history. Driven by oppression and disillusion at home, summoned by the irresistible hope and promise that seemed alive in the New World, they came—family, possessions, cultural heritage—to breathe the air and feel the soil of the land that exclaimed,

> Give me your tired, your poor,
> Your huddled masses yearning to breathe free
> The wretched refuse of your teeming shore,
> Send these, the homeless, tempest-tost to me:
> I lift my lamp beside the golden door.

Poet, freedman, and immigrant—their faith was matched by that of yet another: the leader of American business. Perhaps sparkling with less rapturous phrases, his faith seemed grounded on the solid rock of economic reality. Opposed to his victorious march stood none of those classes whom the European man of capital had been forced to fight and destroy in his ascent to power—no great landed aristocracy, no entrenched clergy, no titled nobility. In the war just concluded had triumphed a social evolution which had removed for all time the constraining force of a hostile planting aristocracy—had done so with a sweep "more complete than the destruction of the clergy and nobility in the first French cataclysm."[3] Now, before the competent, ready hands of the business chieftain, there lay one-half the whole area of the country yet to be exploited: rich in coal, in iron, in timber, in copper, in oil. And by his side stood a solicitous government, fresh from martial triumph, sensitive to the demands of capital, eager for industrial triumph.

To all these men, the promise of the Liberal Society in America seemed infinite. For some of them, promise would become reality; for they would win great economic provinces. The range of the arena was large, for into only that half which lay beyond the Mississippi River could have been placed the whole of the Roman Empire. Hence commensurately great would be the individual provinces of great industrial barons.

Beside the dynastic fiefs of such magnitude as the Standard Oil Company, E. I. du Pont de Nemours, Ford Motor Company, United States Steel—beside these the crown properties of Habsburgs, Hohenzollerns, Hanovers, and Romanovs would fade to mild proportions.[4]

For others—among them, immigrant and freedmen—the harvest was to be less rewarding. But they, as Voltaire had explained, were but the oxen, which need a yoke, a goad, and hay. As the prophet had spoken, so, in truth, it came to pass.

A Yoke . . .

More than a fight for union or a crusade on slavery, the Civil War, interlocking forces with the Industrial Revolution, divided the history of America cleanly in two. It cut "a white gash through the history of the country," Lewis Mumford has written. "It dramatized in a stroke the changes that had begun to take place during the preceding twenty or thirty years. On one side lay the Golden Day, the period of Elizabethan daring on the sea, of a well balanced adjustment of farm and factory in the East, of a thriving regional culture, operating through the lecture-lyceum and the provincial college; an age in which the American mind had flourished and had begun to find itself. When the curtain rose on the postbellum scene, this old America was for all practical purposes demolished: industrialism had entered overnight, had transformed the practices of agriculture, had encouraged a mad exploitation of mineral oil, natural gas, and coal, and had made the unscrupulous master of finance, fat with war profits, the central figure of the situation. All the crude practices of British paleotechnic industry appeared on the new scene without relief or mitigation."[5]

What happened to those men of the dark race in whose name the war had been fought to a successful conclusion? Theirs was not even the status of emancipated serfs, for upon them was a seal of color that could not be removed by legislative fiat. For their vaunted privilege of voting they had no prior education, and on the day of their "liberation" they were propertyless. In the words of Negro leader Frederick Douglas, the Negro "was free from the individual master but a slave to society. He had neither money, property, nor friends. He was free from the old plantation, but he had nothing but the dusty road under his feet. He was free from the old quarter that once gave him shelter, but a slave to the rains of summer and the frosts of winter. He was turned loose, naked, hungry, and destitute to the open sky."[6]

To elevate emancipation above the level of a shallow political gesture, the Negro sought land and he sought education. He was given the franchise. He was given the franchise, in Thaddeus Stevens's words, "to secure perpetual ascendancy to the party of the Union."[7] Since land on which the Negro might sustain himself would be unproductive of anything contributing to the political hegemony of the Republican Party, a government which found it possible to give forty million acres to a single railroad could not surrender one-quarter of that amount for the people it set "free." To all of this the symbolic legal monument was Amendment XIV to the Constitution of the United States. Ostensibly dedicated to protection of the Negro against any effort to deprive him of "life, liberty, or property, without due process of law," the Amendment's true function was to buttress corporate industrial structures: to protect with an unbreachable legal wall the private domain of free business enterprise. To the political technique of the Liberal Society it would be a serious injustice not to recognize the astuteness of those men who succeeded in converting the Negro dream of freedom into a vital pillar of the Liberal Economy.

That economy, and the class who were its masters, obtained immediate and direct support from the post-war government. Financially, it absorbed government bonds whose interest ran up to 7 per cent, and it witnessed reestablishment of a national bank and reassertion of a "sound" money policy, so close to the heart of the capitalist class since the terrible days of Daniel Shays. Industry received its rewards through a swift upward revision of the tariff and a wide-open immigration policy.

Echoing the words of Thomas Paine, the Republican platform of 1864 solemnized America as "the asylum of the oppressed of all nations."[8] The authorities of the asylum therewith lowered their nets into the vast labor reservoir of Europe and emerged with an overflowing haul of cheap labor. Thus immigrant as well as freedman came to serve as an instrument assuring the one true triumph of the day—that of business enterprise.

The extent of the material conquest was titanic. With understandable pride Andrew Carnegie could point to the tangible results of the restoration of man to his sovereignty over nature. "Two pounds of ironstone mined upon Lake Superior," he narrated, "and transported nine hundred miles to Pittsburgh; one pound and one-half of coal, mined and manufactured into coke, and transported into Pittsburgh; one half-pound of lime, mined and transported to Pittsburgh; a small amount of manganese ore mined in Virginia and brought to Pittsburgh—and these four pounds of materials manufactured into one pound of steel, for which the consumer pays one cent."[9] All roads led to Pittsburgh—or its regional equivalent—as Industry moved in giant strides across a continent. The history of this march of the Iron Men is the story of aggressive economic leaders, "akin in spirit," as Charles and Mary Beard have described them, "to military captains of the past, working their way up from the ranks, exploiting natural resources without restraint, waging economic war on one another, entering into combinations, making immense fortunes, and then, like successful feudal chieftains or medieval merchants, branching out as patrons of learning, divinity, and charity."[10]

Industrial pyramids rose as if overnight; their labor base was wide, but their pinnacle was narrow. A single corporation formed at the turn of the century was capitalized at a sum greater than the total national wealth of the United States in 1800. In the last year of the nineteenth century, the capitalization of the consolidations formed in that single year exceeded the total national debt. Twelve years later a government investigating committee revealed, among statistics that startled a nation, the fact that a single banking firm held seventy-two directorships in forty-seven of the country's greatest corporate economic structures. It was the same banking concern which, on a single night in February 1895, had earned a profit of five million dollars in one colossal gold deal with the United States government.[11] Thus "roads from four continents now ran to the new Appian Way—Wall Street— and the pro-consuls of distant provinces paid homage to a new sovereign."[12]

Epitome and strength of the march of Industry was the march of the railroads—long, strong fingers of the hand of the industrial East, reaching across the great plains and over the range of the Rocky Mountains to touch the Western shores, from Puget Sound to the Gulf of California. Much of what the railroads reached they owned, thanks to a beneficent federal government; to them came land grants which together totaled the area of Texas, one company alone receiving grants as large as the state of Missouri. Twenty-five years after the Civil War the capital represented by the railroad business exceeded, in itself, twice the value of all the slaves upon which the whole Southern plantation economy had been built.[13] By the end of the century the major part of the economic power represented by railroads resided with but six groups, absentee landlords whose stream of tribute from the land of the West seemed inexhaustible.

Into this West had come they who had left the Old World to earn freedom and livelihood from the bounteous earth beyond the Mississippi—their ranks enlarged with those who had been hurled from the whirling center of industry in the East. Refugees from the social disasters of the Liberal Society, they had left the shores of Thames, Loire, Elbe, Danube, Dnieper—to bring life to the lands by the Missouri, the Colorado, the Platte, the Columbia. Their labor was without parallel in all history. For what they sought to create was a world of their own within a world that was not their own. All around them the dominion of the Liberal Society was complete—and they turned their backs upon it to fashion an economic way of life whose principles they themselves could dictate. In essence, that system was the economy of the medieval era: its production was for sustenance and use, not exchange or profit: and the psychology of that mode of production was instilled in all the transactions, all the communal affairs and concerns, of these people. The whole was, in reverse, comparable to the cities of the late middle ages: as the latter were isolated economic islands in the social order of the day, so the men of the West in America constructed an economy which spurned allegiance to the precepts of the Liberal Society.

But the march of capitalism seemed ever Westward, too— since the time when the European center of economic gravity had swung to the Atlantic. Now it not only had spanned the Atlantic but maintained its relentless march on into the West of America. Agriculture was sucked into the industrial vortex. Specialization and standardization of crops; conversion of farming as a way of life into farming as a business; evolution of a tenant class, bound to agrarian masters; and the fiscal bondage of almost all agriculture to the economic dynasties of the East—all this came to mean that the dream of a nation sustained largely by free, independent men of the soil was dead. It meant, too, that the refugees had fled in vain.

A half century later, looking back upon the changes that came upon men and ideas in this period, an American writer would find much to doubt in the assumption that the conquest of the West by the forces of industrial civilization was an unqualified social blessing. . . . "In the days before the coming of industry," Sherwood Anderson has reflected, "before the time of the mad awakening, the towns of the Middle West were sleepy places devoted to the practice of the old trades, to agriculture and to merchandising. In the morning the men of the towns went forth to work in the fields or to the practice of the trade of carpentry, horseshoeing, wagon making, harness repairing, and the making of shoes and clothing. They read books and believed in a God born in the brains of men who came out of a civilization much like their own. On the farms and in the houses, in the towns the men and women worked together toward the same ends in life. They lived in small frame houses set on the plains like boxes, but very substantially built. . . . After one of the poor little houses had been lived in for a long time, after children had been born and men had died, after men and women had suffered and had moments of joy together in the tiny rooms under the low roofs, a subtle change took place. The houses became almost beautiful in their humanness. Each of the houses began vaguely to shadow forth the personality of the people who lived within its walls. . . . A sense of quiet growth awoke in sleeping minds. It was the time for art and beauty to awake in the land.

"Instead the giant, Industry, awoke. Boys, who in the schools had read of Lincoln, walking for miles through the forest to borrow his first book, and of Garfield, the towpath lad who became President, began to read in the newspapers and magazines of men who by developing their faculty for getting and keeping money had become suddenly and overwhelmingly rich. Hired writers called these men great, and there was no maturity of mind in the people with which to combat the force of the statement, often repeated. Like children the people believed what they were told. . . .

"Out through the coal and iron regions of Pennsylvania, into Ohio and Indiana, and on westward into the states bordering on the Mississippi River, industry crept. . . . A vast energy seemed to come out of the breast of earth and infect the people. Thousands of the most energetic men of the middle states wore themselves out in forming companies, and when the companies failed, immediately formed others. In the fast-growing towns, men who were engaged in organizing companies representing a capital of millions lived in houses thrown hurriedly together by carpenters who, before the time of the great awakening, were engaged in building barns. It was a time of hideous architecture, a time when thought and learning paused. Without music, without poetry, without beauty in their lives or impulses, a whole people, full of the native energy and strength of lives lived in a new land, rushed pell-mell into a new age."[14]

In that age, before the vast industrial edifices of the day, the masses of labor had to bend their knees, as all the vital and strong economic forces seemed to press toward harnessing to the will of capital the urban as well as the agrarian masses. Increasing mechanization of industry destroyed the individual's sense of creativeness in work, while it exaggerated the capricious character of employment in the industrial world. Giant corporations as employers multiplied labor's problems; impersonal and often almost omnipotent, they could virtually dictate the terms of the labor contract. Immigration that brought millions of new workers every decade sharpened the competition on the labor market, propelling wages on a downward spiral. Immigrants themselves, although welcomed by owners of mill, mine and factory, came to be scorned by men like Thomas Bailey Aldrich—who saw pass Ellis Island only "jailbirds, professional murderers, amateur lepers . . . and human gorillas," until his beloved native country seemed to become only "the cesspool of Europe."[15]

And as the oxen pulled the wheels of industry, men came to perfect a double standard of social morality for master and serf—a standard that explained and vindicated the function and lot of the oxen. For capital to combine was logical business practice; for labor to combine was dangerous to the American tradition of individual freedom. Industrial leaders who organized capital into vast corporate entities were elevated to a station among history's greatest; labor leaders who sought to organize labor were menacing agitators. Business monopoly was the logical fulfillment of natural economic laws; the closed shop violated the sanctity of freedom of contract. Business in politics ensured that the civil authority would be exercised by the most respected members of the national community; labor in politics always could be traced to unwholesome alien instigation. To summon the government to protect by force the interests of property was to guard with zealous vigilance the American way of life; to call upon the government to uphold the interests of labor was to rattle the saber of class hatred. To aspire to a position where one could fix commodity prices which the consuming community must accept was but a slightly circuitous way of working for social welfare; to attempt to bargain with capital to do nothing more than discuss wages was presumptuous and dangerous invasion of the rights of capital management. To use one's economic power to expel a laborer from his job and livelihood was the just and unqualified prerogative of capital; to withhold one's economic power and to strike for clean working conditions or just wages was to challenge the foundations of the Liberal Society. To exalt one's wealth as God-given was to be a Christian; to confuse the precept of charity and radical social reform was to blaspheme.

The yoke was fastened firmly.

A Goad . . .

What purported to vindicate economic maladjustment in the Liberal Society of America was the alleged opportunity for redress through political channels. Since society was not even conceived of as a harmonious unity but as divided into closed compartments of economic, political, and religious realms, it was unreasonable to expect that government should actively dictate to the men who governed the economic affairs of society, for these latter were a private domain and the exclusive property of those who had triumphed in the race for wealth. It was agreed, however, that they who might feel oppressed by real or imagined wrongs in the economic realm could appeal to "their" government for aid. Therefore, the free operation of the franchise would be the salve to heal all social wounds. To no avail did men like Theodore Roosevelt suggest that "a vote is like a rifle: its usefulness depends upon the character of the user."[16] For the faith in the omnicompetence of the franchise was rooted in the Liberal tradition.

The glory of this doctrine was that it served admirably the wishes of the masters of the new economy to have social grievances channeled into the stream of politics, rather than be fought out in the economic arena; while at the same time, the aggrieved were both prodded and subdued by the expectation of political deliverance. Once economic conflicts were converted into political issues, the members of the nation's economic dynasties could inspect and dispose of them at leisure, for their political control was grounded on the firm rock of financial and industrial power. That control they exploited in four characteristic methods: through the judiciary of the nation, through political corruption, through control of both major political parties, and through effective sabotage of independent reform movements.

Legal articulation of Liberal economics resounded from the chambers of the nation's courts, the most elaborate rituals being performed in Washington. Cornerstone to the legal edifice thus constructed was the conception of the corporation as an individual, the most spectacular performance of judicial acrobatics in the circus of the circuits. To an age professing to revere the economic omnicompetence of the individual, it had come as a rude shock to discover that the exigencies of the new-scale business enterprise demanded corporate economic organization: the mythology of capitalism seemed, of its own inner necessity, to have inspired economic heresy. But the reconciliation of economic fact and economic gospel was ingeniously achieved. For the technique which had been so successfully exploited in the realms of religion, ethics and social theory was now invoked in the legal sphere; the nation's law decreed the simple equation of corporation and individual. Perhaps in its whole tradition this technique was never more masterfully employed, for now the equation was one not dealing with philosophical abstractions but economic realities; it successfully baptized as an individual that form of economic organization whose existence was made necessary by the impotence of isolated, mortal, individual economic effort; and it endowed with personality the most impersonal economic agency yet devised by men.

Buttressing the Liberal economy frequently taxed judicial ingenuity to the limit, but they in whose hands were held the scales of justice soon perfected the skill of legal legerdemain. Use of the Fourteenth Amendment alone was competent in the highest degree, for it was invoked to block as many varying legislative invasions of the private realm of business as these: Washington and New Jersey laws regulating private employment agencies, Illinois law providing eight-hour work day for women, Alaskan eight-hour law, innumerable laws prohibiting labor on Sundays, several state laws demanding industrial compensation, and a federal act providing social insurance for railroad employees.[17] The legal mind of the Liberal Society had traveled far indeed since the day when emancipation of Southern slaves laid the groundwork for all this. Quite alone, in effect, was Justice Holmes when he suggested that "the Fourteenth Amendment does not enact Mr. Herbert Spencer's *Social Statics*."[18]

The same legal story was told in the nation's courts on so many occasions as to provoke nothing quite so much as tedium. Use of the Sherman Anti-Trust Act and the Interstate Commerce Act to block expansion of labor unions, while industrial consolidations built their pyramids of interlocking directorates;* perpetuation of the legal fiction of freedom of contract and equality of bargaining power between corporation and employer; indiscriminate use of the injunction weapon against militant organized labor; judicial sabotage of legislative efforts for child-labor reform[19]—there was virtually no end to the list of constitutional hurdles placed in the way of any change in the basic premises of Liberal economics. It was not, then, a matter of great wonder that the capitalist class always paused to genuflect at the bar of law and order.

At the opposite extreme, in a sense, from this sober legal ritual stood the technique of simple and direct political corruption, by which political articulation of economic grievances

* The Sherman and Interstate Commerce Acts were invoked against the unions in the famed Danbury Hatters Case (cf. Commons, J. R. and J. B. Andrews, *Principles of Labor Legislation*, p. 385), the former also in the 1894 Pullman Strike (cf. Josephson, M., *The Politicos*, p. 571). Compare these instances to the Supreme Court's dismissal of the 1895 suit against the American Sugar Trust (cf. Josephson, p. 608).

could be stifled. Railroad baron Huntington deftly summarized an important aspect of this device: "So they are going to regulate the railroads? Well, then, the railroads must regulate the regulators."[20] The corruption which reached its most notorious proportions in the Grant administration was not a sporadic game of caprice. It was, as a friend remarked to Lincoln Steffens, "a process of revolution":[21] a perpetual revolution dedicated to the subversion of all efforts in the sphere of politics to challenge or modify the existing social and economic structure. The most famous journalist of the age, after years of close observation, summarized the matter simply. "In a country where business is dominant," Steffens explained, "business men must and will corrupt a government which can pass laws to hinder or help business." But, he added, "there must be something wrong—unsocial—at the bottom of the organization of businesses which have to control government."[22]

Even more consistent and elaborate than the technique of political corruption was the canalization of political discontent through bourgeois control of both major political parties. As an American historian has remarked,[23] the special utility of the party system consisted of its reversible character: while one of its two constituent parts performed the unpleasant and unpopular necessities of government, the other derived renewed energy from popular misgivings and grievances and thereby harnessed them, preparing to capitalize on them politically at the next election. But the next election merely initiated the same cycle again, this time with party roles reversed. Through the last three decades of the nineteenth century only faint political nuances disinguished the two great political aggregations of the nation: they were evenly balanced, they agreed in their acceptance and regard for the fundamental premises of the Liberal Society, and they alternated with rhythmic regularity in control of the national government. All the while the political tactics of alternation were thus expertly used, the leaders of the nation's economy worked consistently for what one of them aptly described as "the party of business"; the interior and guiding force of both political groups, this party could never lose an election because its principles never were issues in elections.

Throughout the era, thus removed from the revealing glare of the political footlights, these chieftains of industry dominated all—writing the drama, casting the roles, erecting the scenery, and, more often than not, owning the theater. In 1888 the Republican nomination of Harrison was dictated by a telegram from Andrew Carnegie, who was vacationing in Scotland. As Sherman said, it was as if a President were named "at the brisk dictation of the autocratic ruler of the Republican Party as he goes coaching over the Highlands."[24] When in 1892 the same Harrison and the same Republican Party were defeated by Cleveland, the same Carnegie—still in Europe— cabled a high-spirited reply to his friends who had forwarded the news: "Cleveland! Landslide! Well, we have nothing to fear and perhaps it is for the best. People will now think the Protected Manfrs. are attended to and quit agitating. Cleveland is a pretty good fellow. Off for Venice tomorrow."[25] No matter how the political pageant was staged, the party of business always triumphed.

It was a profound development—that which men like Andrew Carnegie were bringing to pass: the total conversion of all political agencies into instruments whose use, in the final analysis, could be dictated by the triumphant bourgeoisie. The greatest middle-class republic of the West therewith reached political maturity, as the institution of the party— from which alone political life was infused into the government—was refashioned to harmonize with and to fulfill the political desiderata of an advanced, world-spanning capitalism.[26] The system was fundamentally simple, the methods precise, the objectives clear, in this political reorientation. The spirit which was victorious has been admirably embodied in these sentences: "It matters not one iota what political party is in power or what President holds the reins of office. We are not politicians, or public thinkers; we are the rich; we own America; we got it, God knows how, but we intend to keep it if we can by throwing all the tremendous weight of our support, our influence, our money, our political connections, our purchased Senators, our hungry Congressmen, and our public-speaking demagogues, into the scale against any legislation, any political platform, any presidential campaign, that threatens the integrity of our estate."[27] More succinctly, the same was said by Mark Hanna when he proclaimed that "all questions of government in a democracy were questions of money."[28]

Against a social organization buttressed in this fashion by legal authority and by control of the major channels of political action, and cemented at the interstices with a judicious amount of graft—against the walls of such a social order the fists of social reform bloodied themselves in vain. In no small measure, the failure followed from the character of the ubiquitous "aesthetic" reformers, distinguished by Roosevelt from the "moral" reformers.[29] Eager to assume the crusading role in political reforms that signified mild administrative reorganization or balanced governmental budgets or extended civil service, this first class of reformers joined the indignant ranks of those who most quickly and vehemently dissociated themselves from any social or industrial reform which cut through the facade of grandiose political gestures to the solid core of social evil.

These "aesthetic" reformers, with their empty efforts at political benevolence, sapped the strength of forces militating for genuine and radical change and fortified what was probably the most characteristic political technique of the Liberal Society in America. That technique was most specifically and aptly described in the words of Attorney General of the United States Olney on the occasion when he addressed the railroad barons of the nation, urging them to see the usefulness to the bourgeoisie of institutions like the Interstate Commerce Commission. "The Commission, as its functions have now been limited by the courts," the Attorney-General explained,* "is, or can be made, *of great use to the railroads.*

* Italics the present author's.

It satisfies the popular clamor for a government supervision of railroads, at the same time that *that supervision is almost entirely nominal.* Further, the older such a commission gets to be, the more it will be found to take the business and rail-road view of things. *It thus becomes a sort of barrier between the railroad corporations and the people* and a sort of protec-tion against hasty and crude legislation hostile to railroad interests. . . . The part of wisdom is *not to destroy the Com-mission, but to utilize it.*"[30] Against political barriers so skill-fully and solidly constructed, was not pathetic the crusade of them who followed the cross of silver into the promised land of bimetallism?

The utility of an institution like the Interstate Commerce Commission to the railroad dynasty was but a minor reflection of the serviceability for the Liberal Society's economic masters of the whole vast popular illusion of political deliverance from social and economic ills. Such an illusion was not the kind of goad which impelled men to action of a grandeur and magnitude which transcended the sober, even plane of daily life and daily life's necessities. It was the kind of goad, half anaesthetic perhaps, which held men to their daily tasks in what were proclaimed to be divinely-ordained vocations, nourishing their powers of endurance in one realm of society with the buoyant hope of deliverance from another. Most effective of the political fables propagated by the masters of the Liberal Society, its true meaning has been explained in another fable of America. . . .

"Modern men and women who live in industrial cities are like mice that have come out of the fields to live in houses that do not belong to them. They live within the dark walls of the houses where only a dim light penetrates, and so many have come that they grow thin and haggard with the constant toil of getting food and warmth. Behind the walls the mice scamper about in droves, and there is much squealing and chattering. Now and then a bold mouse stands upon his hind legs and addresses the others. He declares he will force his way through the walls and conquer the gods who have built the house. 'The mice shall rule. You shall live in the light and the warmth. There shall be food for all and no one shall go hungry.'

"The little mice, gathered in the darkness out of sight in the great houses, squeal with delight. After a time when nothing happens they become sad and depressed. Their minds go back to the time when they lived in the fields, but they do not go out of the walls of the houses, because long living in droves has made them afraid of the silence of long nights and the emptiness of skies."[31]

... And Hay.

This was the Golden Age of the Liberal Society in America —known to a later, less uncritical, generation as the Gilded Age. Old faiths were exploded, old ways of living tossed aside, as men rushed to explore and exploit a continent. The residue of things and ideas of the past was little more than what men could filter through the bars of the dollar sign.

The rich were on the march. As financial dynasties arose with startling suddenness and apparent facility, the whole top stratum of society passed into a state of almost constant flux. Fortunes made in the West returned East to solicit the social benediction of the oldest and most respected clans. "Into the mighty cities of the East," wrote one of the army of the plutocracy, "there moved an ever-growing army of those who had gathered from the mines of California, from the forges of Pittsburgh, from the forests of Michigan, from the metalled mountains of Montana, wealth beyond the dreams of Midas."[32] There came, in short, an army whose leaders and spokesmen exclaimed that their conquest of the political and economic citadels of society should merit the surrender to them of the cultural citadel.

With fabulous flourishes, the captains and lieutenants of business enterprise assumed the cloak of social respectability. As men of Rome once had garnered the treasures of Greece and Egypt, so they ransacked palaces, castles, and churches of Europe. Persian rugs and thickly jewelled Buddhas decorated the halls, rare and costly silver brightened the tables, Renaissance masterpieces smiled from the walls, strains of uncomprehended Mozart and Beethoven passed through the rooms—of the homes of men feverishly engaged in destroying competitors and amassing unsurpassed corporate profits in the production of iron girders, shoes, steel rails, cement, farm implements, glue, tin cans, and toothpaste. Swords of medieval knights were crossed above the mantelpiece, sternly posed portraits of the world's greatest military conquerors were hung on the walls, imposing statuettes of history's most famous kings and tyrants cluttered the tables—in the homes of men whose most daring thrusts were selling short a block of stocks or summoning state militia to break a strike. Culturally undisciplined, these men created a culture little better than depraved.[33]

The power of money claimed dominion over all realms of culture. The arts became businesses: pianos and organs became objects for mass production, were advertised as cultural imperatives, and sold and bought like beds and chairs. Journalism bowed to triumphant technology: printing equipment became elaborate and complex, large capital reserves became prerequisites for newspaper endeavor, and lucratively expanded commercial advertising often signalized the press's obeisance to corporate industry. Education, its system and its principles, was reorganized in the glaring light of the Gilded Age; wealth, seeking absolution through philanthropy, poured into colleges and universities; new institutions of learning multiplied without plan, purpose, or promise; religious overtones to university curricula were subdued or silenced completely, as programs of study veered toward emphasis on the "practical"; and at the end of the century the list of university patrons and trustees was as interchangeable with a roster of corporation directors, as in a different age it would have been indistinguishable from a list of ecclesiastic leaders. A whole nation rose upon the crest of the wave of "pecuniary culture," while its economic leaders performed the appropriate rites of conspicuous consumption, conspicuous waste, conspicuous leisure, and conspicuous philanthropy.[34]

Out of this riotous play of cultural changes, and vindicating all that a cynical observer of the Gilded Age might call tarnished, there emerged the religion of success and the gospel of wealth. A pattern whose fiber was the accepted and undisputed precepts of the men of business, the gospel of wealth rested ultimately on the simple dictum which Senator Platt prescribed as "the right of a man to run his own business in his own way, with due respect of course to the Ten Commandments and the Penal Code."[35]

In the history of ideas, the gospel of wealth assumed for itself the function of stretching an already elastic conception of Christian social ethics to fit the realities of a swiftly expanding capitalist economy. From the divided ranks of religion, Protestantism stepped forth to volunteer to make this reconciliation. As an American historian has summarized the issue, "For post-Civil War Protestantism, the gospel of wealth became a formula which permitted the Church to make peace with popular materialism. The ancient tendency in the Christian religion to withdraw from the world, to stress the warfare between the spirit and the flesh, to think in terms of otherworldliness, was checked in rich America after the Civil War. . . . Protestantism, always sensitive to shifts in the mores, made quick adjustment to the trend of the times. The Christian version of the gospel . . . was, in effect, a Protestant stratagem to retain for itself a place in the new social order, to provide itself with a function, in short, to save itself as a significant social institution. Urban Protestantism cultivated the middle and upper classes who possessed the ultimate power in American society." "The shadow of John Calvin lay across the formulas of common sense."[36]

Thus were reiterated those elements of Protestantism which had been operative centuries before in its initial consecration of the economic virtues—although their restatement now would have shocked and angered men like Latimer and Lever. The rights of property were sanctified in categorical terms, as in the words of President James McCosh of Princeton University: "God has bestowed upon us certain powers and gifts which no one is at liberty to take from us or to interfere with. All attempts to deprive us of them is theft.* Under the same head may be placed all purposes to deprive us of the right to own property or to use it as we see fit."[37] Mark Hopkins, head of Williams College, underscored this doctrine in his treatise on ethics, *The Law of Love and Love as Law*. "The right to property reveals itself through an original desire," he explained in language reminiscent of the Enlightenment. "Without this society could not exist. . . . It will be found too, historically, that the general well being and progress of society has been in proportion to the freedom of every man to gain property in all legitimate ways, and to security in its possession. . . . The acquisition of property is required by love, because it is a powerful means of benefiting others."[38]

Construction of Liberal economics as a moral good was not confined to academicians. To all the initiated it was apparent, as a textbook on ethics widely used in the 1880's declared, that "the Moral Governor has placed the power of acquisitiveness in man for a good and noble purpose." As the human should ever strive to partake of the divine, so then should men seek ever to make more articulate this acquisitive impulse divinely engendered in them. "To secure wealth is an honorable ambition," explained Baptist minister Russell Conwell in his lecture given throughout the nation, "and is one great test of a person's usefulness to others. Money is power. Every good man and woman ought to strive for power, to do good with it when obtained. Tens of thousands of men and women get rich honestly. But they are often accused by an envious, lazy crowd of unsuccessful persons of being dishonest and oppressive. I say, Get rich, Get rich!" His faith derived from such a gospel, it is small wonder that devout Baptist John D. Rockefeller should inform the first graduating class of the university which he founded: "The good Lord gave me my money." Small wonder, too, that this whole Puritan code of economic asceticism should produce the type of economic morality ex-

* An interesting perspective is gained by putting this doctrine alongside the medieval practice of cataloguing property itself under the heading of "theft."

pounded by Bishop Lawrence of Massachusetts. "In the long run," the Bishop generalized, "it is only to the man of morality that wealth comes. We believe in the harmony of God's Universe. We know that it is only by working along His laws natural and spiritual that we can work with efficiency. Only by working along the lines of right thinking and right living can the secrets and wealth of nature be revealed. . . . Godliness is in league with riches. . . . Material prosperity is helping to make the national character sweeter, more joyous, more unselfish, more Christlike."*

With this cool cascade of soothing phrases and absolving dogma tumbling from the pulpits of the nation to wash away its social sins, it is not surprising that leaders of business quickly found it expedient to invoke the name of the Christian God in defense of their estate. Andrew Carnegie, outlining his "true gospel concerning wealth," pointed to the law of competition as basic to economic society, divine and irrevocable "because it ensures the survival of the fittest in every department." Banker Henry Clews pronounced his devout verdict on the use of force by labor in these solemn words: "Strikes may have been justifiable in other nations, but they are not justifiable in our country. The Almighty has made this country for the oppressed of other nations and therefore this is the land of refuge . . . and the hand of the laboring man should not be raised against it."[39] And these sentences of a president of one of the nation's largest railroads might well have been inscribed on the anointed banners of the army of the plutocracy: "The rights and interests of the laboring man will be protected and cared for, not by the labor agitators, but by the Christian men to whom God in His infinite wisdom has given control of the property interests of the country."[40]

Reflected in the more delicately tinted mirror of philos-

* Decades later, the ministers of typical American city Middletown were echoing the same theme: "The church is the 'reason why' of America. . . . The church has made America prosperous. . . . It is no mere happening that church people become well to do. 'Godliness is profitable' even from a business standpoint." (Cited by Lynd, R. S. and H. M., *Middletown, A Study in American Culture*, p. 403.)

ophy, the gospel of wealth shone forth as the doctrine of pragmatism. Deriving strong impetus from the work of Darwin, the pragmatist, in the tradition of the utilitarian, explicitly repudiated the idea of intuitive apprehension of truths, the existence of any moral absolutes. The world of reality was a world of contingency, a world of change, of adjustment and readjustment; in such a world only that was true which was useful. As William James described the pragmatist: "He turns away from abstraction and insufficiency, from verbal solutions, from bad *a priori* reasons, from fixed principles, closed systems, and pretended absolutes and origins. He turns towards concreteness and adequacy, towards facts, towards action and towards power."[41]

Concreteness, facts, action, power: to men of business there could seem to be no more accommodating philosophical fortification for the principles on which they wished to run the affairs of the market place. Such a philosophy, to such an age, quickly and logically came to mean "pragmatic acquiescence," as one historian has stated it[42]—acquiescence which signified acceptance and ultimate vindication for the *faits accomplis* of the realm of economics. As another of the pragmatic school put the issue, the necessary goal in the art of living was to substitute for "realizing the ideal" the more facile method of "idealizing the real."[42] And idealizing the real was precisely what the gospel of wealth sought to achieve.

The pragmatism of America as popularly conceived in this era was the culmination, in a sense, of a long and historic tradition—that tradition which has been summarized as "the protestantism, the individualism, the scientific distrust of 'values,' which had come down in unbroken succession from Calvin and Luther, from Locke and Hobbes and Hume and Bentham and Mill."[43] It was the tradition which James himself described as "philosophic protestantism."[44] And the final effective resolution of that tradition was the amoral abandonment of all social disciplines, the frank undisguised surrender to the triumphant fact. The Liberal confessed that from his faith he could deduce no system of social ethics which could make an intelligent and rational claim to men's allegiance.

The great Liberal adventure thus ran its course. The economic yoke was fastened tightly. The political goad—half sedative, half incentive—was perpetuated in the folklore of Liberalism. The intellectual fodder of exculpation and absolution was fed by the masters to the oxen.

The illusions of poet, of immigrant, and of freedman came to appear somewhat ungrounded in fact. But the age's philosophy offered some consolation, because, as the standard of the pragmatist was construed by men, those illusions were "true" —because they had been useful.

Of the three, first to experience disenchantment was the poet. And disenchantment was quickly made vocal, as the poet Whitman spoke. . . . "Society in these states is cankered, crude, superstitious and rotten. . . . Genuine belief seems to have left us. . . . The great cities reek with respectable as much as non-respectable robbery and scoundrelism. In fashionable life, flippancy, tepid amours, weak infidelities, small aims, or no aims at all, only to kill time. . . . I say that our New World democracy, however great a success in uplifting the masses out of their sloughs, in materialistic development, products, and in a certain highly deceptive superficial popular intellectuality, is so far an almost complete failure in its social aspects, and in really grand religious, moral, literary and aesthetic results. In vain do we march with unprecedented strides to empire so colossal, outvying the antique, beyond Alexander's, beyond the proudest sway of Rome. . . . It is as if we were somehow being endow'd with a vast and thoroughly appointed body, but then left with little or no soul."[45]

The Church Militant

THE Catholic Church, for these many centuries, had watched the building of the Liberal Society—had watched and fought against it, from the time in the sixteenth century when the initial and essential Liberal triumph had been won in the religious arena. After that time, it had seen the depersonalization and then the denial of the Christian God: first, the conversion of Him into a mechanical Prime Mover, setting in resolute motion the Newtonian world-machine; then—inevitably—His complete exile as men's infatuation with the simple mechanics of the machine had become a self-sustaining ideal. It had seen the men who denatured God move on to deify Nature: some to become lost in their own confusion of the ideal and the actual; others—hopelessly caught in the net of their own axioms—to conclude grimly that whatever was, was right. It had seen, consequent to the denial of the real personality of God, what seemed to be the annihilation of the personality of man; for the same mechanistic creed which dictated the first swiftly produced the second consequence, once it was translated into the all-encompassing reality of industrialism. It had seen the categorical denial of absolute truth, value or morality—the supple insinuation of relativism and pragmatism into the whole texture of Liberal thought. It had seen the birth and coming-of-age of that strange new being known as Economic Man: he who lived on bread alone. It had seen the minds of men become frenzied with what it regarded as the power-lust—power over nature and power over fellow-men—vindicated by a miracle of insensitivity: the modern conscience. . . . It had seen all this—and had repudiated it.

In so doing, the Church had made reference to its own body of traditions—its own legacy of faith and ideas—from which single arsenal it had sought to draw its intellectual weapons in fighting the Liberal faith in its myriad forms, from a non-Christian humanism to an amoral pragmatism. In that tradition, it could refer back to Bellarmine and Suarez: they who had startled an age by their declaration of the Christian rights of man, rights which derived from man's creation in the image of God and the equality of all men before God's just judgment. . . . To Suarez, again, and to Vittoria: they who had most signally laid the foundations for international law, logically articulating their heritage of a Christianity which knew of no nationality. . . . To Thomas More: he who had written bitter words about the early surge of the new economy—words which could speak with the same anger centuries later—"They pluck down towns and leave nothing standing but only the church to be made into a sheephouse."[1] . . . To St. Thomas Aquinas and John of Salisbury: they who had most eloquently expressed the medieval conception of a society in which humanity was not divided against itself, which proclaimed allegiance to a moral purpose towards the fulfillment of which all men must strive. . . . To St. Basil and his fellow-leaders: they who had cried out against men who covered their walls with tapestries and clothed not the nakedness of their fellow-men. . . . Finally, far back to the time when a world order was disintegrating: when known, inherited intellectual habits and political forms were breaking apart: when traditions and legends were passing from mouth to mouth among the illiterate Roman masses about a certain Man of Nazareth: when these men were inspired with renewed hope by the spirited exclamation of Paul of Tarsus—"It is sown in corruption, it is raised in incorruption; it is sown in dishonor, it is raised in glory; it is sown in weakness, it is raised in power." This was the time when oppressed, beaten men took as their own the cry of the Son of Man:—"The foxes have holes and the birds of the air have nests, but the Son of Man hath not where to lay his head."

For decades, for centuries, the Church which maintained

itself to be the true historic repository of that tradition had retreated before a world of ideas with which it could make no compromise that would not jeopardize the integrity of its heritage. That world, in the militant person of the army of the French Revolution, had marched on Rome, stuck the Jacobin cap upon the head of the Archangel Michael, planted the Tree of Liberty on the Capitol, and placed before the Castle of San Angelo a statue of the Goddess of Reason with its foot upon the papal tiara lying in the dust.[2] The age which believed, with Gibbon, that the Cross had been planted on the ruins of the Capitol was resolved to plant the Tricolor in the same place.

Almost a full century from that time,* the Church yet stood against a complex background of seething religious and political forces. Intellectual and philosophical problems of serious proportions were multiplying with the popularization of Darwinism, the rise of schools of thought around men like Lamennais, Strossmayer and Döllinger, and the whole surge of the Modernist movement. In addition to these essentially internal problems, there came the open clashes with the sovereign national states of the Liberal Society. In France there was the anti-clerical crusade of the Third Republic and the fight to convert the last great social function of the Church— education—into a department of the secular state, all this aggravated by the association of Catholic and royalist political parties. In Germany, now on the threshold of fulfillment of the dream of Herder and the achievement of national unity, there was to follow the bitter struggle revolving around Bismarck and Windthorst—the *Kulturkampf*. Even in sober, rational England there was Gladstone, corresponding at length with Bismarck in their joint attack on the Church and denouncing centralization of control within the Church as "an anti-social power."[3] And militantly crusading in Italy there

---

* The Papal succession in this period was as follows: Pius VII (Gregorio Chiaramonte): 1800-1823; Leo XII (Annibale della Genga): 1823-1829; Pius VIII (Francesco X. Castiglione): 1829-1830; Gregory XVI (Mauro Capellari): 1831-1846; Pius IX (Giovanni Mastai-Ferretti): 1846-1878; Leo XIII (Joachim Pecci): 1878-1903.

were Mazzini and his "Young Italy," Cavour and his "Libera chiesa in libero stato"—leading the armies of Italian nationalism through the lands which were the last vestigial remains of Papal temporal rule, on to the final storming of the gates at Porta Pia.

It was against this background that men of the Church went to the task of reforming the intellectual lines of faith, reorganizing forces which for more than a century had been falling back, often in serious disorder. That task demanded first a clear and explicit indictment of the foundations of the Liberal Society; and secondly, a positive and compelling affirmation of the social philosophy of the Church.

December 8 is the anniversary of the three declarations of the pontificate of Pius IX which constituted the categorical denial of the Liberal faith. Those three declarations were: *Ineffabilis Deus*, promulgated in 1854 and defining the doctrine of the Immaculate Conception; ten years later, the Syllabus of Errors; and finally the declaration of Papal Infallibility by the Vatican Council, convened December 8, 1869. Conceived as a unit, they presented "an ultimatum to the world."[4]

Promulgation of the doctrine of Mary's freedom from the legacy of original sin was much more than a remote theological pronouncement, more than a testimony to the simple piety of the Pontiff who proclaimed the doctrine. It achieved, in short, two objectives. First, it reiterated and underscored the Church's insistence on the reality of the supernatural and the validity of religious mysteries; it repudiated all that was associated with the dictum of Holbach, that matter acts because it exists and exists to act, beyond which aphorism there could be nothing but the fanciful fabrications of priestcraft. In the second place, implicit in the sentences of *Ineffabilis Deus*, was the reaffirmation of the fact of man's legacy of sin, she who had been the Mother of Christ alone having been untouched by that human heritage. Such a doctrine struck directly at the foundations of the Liberal faith: it discarded as

sanguine fantasy the idea of immutable and boundless progress and of the innate goodness of man. Simply and directly
was herewith denied the Liberal conception of man's nature.

The second pertinent proclamation of the pontificate of
Pius IX, the Syllabus of Errors, was drawn up by a commission of Cardinals in an effort to summarize his indictment of
contemporary thought and faith. Composed of statements
garnered from the Pope's several encyclicals and addresses
to the clergy, the Syllabus was the most extreme and frankly
belligerent condemnation of Liberalism that had ever been
issued from the Vatican. Divided into ten sections, it sought
in its narrow compass to discuss and dispose of as many and
diverse issues as pantheism, naturalism, and rationalism; in-
differentism and latitudinarianism; socialism, communism
and secret societies; the State and the Church; natural and
Christian ethics; Christian marriage and Liberalism. Among
the basic "errors" assailed were the following:

1. There exists no supreme, all wise, most provident divine Being,
distinct from the universe; God and nature are one, and God is therefore subject to change; actually God is produced in man and in the
world; God and the world are identical, as are spirit and matter, true
and false, good and evil, just and unjust.

3. Human reason, without any regard whatsoever to God, is the sole
judge of the true and the false, of good and evil; it is a law unto
itself, and suffices by its natural powers to secure the welfare of men
and nations.

16. Men may, in any religion, find the way of eternal salvation and
attain eternal salvation.

19. . . . It belongs to the civil power to define what are the rights
of the Church and the limits within which she can exercise them.

45. The entire direction of public schools in which the youth of any
Christian state are educated, except to some extent in the case of
episcopal seminaries, may and must belong to the civil power.

54. Kings and princes are not only exempt from ecclesiastical rule
but are even superior to the Church in disputed questions of jurisdiction.

55. The Church should be separated from the State, and the State
from the Church.

59. Rights consist in the mere material fact, and all human duties are an empty name, and every human deed has the force of right.

80. The Roman Pontiff can and should reconcile and align himself with progress, Liberalism, and modern civilization.

By virtue of its character as a collation of more or less isolated extracts, there was much in the Syllabus, as even the most orthodox Catholic apologists admitted, which lent itself to exaggerated misconstruction. As a social document, it lacked any organic unity, inner logical consistency, or eloquence in the presentation of its position. Yet it did serve its immediate purpose of furnishing the clergy of the Church with a convenient manual summarizing the Pontiff's broad indictment of the intellectual and political operations of the Liberal Society. It denounced in firm tone the breaking-down of social organization into closed compartments which prohibited the investiture of the whole unity of society with a single, transcendent moral purpose. It forthrightly assailed the secularization of politics, the unharnessed freedom of economic appetites, the abrogation of social duties as the contingent basis for rights in society, and the predication of human right on no firmer or juster a foundation than material expediency. Its essence was to be found in the words of a letter of Leo XIII, written in 1887 to his newly appointed Secretary of State. . . . "Fundamentally . . . only that can represent real progress for man, which leads to his spiritual and moral perfection or at any rate does not oppose it."[5] The final significance of the Syllabus—its affirmation of a conception of man's nature which could in no fundamental sense compromise with the Economic Man of the Liberal Society—was clearly perceived by Gladstone. He called the Syllabus "the gravest event since the French uprising in 1789."[6]

Final and expressive articulation of all these forces was to come five years later. Then, at nine o'clock on the morning of December 8, 1869, cannon fired their salutes from Monte Aventino and the bells of every church in Rome announced the opening of the Twentieth Ecumenical Council: fifteen centuries after the first so recognized by history, the Council of Nicea, eighteen after that of Jerusalem, and three centuries after the most recent, the Council of Trent.[7] More than eight hundred bishops, patriarchs and abbots had assembled in the great hall above the portico of the Vatican Basilica, arranged on this occasion as a chapel. From there, in procession, the assembled passed through the hall which gives access to the Sistine Chapel; then descending the grand staircase of Bernini, they turned to the right through the portico and entered the Church of St. Peter. In front walked the choir of the Sistine Chapel, followed by cardinals, abbots, archbishops and bishops. Then, in their picturesque robes, appeared the patriarchs of the East—Bulgarian, Armenian, Coptic, Chaldaic and Syrian prelates—followed by Pius IX. Into the right transept of St. Peter's the procession turned, under the cupola of Michael Angelo. Guarding the door to the transept were the Knights of Jerusalem and Papal Zouaves. Above the door through which the procession turned was the text: "Go ye, and teach all nations; I am with you always, even unto the end of the world."

Thus the Vatican Council convened, to debate the proposed declaration of Papal Infallibility. Seven months were demanded to proceed through even the first part of the prescribed agenda. In fourteen secret general congregations and twenty-two special discussions, the issue was debated. Leading the forces opposing the declaration were such dignitaries as Newman, Ketteler, Strossmayer, Dupanloup, MacHale, Mathieu and Darboy. Leaders of the majority group were Deschamps of Belgium and Manning of England. When the debate was concluded on July 4, advocates of the declaration had a majority of more than six to one. The final meeting on July 18 found only two who cried *"non placet!"* to the last.* When the issue was finally decided, even these two joined the whole body in pronouncing the same simple *"Modo credo"* by which each had signified his acceptance and allegiance.

* Formally and officially, the Vatican Council has not to this day dissolved.

The Vatican Council made articulate the principle which as long ago as Tertullian had been expressed in the words: *Ecclesia ab apostolis, apostoli a Christo, Christus a Deo*. In the same stroke the Council reaffirmed the historic faith in the supernatural origin and reasserted the supra-national character of the Church it represented. It was a pronouncement, however, more striking and more historically far-reaching in implications than any made in times such as those of Tertullian; for, while the central principle might be the same in both cases, that principle was now reiterated after a sustained, centuries-long assault upon it and its associations—was now more firmly and explicitly stated than ever before in an historical context that was militantly hostile. It was these facts which underlay Cardinal Manning's depiction of the Declaration as "the widest and boldest affirmation of the supernatural order that has hitherto been thrown in the face of the world."[8]

Consequent to the Declaration the divisions which many leaders had forecast within the Church did not materialize,* but the vehemence of the denunciations from the secular powers measured up to expectations. The government of Austria condemned the proclamation and immediately annulled the Concordat of 1855. Bismarck—of all European statesmen, perhaps the most sensitive to any idea or event compromising the immutable autonomy of the national state—soon launched his attack on the Church in Germany. The French government, the day after the proclamation, withdrew its garrison of troops stationed at Rome and cleared the road for the insurgent armies of Italian nationalism which were pressing ever closer to the Tiber. In England, Gladstone—moving on momentum whose initial impetus was his denunciation of the Syllabus—launched a swift verbal attack on this, "the most portentous (taking them singly), of all events in the history of the Christian church."[9] Exclaiming that "Rome . . . has refurbished and paraded anew every rusty tool she

* The only conspicuous defection, of several thousand, was that of Döllinger and the "Old Catholics" of southern Germany.

was fondly thought to have disused" and that "the claims of Gregory VII, of Innocent III, and of Boniface VIII have been disinterred in the nineteenth century, like hideous mummies picked out of Egyptian sarcophagi"—so crying, the English statesman called upon his Catholic subjects to state clearly their allegiance—to London, or to Rome.[10]

Extreme symbolic representation of such vigorous dissent was provided by the Anti-Council of Free-Thinkers, who met in Naples at the same time that the leaders of the Church were meeting at St. Peter's. Here the assembled company cheered lustily as President Ricciardi exclaimed: "The only means of combating the fresh efforts of the old and irreconcilable enemy of every freedom is a holy alliance of the enlightened of all nations." The militant platform of the Anti-Council therewith reaffirmed the Voltairean spirit of *Deleatur Carthago*, although now it was evidently conceded that somewhat more than five or six philosophers were needed to destroy the colossus. . . . "Seeing that the idea of a God is the source and fulcrum of every despotism and of every wickedness, and seeing that the Catholic Church is the most complete and most formidable personification of this idea and that the total content of her dogmas presents a true denial of human society, the Free-Thinkers of Paris bind themselves to work actively for the speedy and radical overthrow of Catholicism, and to strive for its destruction by all legitimate means, not even excluding revolutionary violence, which is nothing but the justifiable right of defence applied to society."[11]

The Anti-Council was an extreme but not much exaggerated expression of an age's beliefs: an age in which Schopenhauer wrote that religion would soon leave European humanity "like a nurse whose fostering care the child has outgrown": an age in which Flaubert prophesied joyously that "the nineteenth century will see the end of all religions. Amen! I shall not weep for any of them": an age in which, in the same year as the Vatican Council, the President of the Vienna Academy of Sciences proclaimed, "Only after the destruction of the divine can humanity prosper."[12]

To such an age the work of the Vatican Council was an un-equivocal challenge, proclaiming at once the reality of an intellectual and spiritual level above the realm of matter—and an institutional level transcending the plane of national sovereignty. The day on which the Declaration of the Council was finally promulgated had been a day of tremendous storms. With the leaders of the Church gathered in the *Aura Conciliaris* of St. Peter's, thunder had pealed above and light-ning had flashed by every window and illumined every small cupola. The "placets" of the prelates had been barely audible above the raging storm. Many, like Strossmayer and Döllinger, who feared the consequences of this day must have wondered if the descending darkness without were not, for their Church, like a tempest to another Lear. When the result of the voting was taken up to the Pope, the darkness was so dense that a huge taper was brought and placed by his side as he announced in the language of the Church the result of the work of the Council. And in the midst of that darkness the long shadow of Canossa seemed to fall across the Liberal Society.

The following day, the outside world read and learned of these ceremonies in their morning papers. The evening brought news of a correspondingly appropriate ceremony in-augurated by other men and forces: the Franco-Prussian War was begun—that war which was to assure the triumph of the national state in Europe and the Western world.

In February of 1878, after but two days' deliberation, the College of Cardinals elected a successor to Pius IX. While in the Sistine Chapel the new Pope for the first time received the homage of the College, the senior Cardinal-deacon, from the outer loggia of St. Peter's, to the multitude assembled below announced that *"Habemus Papam,* the most eminent and holy Joachim Pecci who has assumed the title of Leo XIII." The sum of this man's work was to be the positive affirmation of the social philosophy of the Church.

The foundation to this labor was laid with Leo XIII's reinstatement and reiteration of the work of St. Thomas Aquinas, and in *Aeterni Patris* he called upon all the prelates of the Church to summon the attention of all men once again to that philosophical synthesis which had been the climactic accomplishment of the medieval era. To turn thus to Aquinas was peculiarly appropriate; for he too had faced an age in which the inherited Christian tradition and way of thought had been threatened—then, by the revival of Aristotelian learning and logic. Unafraid of the new intellectual forces while retaining unqualified allegiance to the historic precepts of Christianity, Aquinas had accomplished what was tantamount to a theological revolution: he had demonstrated that reason, far from signalizing the denial of faith, could—in fact, must necessarily—fortify and fulfill faith. To revive this philosophy in the nineteenth century was in itself almost as revolutionary a development as had been the construction of that philosophy, for an intellectual venture without parallel in the intellectual history of the West was herewith inaugurated. A philosophical and theological system was resurrected in the center of an intellectual world to which it was virtually antipodal; in the midst of a scientific thought and non-Christian scale of values whose sovereignty was regarded as absolute, a system of theology and philosophy which had come from the brain of a Dominican friar five centuries before arose to contest that sovereignty and to influence at countless critical points the historical and intellectual evolution of the age.

From this general foundation, Leo proceeded quickly to a succession of positive and explicit expositions of the social philosophy of the Church. He condemned what seemed to him to be the anarchic, atavistic individualism of the Liberal Society and sought to reconstruct the nature of man in terms which demanded for their fulfillment the communal life. . . . "Man's natural instinct moves him to live in civil society, for he cannot, if dwelling apart, provide himself with the necessary requirements of life, nor procure the means of developing his mental and moral faculties. Hence it is divinely ordained that he should lead his life—be it family, social, or civil—with his fellowmen, amongst whom alone his several wants can be adequately supplied."[13]

With the fundamental character of social organization so conceived, Leo reiterated the principle that the only just and proper end of government was the securing of the welfare and the fulfillment of the social needs of the whole people: fighting against the tragic end for which the puissant and conflicting forces of absolute national sovereignty seemed preparing. . . . "The right to rule is not necessarily . . . bound up with any special mode of government. It may take this or that form, provided only that it be of a nature to insure the general welfare. . . . They who govern others possess authority solely for the welfare of the state. Furthermore, the civil power must not be subservient to the advantage of any one individual, or of some few persons; inasmuch as it was established for the common good of all. But if those who are in authority rule unjustly, if they govern overbearingly or arrogantly, and if their measures prove hurtful to the people, they must remember that the Almighty will one day bring them to account, the more strictly in proportion to the sacredness of their office and preeminence of their dignity. *The mighty shall be mightily tormented*."[14] . . . Such pronouncements were clearly not concerned with furnishing pleasant, casual reading in the state houses of Europe.

Finally, Leo came to his direct encounter with the central social and economic postulates of Liberalism, appealing directly to the laboring masses. . . . "Some remedy must be found and quickly found, for the misery and wretchedness which press so heavily at this moment on the large majority of the poor. . . . Working men have been given over, isolated and defenseless, to the callousness of employers and the greed of unrestrained competition . . . so that a small number of very rich men have been able to lay upon the masses of the poor a yoke little better than slavery itself. . . . To exercise pressure for the sake of gain, upon the indigent and destitute, and to make one's profit out of the need of another, is condemned by all laws, human and divine. . . . The blessings of nature and the gift of grace belong in common to the whole human race. . . . It is only by the labor of the working man that states grow rich. . . . The first concern of all is to save the poor workers from the cruelty of grasping speculators, who use human beings as mere instruments for making money. . . . The state must protect the laborers' rights."[15] . . . It is pertinent and necessary to recall that these words were written in the same age which heard the vaunted science of economics proclaim the inevitability of the poverty of the laboring masses—the same age that reverently heeded the gospel of wealth as it proclaimed that "material prosperity is helping to make the national character sweeter, more joyous, more unselfish, more Christlike." These words of Leo would certainly have sufficed to have found him a place in the ranks of Macaulay's "illiterate, incapable, low-minded flatterers" of the poor.

The pronouncements of Leo XIII at once reflected and reinforced the traditional social doctrines of the Church. They were nonetheless only papal encyclicals, whose merit or success could be little more than as literary exercises, unless and until their doctrines and manifold implications were comprehended by the body of the Church and their words implemented by action. But men like Frederic Ozanam, founder of the Society of St. Vincent de Paul, had, even before the time of Leo, actively entered the arena where the great social issues of the day were being fought. It was Ozanam who, so far in advance of his time, had scorned the empty political gestures of the benevolent bourgeosie and demanded that men cut through to the rock-bed of social and economic issues underlying the Liberal Society. "We must not imagine," he declared, "that we can escape these problems. If men think that they can satisfy the people by giving them primary assemblies, legislative councils, new magistrates, consuls or a president, they are sadly mistaken. Within a decade of years, and perhaps sooner, the old difficulties will return."[16]

The pronouncements of Leo, in short, were far from being isolated outbursts of a peculiarly voluble pontiff whose sense of social decency came as a shock to an apathetic hierarchy. For the doctrines of Leo were not only embodiments of a tradition of social thought that had deep roots in the past: they were expressions of a social gospel which in this age had forceful ecclesiastical propagators throughout the Church. On the continent of Europe probably the most distinguished of the clerical social leaders was William Emmanuel von Ketteler, who had earned for himself the familiar title of "Bishop of the Workingmen." It was in 1869 that he had addressed this warning to the assembled hierarchy of Germany at the Fulda Conference: "Interest yourself in the laborer, or others will do it in your stead who are hostile to the Church and to Christianity. . . . The Church must help to solve the social question, because it is indissolubly bound up with her mission of teaching and guiding mankind."[17]

With clear historical perception, Ketteler traced the evolution of the working classes in the course of the ascent and triumph of the Liberal Society. "The working classes have passed through the same phases as the state and the old social order," he declared. "The Physiocrats of the last century made the organization of labor responsible for all the economic ills of the people, instead of looking for their true origin in its degeneration, its egotistical ossification and in the patent fact that this organization had not been developed to meet changed conditions. And so they annihilated the grand constitution of labor handed on to them from the Middle Ages. . . . This demolition they recalled restoration of the natural order—*le gouvernement de la nature*. . . . Complete disorganization of the state, of society and of labor; the powers of the state vested in a bureaucratic officialdom on the one side, and on the other, unbridled competition amongst the people dissolved into isolated individuals under the sole control of an absolute monarch or an equally absolute National Assembly—this is the natural law of the Revolution. Such too is the spirit of Liberalism, not merely the spirit of its economic teachings but also of its politics and its social theories. The tendency of our times to return to corporative forms, far from being a product of Liberalism, is on the contrary a reaction against the unnaturalness of its pretended natural law."[18]

At the same time and working in the same spirit, there rose in America men like Hecker and Ireland, the former the founder of the Paulist Fathers and the latter Archbishop of St. Paul. It was Archbishop Ireland who, in 1889, at the Centenary of the Institution of the Ecclesiastical Hierarchy of the United States, addressed the assembled dignitaries in strong, clear phrases. . . . "Have no fear of the new. Well based principles are always able to defend themselves. But . . . in order to keep pace with the age, religious action must adopt new forms and methods. . . . There is no necessity that the layman should wait to follow the lead of the priest, nor the priest that of his bishop, nor the bishop that of the Pope. . . . We are each bound to live with the age, to know it, to keep ourselves in touch with it. . . . The world has entered upon an entirely new phase. The past can return no more. Reaction is the dream of men who can neither see nor comprehend, of men who, seated at the portals of a necropolis, weep over tombs that can never be reopened, and forget the living world around them. Let us, therefore, speak to our age of things that it feels, and in language that it understands."[19] . . . And conversion of words into actions came with such instances as Cardinal Gibbons' defense of the Knights of Labor.[20]

Of all these men, however, he who most distinguished himself as a militant propagator of the Church's social gospel was the English Cardinal Manning. In addresses, in pamphlets, in communications to the great newspapers of the realm, in books marked by succinct and vigorous language, Manning distinguished himself as one of the age's best protagonists of the cause of labor. It was not strange that on the fourth of May 1890, the day when the great London dock strike reached its climax in the demonstration for the eight-hour work-day, even the Socialist banners of the marching workers bore, side by side with the portrait of Marx, that of Cardinal Manning.

Manning vigorously assailed what he regarded as the cold prescriptions of an economic science which created an Economic Man in its own deathlike image. . . . "Political economy . . . is circumscribed by higher moral laws to which, if it come in collision with them, it must at least for a time give way. If on the sound and strict principles of political economy, poverty and sickness could be remedied by thrift and provident dispensaries, I should rejoice; but knowing, as we all must, that thrift and providence have as yet made but little impression upon the multitudes who are poor, hungry, sick, and dying, we are compelled to relieve human suffering for which no sounder or more disciplined relief as yet exists. The Good Samaritan did not delay to pour oil and wine into the wounds of the man half-dead until he had ascertained whether he was responsible for his own distress. Necessity has no law, nor has present distress, except a claim for prompt relief."[21] . . . Revealing indeed would have been a discussion of these points by Manning and Arthur Young.

For the legal fictions which threw a veil of legitimacy around the abuses of Liberal economics Manning had only impatient anger. . . . "We speak of freedom of contract, and a few ask, whom have we defrauded? were not our contracts freely made? and if free are they not legal?—But what liberty can there be between irresponsible wealth and needy poverty? Is it not 'to accept or not to eat'? . . . In these conditions freedom of contract does not exist. It is but a cruel deceit."[22]

To Manning, the removal, or at least the control, of such relentless economic forces demanded the radical curtailment of the unlimited autonomy which the realm of private business claimed as its just prerogative. . . . "So long as the hours of labor have no other limit than the gain of the employer, no workman can live a life worthy of a human being. The humblest workman, no less than the man who is rich and literate, has need of certain hours wherein to cultivate his mind and soul; and if such hours are not permitted him he is lowered to the state of a machine, or to that of a beast of burden. What manner of nation will be formed by men living in such conditions? What must be the domestic, social, or political life of such men? Yet it is to this that the individualism of the last fifty years is leading us. . . . I do not believe that the powerful relations of employers and employed will ever be safely and solidly secured until the just and due proportion between profits and wages shall have been fixed, recognized, laid down, and publicly known to govern all free contracts between capital and labor."[23]

Eloquent and incisive was Cardinal Manning's summary of his social faith. . . . "Human society has no use for the imaginary 'economic man' of our political economists, but needs the human being in the full reality of the divine breath of life that animates him; it needs the man of the family of Adam . . . invested with all the sympathies, all the dignities of our human race. . . .

"We have been strangled. We have been strangled by an exaggerated form of Individualism. But the coming century will show that human society is grander and nobler than anything merely individual. . . . The future will call forth into the light of reason the social state of the world of labor. We shall then see upon what laws the Christian society of humanity rests."[24]

Thus did the Church, in the hour of the most complete Liberal success and glory, attack the entire Liberal faith. The Liberal Society's conception of man's nature it denied with *Ineffabilis Deus* and the Syllabus of Errors, asserting the corrupting force of the legacy of original sin and the incompetence of naked reason to aspire to all knowledge and truth. The Liberal conception of man's relationship to his God the Church challenged with the work of the Vatican Council. The Liberal conception of man's relationship to fellow-man it repudiated with the social encyclicals of the popes, enforced by the words and actions of the hierarchy of ecclesiastics: no longer, these men declared, could the realm of the affairs of society be construed as a sanctuary of acquisitiveness from which the disciplines of religion and ethics could be banished.

It was on the fortieth anniversary of the issuance of Leo XIII's famous *Rerum Novarum* that another man who wore the Fisherman's ring set himself to the task of commemorating that work. The result was the most logical arraignment of the social realities of the Liberal Society, the most succinct and incisive statement of the Church's social doctrine, to issue from the Vatican in the whole era of Liberal triumph. . . .

"Towards the close of the nineteenth century, new economic methods and a new expansion of industry had in most countries resulted in a growing division of the population into two classes. The first, small in numbers, enjoyed practically all the advantages so plentifully supplied by modern invention; the second class, comprising the immense multitude of workingmen, was made up of those who, oppressed by dire poverty, struggled in vain to escape from the difficulties which encompassed them. . . .

"Not wealth alone is accumulated, but immense power and despotic economic domination are concentrated in the hands of a few, supplying, so to speak, the life-blood to the entire economic community, and grasping in their hands, as it were, the very soul of production so that no one can breathe against their will. The whole economic regime has become hard, cruel, and relentless. . . .

"The state, which should be the supreme arbiter, intent only upon justice and the common good, has become instead a slave, bound over to the service of human passion and greed. The clash between states arises because the nations apply their power and political influence to promote the economic advantages of their own citizens. . . .

"Society today still remains in a strained and therefore unstable and uncertain state, because it is founded on classes with divergent aims. The wage system divides men on what is called the labor market into two sections, resembling armies, and the disputes between these sections transform this labor market into an arena where the two armies are engaged in fierce combat. Moreover, just as the unity of human society cannot be built upon opposition between classes, so the proper ordering of the economic life cannot be left to free competition. . . .

"Free competition cannot be the guiding principle of economic life. . . . The civil power is more than the mere guardian of law and order. It must strive with all zeal to 'make sure that the laws and institutions, the general character and administration of the common wealth, should be such as of themselves to realize public well being and private prosperity.' . . . Freedom of action should be left to individual citizens and families—but only as long as the common good is secure. When civil authority adjusts ownership to meet the needs of the public good, it effectively prevents the possession of private property . . . from creating intolerable disadvantages and so rushing to its own destruction. . . .

"Is it not apparent that the huge possessions which constitute human wealth are begotten by and flow from the hands of the workers? Wealth, therefore, which is constantly being augmented by social and economic progress, must be so distributed amongst the various individuals and classes of society, that the needs of all thereby be satisfied. . . .

"Unless serious attempts be made, with all energy and without delay, let nobody persuade himself that public order and the peace and tranquillity of human society can be effectively defended against the forces of revolution. . . .

"This is the necessary object of our efforts: the uplifting of the proletariat. It calls for more emphatic assertion and more insistent repetition. . . . For then only will the economic and social order be soundly established and attain its ends, when it secures, for all and each, all those goods which the wealth and resources of nature, technique, and the social organization of economic affairs can give."[25]

It was, appropriately, a man of peasant stock who proclaimed this social faith from the highest office of Christendom.

The tradition of Bellarmine, of Suarez, of More, of Thomas Aquinas, of John of Salisbury: that tradition was finding new vigor and new fulfillment.

Part IV · The Crisis of the West

Weimar, Versailles and Munich

IN THE latter part of the eighteenth century, the intellectual center of the German states was at a place called Weimar. The Germany of which it was thus the center was inhabited by a disunited and distracted people. They were burdened with the bitter legacy of religious wars which had almost completely dismembered the body politic. They were divided into eighteen hundred separate territories over which the formless shadow of the Holy Roman Empire fell ineptly. They lacked any economic unity such as the commercial nations on the Atlantic had securely established. They were stripped of any warming or protecting cultural tradition—their masses spoke one language and the intellectual elite another, the literary and philosophical past of their nation was scorned, and blind, boundless imitation of all things Gallic became the prevalent, if not exclusive, cultural exercise.

The Weimar of this era was the refuge of men of learning. It was to this town that there came men like Goethe and Schiller. And here, in the year 1776, there came a man who knew intimately the forces that were to make the future of his nation. He was a Lutheran minister with a rare gift for forceful language. Intellectually he stood virtually at the terminus of the evolution of the Pietist movement, which had swept his land through the eighteenth century, and almost in the first flickering light of the Romantic movement of the next century. His name was Johann Gottfried Herder—and he came with a gospel for his people.

The gospel of Herder proclaims that humanity is divisible, not into units of isolated individuals, but only into units of nationality. He announces that "every human perfection is national."[1] He talks about the "national plant" and the "national animal"—invested with the organic attributes of growth, maturity, decay.[2] He sees the division of humanity into national units as part of a divinely ordained scheme. For within each nationality is a national "soul" which "is the mother of all culture upon the earth . . . singular, wonderful, inexplicable, ineradicable, and as old as the nationality."[3] Each nationality is thus a collective individual with a peculiar and distinct personality. Not less than the individual human being is the nationality made in the image of God. With Schleiermacher, Herder sees that "every people is appointed to present a particular side of the divine image."[4]

But the prophet sees more than this—something ominous and disturbing. He sees his nation "torn and divided into religious factions"—and he asks, he cries aloud: "Are we not all Germans? Are there Catholic and Protestant physics, mathematics, morals, etc., which are different in principle? Should they exist? And again I say it, are we not all Germans?"[5] In similar fashion, he sees Germany divided into social classes. He denounces them and exclaims—"There is only one class in the state, the *Volk* (not the rabble), and the king belongs to this class as well as the peasant."[6] He perceives, too, the cultural disunity of his country and he denounces those who pervert the natural articulation of the national soul through its native language—and to his fellow-countrymen who would speak French he cries out,

> O spew it out, before your door,
> Spew out the ugly slime of the Seine.
> Speak German, O you German![7]

He castigates those who prevent literature from being the handmaid to nationality, for "literature is significant only in so far as the author permits the national soul to work through him."[8] All must be enlisted in the service of the salvation of the national soul.

And to Joseph II, Herder turns to implore,

> . . . O give us what we thirst for,
> A German fatherland. . . .
> And one law and one beautiful language,
> And one honest religion.[9]

And the nationalist prophet of the eighteenth century, for all the Pietist and humanitarian overtones to his thought and speech, yet echoes strangely almost the exact words of Machiavelli, as he warns—"It is easy to become the slaves of others, but not always will a Moses appear to free his people and to reward them for their servitude with the spoil of Egyptian legislation."[10]

Thus—often with dignity of expression and loftiness of thought, yet not fundamentally unlike the gospels of the Bolingbrokes of England or the Fouchés of France—the faith of Johann Gottfried Herder was proclaimed. A half century later, the words of the leader of the forces of Italian nationalism testified to the fact that the new religion of nationality itself recognized no national lines, but had woven itself into the whole texture of thought of the West. Thus did Mazzini solemnly speak: "Each nationality has its special mission, which will contribute towards the fulfillment of the general mission of humanity. That mission constitutes its nationality. Nationality is sacred."[11]

The gospel of nationalism was quick to be received and propagated by the prophets of the Liberal faith, for in many senses it was a fulfillment of basic ingredients of that faith. The very conception of nationality—of national individuality —could be understood only by men reverent of the primary concept of individuality: individual freedom, men of the Liberal faith perceived, could and in justice must be written in the larger letters of national freedom. At the same time, the conception of the necessary multiplicity of nations, each expressing and fulfilling a peculiar native genius, was little more than a political translation of the doctrine of religious toleration and latitudinarianism; as each of many religions possessed individual worth in expressing some aspect of ultimate religious truth, so men conceived that each nation was the unique embodiment of some distinctive attribute of humanity at large. As many religions must all be tolerated as equally valid, so must all nationalities be allowed to make articulate their native genius.

An integral part of the Liberal faith, the gospel of nationalism soon developed the accretions of ceremony and ritual, along with the general religious overtones, which all such movements seem to demand.[12] Like the medieval Church, the national state of the Liberal Society was endowed with a transcendent mission and ideal: it lived beyond the paltry lifespan of the men who proclaimed allegiance to it, and it demanded of these men every sacrifice, even death, which might enhance the glory of its mission. Into the national state the individual was born as he was once born into the Church; and the individual of the Liberal Society who had no national allegiance was as isolated and ostracized as the heretic who suffered excommunication by the medieval Church. The national entity—the deathless national spirit—was conceived to be as essentially infallible as a "true" religion: while its many magistrates might err or betray their trust, the "nation" could not do wrong. Each national state developed its canon of sanctified national documents: its great constitutions, its historic declarations in time of crisis, the eloquent addresses of its great leaders. It supervised education of its youth in much the same manner and with much the same ends in view as had the Church: its patriotic Boards of Education uncovered "alien" influences, dismissed "radical" academicians who lacked sufficient reverence in their discussions of the nationalist icons, and prohibited by a sort of nationalist *Index Librorum Prohibitorum* the use of "dangerous" textbooks in the school systems of the nation. It evolved characteristically religious use of ritual and symbol: the flag and the reverential proprieties associated with it became such a symbol, as did the national anthem; and the nationalist viewed a literalist's criticism of the color-harmony of the flag or the poetic caliber of the anthem in much the same way that a priest of the sixteenth century regarded textual criticism of the Scriptures. The nationalist mythology was enriched with fables just as the medievalist delighted in stories of the great saints: the national hero was recreated in the popular imagination with all the personalized legends about his youthful exploits, his untarnished virtue, his gentle and delightful wit, his valor, his unstinted devotion to his country.

It was in the light of this faith that men undertook the Crusades of the nineteenth century—the succession of wars by which each nationality set forth to reclaim and recover the Holy Lands which were their ancestors'. The great political and military energies of this era of Liberal triumph were expended in the task of converting, for all peoples, the nationalist gospel into the national state. When that was achieved, the newly established nation of course discovered that neither nationalism nor the autonomy of the national state was a static thing; rather, men who loved their nation had ever to seek to increase its power, fortify its security, enhance its prestige and rank among the great competing imperialist nations. Thus, as the surge of technology and industrialism had virtually encompassed the globe, so now the national state guided men in their imperialistic conquests. From the Sudan to the Shantung peninsula, from the Panama Canal to the Persian Gulf, political triumph and acquisition followed economic.

Then finally, out of the globe-spanning contest of competing imperialist systems; out of the dread and fervent race in amassing the weapons of conquest; out of the subdued fires of national hatred which flamed bright in Alsace-Lorraine, in the Balkan peninsula, in Korea, the national state led men into the War of 1914. . . .

Apparently unstained by a five-year flow of blood, the legacy of optimism from the age of the Enlightened remained intact, as men faced the task of creating a durable post-war order. While the central political fact of the ante-bellum world had been the preeminence of the national state, few if any considered the possibility of redefining it or circumscribing its power; for the national state was rooted in the ground of the Liberal faith. Yet men were supremely confident that a sound international order could be established on virtually the same premises as the old. This spirit, which was to surround the inauguration of the meeting of the victorious Western nations in Paris in 1919, was profoundly felt by a young diplomat from England, Harold Nicolson, as his train was swiftly carrying him toward that place where all wounds were to be healed. . . .

"I felt, as the train approached St. Denis, that I knew exactly what mistakes had been committed by the misguided, the reactionary, the after all pathetic aristocrats who had represented Great Britain in 1814.

"They had worked in secret. We, on the other hand, were committed to 'open covenants openly arrived at'; there would be no such secrecy about proceedings: the people of the world would share in our every gesture of negotiation.

"At Vienna, again, they had believed in the doctrine of 'compensations': they had spoken quite cynically about the 'transference of souls.' We for our part were liable to no such human error. We believed in the self-determination of peoples. 'Peoples and Provinces,' so ran the 'Four Principles' of our Prophet, 'shall not be bartered about from sovereignty to sovereignty as if they were but chattels or pawns in the game.' At the words 'pawns' and 'chattels' our lips curled in democratic scorn.

"Nor was this all. We were journeying to Paris, not merely to liquidate the war, but to found a new order in Europe. We were preparing not peace only, but eternal peace. There was about us the halo of some divine mission. We must be alert, stern, righteous and ascetic. For we were bent on doing great, permanent and noble things."[13]

Reason for hope and embodiment of this faith was Woodrow Wilson. Like a religious prophet who had arisen in a distant land, so men in France awaited his arrival. Key figure in the attainment of the victory of the Western powers, representative of the New World and its most powerful nation— he was on his way with the Fourteen Commandments. And when he would come, he would receive the liberated Poles, Slavs and Belgians as the lost sheep over whom there was much rejoicing. He came, too, with the sword as well as the Scriptures, for his nation—with its money and its food—was in an unassailable position, a position from which it could demand that its principles be accepted by the statesmen of the Old World. "Never had a philosopher held such weapons wherewith to bind the Princes of the world."[14]

When he stepped on the shores whence Lafayette had come, his first words spoke conviction. "If we do not heed the mandates of mankind," he exclaimed, "we shall make ourselves the most conspicuous and deserved failures in the history of the world."[15] And a caustic Parisian journalist echoed that sentence—with a more ominous emphasis: "President Wilson has lightly assumed a responsibility such as few men have ever borne. Success in his idealistic efforts will undoubtedly place him among the greatest characters of history. *Mais il faut dire hardiment, que s'il échouait il plongerait le monde dans un chaos dont le bolschevisme russe ne nous offre qu'une faible image: et sa responsabilité devant la conscience humaine dépasserait ce que peut supporter un simple mortel.*"[16]

The issue was decided against a chaotic background of milling masses of people, strident emotions, discordant national hates. There were newspapers calling for demobilization and treaty-action; starving masses in central Europe; the English *Daily Mail* screaming hoarsely about "the impudent Hun" and "Germany's whines for food";[17] long slouching lines of prisoners still behind barbed wire; in Munich and in Budapest the Communists on the march.—And in Paris there were Lloyd George, Wilson, Balfour, Clemenceau, Orlando; conferences, typewriters, delays, disagreements, boards of experts, telegrams, racing bicycles, rushed messages; the impudent cry of newsboys, the cold drone of the interpreter; Clemenceau at Plenary Conference sessions at Quai d'Orsay, chattering like a machine gun—"Y a-t-il objections? Non? ... Adopté."[18] There were weeks spent in empty temporizing, while the prophet from America knelt before the Covenant of the League of Nations. And after this there was frantic activity —the frenzied conversion of Preliminary into Final Treaty, without any of the anticipated revisions. Haste, confusion, disorganization, while the uniforms of twenty-seven armies and nations brightened the sidewalks of the French capital. . . . "Paris, for those few weeks, lost her soul. The brain of Paris, that triumphant achievement of western civilization, ceased to function. The nerves of Paris jangled in the air."[19]

Then came the tragedy.

The Fourteen Commandments were broken.[20] The prophet from America lost honor in his own country. In Paris he capitulated too, as the secret agreements of Old World diplomacy took precedence over the nobly-conceived principles of the New. At the same time, presence of the prophet removed the halo that had surrounded the head of the absent oracle. Disillusion raced like fire among the diplomats, as they scrambled back to old landmarks—familiar signs of victorious nations at work.

Why did it happen so? One of the keenest witnesses answered quickly: "deterioration of our moral awareness."[21] Given the task and the privilege of reconstructing a world, men found that they had no universally accepted standards, no prior and constant principles, no frame of reference or scheme of values which all might understand and accept. They groped desperately for some final objective to transcend the petty plane of recrimination and shifted lines on a map. They found they had no such objective.

Versailles signified more than the meeting of old and new diplomatic methods; it denoted the uniting of the intellectual and moral powers of the New World and the Old World. And the combined force failed. The sins of each's heritage broke through the thin crust of a transient idealism. To men from Rome, demanding territorial reward for services rendered, the men from London had no answer when the finger was pointed at Ireland, at Egypt, at India. And the men of America could not subdue in the statesmen of the Old World the rising consciousness that America had achieved puissant nationhood through the practice of the same imperialistic devices it was now so eloquently discountenancing. The lines of an idealist became caught in the throats of men—and they returned to and welcomed the more familiar role.

On Saturday, June 28, 1919, the curtain drops. Ushers in the Galerie des Glaces respond promptly to Clemenceau's crisp order: "Faites entrer les Allemands." Immediately the ceremony proceeds, as the two unhappy, very unmilitaristic German representatives confirm their country's capitulation. The officials of the Quai d'Orsay blot the signature with neat, small pads. The crash of guns from the courtyard below announces to Paris and to the world the signing of the second Treaty of Versailles.

The spiritual and political resources of two continents have been united in joint effort. The result has been the drama of Versailles—the last glamorous gestures of a Liberal Society spiritually bankrupt.

Less than twenty years later, in the land east of the Rhine, the land of Herder, men were again talking of the *Volk*, of the national soul, of the division of humanity into units larger than individuals, units whose dominion over the individual was absolute. And these men armed themselves as never men had been armed before. At first they turned these weapons upon some of their own ranks—those whom they distinguished as of the race into which Christ had been born. Then they turned their weapons outwards, advancing a little to the west, thrusting directly south into the country of the Danube, finally facing to the south-east and demanding yet more land.

Men who were leaders of the Western nations were bewildered. They were confused by this talk of national rights and national freedom. Had not the leaders of their world long ago exalted these ideas? They were perplexed by this oratory which spoke of the self-determination of peoples, the inalienable rights of a nationality for self-expression. Had not one of their own prophets pronounced this a sacred doctrine? They were distracted by the proportions which these ideas across the Rhine seemed to be assuming—the proportions of a faith. But had not they too constructed a faith from the great substance of nationality?

And so these men surrendered. They betrayed the trust of a nation which they themselves had brought into existence but twenty years before, a nation which had been a living monument to their own principles, a nation which had adhered to those principles with perhaps more fidelity than they themselves. They betrayed this nation because, in the final analysis, they knew of no reason why they should not: they believed in no sanction which could be invoked against them for this betrayal.

It all came to pass on Thursday, September 29, 1938. Then the leaders of four nations met in the Brown House in Munich. Two of them sold to the other two the integrity of a fifth nation. In Prague, capital of that fifth nation, men called this the basest surrender and betrayal in history. But the men in the Brown House finished their work, and the two from the West returned to their own countries.

In Prague, for the few tense days preceding the meeting at Munich, men had stood and faced the imminence of war. Grimly they had turned their faces toward the sky which, at any moment, it had seemed, might be thronged with planes coming from the north. During the nights, the city had been like a town of the dead. There were no street lights; shades were drawn across windows; streets were deserted. In that silent darkness, the last, pale light of the faith that had made the Liberal Society flickered quietly and died.

XIV

Liberalism: An Autopsy

THE wheel of the Liberal Society has turned full circle.

The Liberal Society had been erected on intellectual ground from which men had exiled the conception of society as a *communitas communitatum*—with its insistence on the attachment to social organization of a transcendent moral purpose, its functional unity of individuals and classes, its established dominion of ethics over economics.

It had replaced this with a society conceived as a joint-stock company rather than a spiritual organism—a company in which the liabilities of shareholders were strictly limited: a society entered by men only to secure more firmly those rights with which they were already invested by a beneficent Nature: a society in which the state was a matter of convenience, not of supernatural sanctions, existing only to protect those preordained rights of men and to allow their unfettered exercise.

It had propagated—itself was predicated upon—a wholly new conception of man's nature and his relationship to his God, his universe and his society. In the large it dismissed from its community mind the conception of duties to either God or fellow man as defined by any system of religious ethics. It affirmed the innate goodness of man and the perfectibility of his character through secular education and legislative fiat. It finally consecrated a conception of man toward which it had pointed virtually from the beginning—Economic Man: a man whose salvation was in the future of this world, to be realized by no sudden vicarious redemption and no adherence to a religious system of morality, but through the resolute and relentless power of material accumulation.

It had, in the propagation of this conception of man, evolved a philosophic technique which leveled to the ground of Utility the vast Christian superstructure of moral absolutes and ethical disciplines. In the realm of religion, it had equated the prescriptions of Christian social morality and the exigencies of business enterprise. In the sphere of ethics, it had equated virtue and desire, exalting the native passions and making morality painless and empty. Finally translated into terms of a social philosophy, it had discovered the infallible alchemy by which pursuit of self-interest was transmuted into attainment of social well being.

It had, in its day of triumph, evolved an institutional tech-

nique by which the illusion of man's salvation through unin-
hibited economic competition was fostered and perpetuated—
at the same time that the proprietorship of the economic citadels of society was surrendered to an aristocracy of wealth.
This it achieved by proclaiming the doctrine of political dis-
pensation of economic grievances—while at the same time it
allowed political operations to run a free course only so long
as they did not jeopardize the basic economic premises of the
established social order.

The outward signs of the collapse of the Liberal Society
have come with a succession of economic debacles and international wars, but these do little more than signalize the final,
tragic outworkings of forces within which have long pressed
inexorably toward this conclusion. It is not a matter of sur-
prise that this should be true of a society whose philosophic
foundations were constructed by the tenuous expedient of syn-
thesizing antitheses—a society whose institutional maintenance demanded a capricious, dynamistic and unprincipled
policy of sporadic social concessions to the laboring masses
whenever the central economic citadel seemed in danger of
attack. The process of inner deterioration which thus worked
its way through the whole structure of Liberalism is of two
natures: first, those forces within Liberalism which, in their
changing form and content, confused and disrupted the faith
of the Liberal, invalidating premises they had once been
believed to uphold; secondly, the germination within the
framework of Liberalism of ideas which, in the hands of
hostile forces, became instruments for assault upon the Liberal
structure from without.

However dubious may be the *a priori* premises of a definition of man's nature or a social philosophy, that philosophy
yet can maintain its standing if it can retain the virtue of inner
consistency. But when its rationale comes to evolve mutually
exclusive and contradictory doctrines, when its inner logic and
persuasiveness is gone, from that time its existence becomes
precarious and its ultimate collapse certain. It is this which

came upon the faith of the Liberal Society, in at least four ways which, in combined force, proved fatal.

I. The spirit of nationalism, in either its dynastic or its territorial signification, had sprung logically from the Liberal faith; for, in the final analysis, post-Enlightenment nationalism signified nothing so much as the projection of an atomistic individualism upon a national scale. The Roussellian cry for individual self-development and "natural," unfettered self-expression was the essential basis for Herder's conception of a nationality which must develop its native literature, language and cultural traditions—that is, express totally and freely the national individuality, the national soul. Both concepts had, in fact, been indistinguishably fused in the Machiavellian Prince—at once the symbol of resurgent Italian nationalism and the supreme expression of Italian individualism.

There were yet other bonds between Liberalism and nationalism. In the simple terms of political history, it was the bourgeoisie—agents and propagators of the Liberal faith—who initially ensured by their financial support the triumph of the absolute monarch who would bring national peace and unity; and it was the same middle class who, on through the nineteenth century, fortified and directed the forces of nationalism along the lines of economic conquest and imperialistic competition. Again, it was the Liberal faith which successfully achieved the emancipation of political as well as economic affairs from the dominion of historic Christian social ethics; and without this liberation, the phenomenon of modern nationalism would have been impossible.

Thus a logical corollary of Liberalism—in fact, the institution which most nearly in itself served as a religion for men of the Liberal Society—yet the national state evolved in such a way as to imperil and finally uproot much of the Liberal faith. Infatuated with the prospect of writing individual liberty in the larger letters of national self-determination, the Liberal produced a sovereign national state which, in its own domain, came frequently to threaten the most elementary civil liberties, and which, reaching far beyond its prescribed limits, carried men into a vast and uncharted field of colonial and imperial exploitation. Here the exigencies of the competition of nation with nation and the rewards of unstinted exploitation of colonial resources together proved so strong that in these subject countries the Liberal frankly abandoned those principles of political freedom saluted with such flourishing rhetoric on the floor of Senate, Parliament, Chamber, and Reichstag.

When the tragic cost of competitive national and imperialist systems was apparent even to their creator, the Liberal stumbled confusedly over successive institutional reforms by which he hoped to check the manifest destruction. In the early nineteenth century there was the Holy Alliance, by which statesmen tried to resolve national hates by ostentatious subscription to pious and innocuous platitudes: it constituted, in fact, a subversion of religious principles, an enlistment of them in the service of national self-interest—in much the same way that other men had invoked religion to blunt the edge of class grievances and thereby exploit class self-interest. At the conclusion of another century in which men could observe the ways of nationalism, there was the League of Nations—venturing no modification of state sovereignty, making no intelligent effort to inaugurate any basic community of feeling from which the bare forms of international institutions might derive life and spirit.

This League, monument that it was to the combined intellectual and political power of two worlds, was, in fact, nothing more pretentious than what has been described as "Bourgeois society's own administrative instrument *par excellence*."[1] Its operations and its standards of value were dictated by the world-spanning economic necessities of the Liberal Society. Its basic aim was the maintenance of that condition of affairs most desired by the great economic dynasties: on the one hand prevention of international politics from becoming inimical to uninterrupted world trade, and on the other hand establishment of the world economic system on as freely competitive and lucrative a basis as possible. Just as the "party of business" perpetuated its dominion in the Liberal national state, regardless of the ostentatious clash of political parties on the national stage, so in like manner the international bourgeoisie's hegemony was never in serious jeopardy, however world-shaking might seem the wars in which their many national governments indulged.

In this text of conditions, the League of Nations commended itself to maintenance of the status quo regardless of its intrinsic worth or justice. The devices for political dominion over fields of imperialistic interest were modified but remained essentially the same: mandates, dominions, customs unions and the like were concessions to the era's political conscience which yet in no essential way altered the economics of international conquest. The world-perspective of the Liberal Society was unmistakably stamped on the whole pattern of devices used to bring peace to the world; a formalistic and quantitative march toward lasting peace was conceived as feasible through mechanical reduction of naval ratios expressed in tons and of army maintenance described in heads and pieces. In short, this system of the League was "functionally conditioned by the dynamics of a bourgeois and acquisitive society, by the atomistic structure of its philosophy, by the role of money as its scale of measurement, and by its reduction of all social relationships to formal quantities."[2]

From its initial conception in the mind of the Liberal, the national state had been looked to as an agent to end feudal internecine strife, to stop the costly disruptions of religious wars, to bring peace and order, to secure the opportunity for the sober undisturbed pursuit of business enterprise. It soon, however, assumed less docile a function and evolved to serve as a militant force in sustained economic conquest. From that point in history, enlisted in the service of communal acquisitiveness, it proceeded to take new form again, until at the terminus of its evolution it became in itself at once the provocation, the instrument, and the combatant in wars of such magnitude that the religious strife of an earlier age became a pale frolic by comparison. Efforts to harness this creature of his own making proved shallow—because the Liberal was never willing to cut beneath the surface of political maneuvers and examine the foundations on which his own political thought was predicated. The doctrine of Thrasymachus maintained almost undisputed sovereignty. And Liberalism's eldest child became a fierce progeny which it could neither control nor understand.

II. It had been the new science which had furnished the essential substance for both the theoretical elaboration and the material conquests of Liberalism. Its revelation of a world of unexplored but controllable natural forces had inspired men to consecrate as an ideal the restoration of man to his sovereignty over Nature, while Nature herself was conceived as an animate, personalized and omniscient dispenser of the good things of life. . . . But, in the course of a century and a half the changing elements in the scientific revelation made insubstantial and unstable that foundation upon which so great a part of the Liberal faith had been erected.

In the eighteenth century men who were eager to banish the Christian God and His precepts from the immediate world of daily affairs, but who were anxious to display some passing deference for things religious—these men had found it a simple matter to attach a mechanical Prime Mover to a universe conceived like the Newtonian world-machine, a static unity governed by inflexible natural laws. But the revelation that came with Darwin upset all this. With scientific propagation of the theory of natural selection, instead of a fixed and changeless pattern of natural laws, men saw only growth and motion and change. Now, instead of a Nature whose laws and works were ever beneficent, men saw an interacting process of growth and decay. Now, instead of a precisely articulated natural mechanism which pointed directly to some ingenious Initiator, men saw the domain of nature governed by its own laws of natural selection. From all this the result was logical: whatever foundation the new science had formerly appeared to the Liberal to lend to the belief in a God, that foundation now was gone. A God there might yet be—but there was no longer anything in the gospel of science which supported such a conclusion for the Liberal.

In the course of the same period, the mature accomplishments of science themselves proved to be considerably less automatic and unqualified social graces than the Enlightened had anticipated. Successive wars in which the art of mass killing became ever more refined and elaborate soon suggested to some men the thought that the social worth of mechanical advance might, in the final analysis, depend not on the quantitative multiplication of inventions, but on the service in which men themselves enlisted these new weapons. One of the most signal applications of the new physiological knowledge was the examination of prospective candidates for war, so that now as never before nations were certain that the human sacrifices they demanded were of the strongest and healthiest human material they could find within their ranks. And while the psychologists of the eighteenth century had affirmed that man's character was innately neutral, men now began to wonder if it were not the scientific triumphs which were neutral in worth—triumphs not in themselves but only as men made them such.

Even in the affairs of peacetime, in the industrialization of society, it was soon evident that the massed power of mechanical inventions could not be automatically converted into benefit to humanity at large. "While much good came through invention," as Lewis Mumford has written,* "much invention came irrespective of the good. If the sanction of utility had been uppermost, invention would have proceeded most rapidly in the departments where human need was sharpest, in food, shelter, and clothing: but although the last department undoubtedly advanced, the farm and the common dwelling house were much slower to profit by the new mechanical technology than were the battlefield and the mine, while *the conversion of gains in energy into a life abundant took place much*

* Italics the present writer's.

[241]

slower after the seventeenth century than it had done during the previous seven hundred years."[3]

Finally, the application of scientific principles to the study of man and his society—application so eloquently urged by the Liberal of the Enlightenment—has itself tended increasingly to undermine, if not to destroy, basic dogmas of the Liberal faith. The empirical study of psychology has ultimately come to demand the repudiation of the essentially all-rational man which the Enlightened had envisioned: it has reaffirmed the importance of the non-rational and the irrational in men, the complex emotional and group patterns revolving around impulses like loyalty, enthusiasm, eagerness to lead, willingness to be led, self-esteem, convention, and anxiety for some unchanging faith to rationalize social activity and explain social disaster.[4] Following the principles of the Enlightened's faith that natural laws would govern social phenomena, there have come, also, that seemingly endless succession of natural scientists whose regard for their own authority in the field of social science is boundless. And when these oracles speak, as often as not theirs is a program for a biological and intellectual elite which is difficult to reconcile with the announced political gospel of Liberalism. Thus has one of them written: "A choice must be made among the multitude of civilized human beings. . . . The only way to obviate the disastrous predominance of the weak is to develop the strong. Our efforts to render normal the unfit are evidently useless. We should, then, turn our attention toward promoting the optimum growth of the fit. By making the strong still stronger, we could effectively help the weak. For the herd always profits by the ideas and inventions of the elite. Instead of leveling organic and mental inequalities, we should amplify them and construct greater men. . . . It is imperative that social classes should be synonomous with biological classes. Each individual must rise or sink to the level for which he is fitted by the quality of his tissues and of his soul. . . . Modern society should be given an immortal brain."[5] This, indeed, is a far scientific cry from the gospel of the Enlightened who proclaimed that education could and should establish complete intellectual equality.

And finally has come the sociologist. He has denied *a priori* assumption of and investiture of men with natural rights. He has exclaimed that man is not, as Rousseau maintained, born free but becomes free in society, from which he derives those civil rights consistent with his acceptance of obligations imposed on him by the social order.[6]

In these many ways the basic ingredient of the Liberal faith of the eighteenth century has turned upon its intellectual sponsor. The Liberal's conception of the universe and the God he derived therefrom; confidence in the positive good implicit in scientific invention; conception of man's rational nature, his essential equality with fellow-man, his inalienable natural rights—all this the changing content of the scientific revelation has ultimately not only failed to sustain, but in many cases has actively attacked. Having climbed skyward on the golden rungs of the ladder of the new science, the Liberal faith came to rest upon a cloud—suddenly to find itself without any means of descending again to the realm of reality.

III. Consecration of the individual as the supreme judge of truth and the final arbiter of all social issues has left the Liberal Society powerless to defend its own faith. Satisfied with a definition of liberty in terms of emancipation from social or religious disciplines, the Liberal has felt obligated, by the phraseology of his own creed, to accord to others the right and freedom to destroy what he himself maintains to be true.

From men conceived as ever rational and innately good, with the prescriptions of virtue indelibly inscribed upon their hearts—from men such as these there was no just reason for withholding the right to sit as final judges on all social action. There could not exist for them, nor could they be bound by, any superior standard of moral absolutes or any uncontingent code of social ethics. And it followed that, in the economic affairs of society, there was no valid reason for the state to grasp the wrist of that "unseen hand" which led men to enlist in the service of social needs to satisfy their own. All this followed logically from the Liberal's conception of the political nature of man, either cast in terms of innate natural rights antedating social organization, or constructed from the flexible tissue of that utilitarian doctrine which marvelously perceived the mysterious identity of self-interest and social welfare.

The political logic of the Liberal creed was as tragically constructed as its economic dialectic. The Liberal was traditionally militant in his opposition to political tyranny, his support of representative government. Having effectively denied the Christian conception of original sin and the concomitant doctrine of man's corruption and fallibility, the Liberal could defend representative government only by his assertion of the virtual infallibility of the individual (and the "common man"). It was by exactly the opposite doctrine that Christian social thought measured and denounced political tyranny— the fallibility of all men, and the consequent necessity of circumscribing the political authority of society's leaders. Beside this, the Liberal doctrine of ubiquitous human infallibility was wistful and wishful. More than that, it was fatal: as the fallacy of insistence on the infallibility of the "common man" became ever more evident, extreme reaction was bound to develop—in the form of Fascism. The terrible, repetitious tragedy of the Liberal faith was enacted here again: not its announced political doctrines, but the philosophical premises on which the Liberal sought to predicate them, proved insubstantial and essentially false.

Working from within the framework of the Liberal Society, these political and economic ideas propelled the process of attrition in three ways. First, the individualism of Liberal economics degenerated into a chaos of competitive greeds; economic inequalities multiplied, avarice became chronic. With freedom converted into a cloak for economic anarchy, the day was fast approaching when men would tear that cloak to shreds—and care little how fine might have been the cloth from which it once was cut. Secondly, with civil liberty accepted as the natural right of all men, uncontingent upon their respect for positive and explicit social ideals, that liberty allowed itself to become the medium by which its own destruction might be assured. Finally, with the individual accepted as the final judge and a majority of individuals acting as the infallible medium by which such judgment was made articulate, the Liberal, in effect, welcomed the possibility that a majority expression of opinion through the electoral process might vote the Liberal state out of existence. In Germany in 1933 there was an unquestionable and highly articulate majority favoring the death of the German Republic and the ascent to power of Adolph Hitler. When war came in 1939, the Third Reich's military effort was powerfully fortified by the Roussellian "general will" of the people. Unwilling to assume the arduous intellectual labor of positing specific and clearly defined ideals as the necessary and immutable ingredients of the good society, the Liberal faith, by its own definitions, could not condemn even its own annihilation.

In Christian thought, the supreme fact in the life of the individual was death. In the life of the Liberal state, the climactic experience was suicide.

IV. In its earliest and most militant days, the last indictment that could be made of the Liberal faith was that it failed to carry the fight to its opponents with the necessary courage and resolution. As the creed of an aspiring and ascendant bourgeoisie, the Liberal faith had, by force of intellectual or military arms, claimed the world for its own. But, in its evolution through the nineteenth century and in its conversion into the defensive and self-exculpating creed of a triumphant social class, Liberalism's primitive resolution became sicklied o'er with the pale cast of the dogma of inevitable progress.

Even the World War that began in 1914 could not erase the smile that the Liberal had worn since the days of Condorcet. Writing in 1924 on the significance of the conclusion of the War, one of the University of London's most distinguished historians exclaimed: "It seemed to symbolize the overthrow of antiquated despotism, the dethronement of militarism, the final defeat of dynastic ambition, the deliverance of a troubled world from diplomatic intrigue and imperialist aggression. It held out the hope of the advent of a new age marked by international amity, established peace, federated peoples, and universal law. The nightmare menace of German world-dominion was over; the hectic era of the race for armaments that reached its limit; the day of liberty, equality and fraternity had at last arisen."" And in the same period, H. G. Wells, at the conclusion of his popularized study of man's history, was convulsed by a spasm of optimistic prognostication: "Life begins perpetually. Gathered together at last under the leadership of man, the student-teacher of the universe, unified, disciplined, armed with the secret powers of the atom, and with knowledge as yet beyond dreaming, life, for ever young and eager, will presently stand upon earth as upon a footstool, and stretch out its realm amidst the stars."[8]

Men whose faith in the immutability of progress was infinite were spiritually and intellectually unequipped to face social realities which seemed unsavory. When in 1939 Europe's marching armies signaled the end of a world, the Liberal—ever thinking in terms of the rational man who was the creature of his own imagination—was still incapable of understanding a philosophy to great degree built upon the *non-rational*. Because his creed told him that all men were innately good, the Liberal could not comprehend the threat of armed men who clearly were not so. Because neither the Fascist nor the Communist ideologies were palatable to the Liberal, he assumed that both were essentially weak, victims of their own inner deterioration, from which followed the gross underestimation of the power of both the German and Russian states. Because his chronology did not include an era of regression and disaster, the imminence of such a period in man's history could not stir the Liberal to action. Because he could not conceive of decay or degeneracy in his own mature civilization, the Liberal insisted on disposing of Fascism as a simple "reversion to barbarism"[9]—thereby reflecting his tragic belief that only the primitive past could nourish evil, and his equally tragic moral and intellectual incapacity to fight out the issues of the present in terms of the present.

When Marx wrote that the bourgeoisie of capitalist society would finally prove to be their own gravediggers, he was thinking in terms of economic dialectic. But the statement was even more valid in reference to the fact that vast segments of the Liberal rationale would finally come to serve as intellectual springboards from which could be launched assaults upon the whole Liberal Society. It was this development—as much as the inner decay of the creed—which proved fatal to the Liberal faith.

Marxism itself furnished the first instance of this—although few suggestions so irritate the Marxist as that which questions the really revolutionary character of his doctrines. The broad historical basis for the rise of an insurgent proletarian social philosophy was the fact that the laboring masses betrayed the Liberal's trust in their ignorant apathy and actually took to heart and mind the doctrines of liberty and equality. When the dynamic economic forces behind the Liberal Society had finally frozen into the capitalistic structure, when the injustice and inhumanity of bourgeois society revealed the gulf between Liberal gospel and capitalistic fact—then it was that the working masses took hold upon the pliable concepts of liberty and equality, refashioned them with their own hands and in the light of their own demands, and, with Marxism, set forth the text of conditions in which they believed the ideals so defined could be realized.

Having accepted the same basic ideal as the Liberal Society, the Marxist crusade appealed to the same instrument and criterion of progress—material accumulation. While the Marxist system of the organization of production and the distribution of wealth might be revolutionary, yet it conceived its ideal society as realizable through action confined to that same economic realm which the Liberal had exalted and hallowed as the ground—the only ground—on which man's salvation could be fought for and won. The realm of the spiritual, at the same time, was just as imaginary and fruitless a product of oppressive priestcraft for the Marxist as it had been to the Liberal of the Enlightenment—and fundamentally no more so. Marx's exultant claim that the social gospel of Christianity was "mealy-mouthed" while his was "revolutionary" signified an attitude of mind that was in no wise revolutionary, because it had been fully articulated a century before by the men who also regarded themselves as the Enlightened.

The Marxist faith not only postulated man's salvation as an earthly event of the future and one to be realized through the same grace of material acquisition which the Liberal had revered, but also it followed an analogous technique to secure the fidelity of the faithful through all the trials and vicissitudes of class warfare. There was more than adequate precedent in the Liberal experience for this technique—most conspicuously in the Calvinist doctrine of predestination which assured victory to the religious elite and in the Liberal faith in inevitable progress under the aegis of the bourgeois elite. With Marxism, the final working-out of dialectical materialism produced the same happy result: the collapse of bourgeois society was inevitable, the great and good forces of the universe were now resolutely working side by side with the new revolutionaries, and the ultimate victory of the Marxist-proletarian elite was an event which the combined force of all the tyrannous practices of the bourgeoisie could never prevent.

The simple issue which underlay this correspondence between the intellectual habits of Liberalism and Marxism was the fact that both accepted, in the final analysis, the same definition of man's nature and final destiny. Although the Marxist might argue that his was a system of thought concerned only with the process of social change and one which cared not a whit for pietistic-sounding phrases like "the nature of man," yet his doctrines ultimately had to rest upon a definition of man's nature. In other words, the Marxist dialectic might prove to everyone's complete satisfaction that the Communist organization of the means of production was the only intelligent one—and still it would have proved nothing. It had to prove first that *any* organization of production was *important to man*, that man's *nature* was such that his salvation or welfare could be achieved by even the most perfect economic organization. The Marxist creed, in short, had to accept—and did accept—the same Economic Man which the Liberal faith had made the human substance of its society.

The advent of Fascism signalized the passing of a world order—testified to the fact that war and economic chaos had finally disemboweled Economic Man. With the failure to realize liberty, equality or the good society through the infinite process of accumulation of economic wealth, the rationale of the Liberal Society proved itself no longer tenable. The promise of capitalism was proven false. The social and economic organization of society was divested of any rationalizing purpose or excuse, and there remained only the unchained, uncomprehended shock and clash of inchoate social energies. "The demons," as one writer has expressed it, "returned to haunt men and to present themselves as, after all, the real masters of human destiny. . . . These new demons— poison gas and bombs from the air, permanent unemployment, and 'too old at forty'—are all the more terrible because they are man-made. The demons of old were as natural as their manifestations in earthquakes or storms. The new demons, though no less inescapable, are unnatural. They can be released by man only; but once they have been turned loose, man has no control over them."[10] . . . Man had, indeed, reclaimed his sovereignty over nature and enlisted nature in the service of human convenience. He was no longer the helpless, inept being he had once been in the face of riotous, untamed forces of nature. But he was now the victim of forces equally cataclysmic in proportions, forces which ran their riotous course through the whole of his society—and forces which his fellow men had created. The skies had darkened, the earth had shaken, and the Liberal temple of the natural harmonies had come down in ruins.

Such a collapse of the Liberal rationale necessarily created an imperative demand for a new creed which could invest men's life in society with an immediately apprehensible purpose. This was the service and function of Fascism—which came first to those countries where the bourgeois ideals of the Liberal Society had taken weakest root, where the purpose-giving and rationalizing service of the Liberal social faith first proved mortal. To the immediate, unordered needs of the moment Fascism responded with the exaltation of a non-economic standard of values, a way of living whose horizon extended beyond the massing of material possessions. Men who had been failures so long as their worth was measured in terms dictated by Economic Man were liable to elevation to the stature of national heroes, when their worth was judged by a different standard. For an equality that had been proven unattainable in the economic realm, the Fascist rationale idealized an equality stated in terms of service to the national entity. It exorcized the demon of irrational unemployment and exalted (thereby rationalizing) the fact of war. It explained what Liberalism could not explain: it gave an immediate, swift and exhilarating resolution to issues which left the Liberal only confused. "Man's material interests," the Bible of Fascism explained, "are able to thrive best as long as they remain in the shadow of heroic virtues."[11] And the Fascist faith was built upon the construction of a new scheme of values, a new rationale of social organization, which would incorporate those "heroic virtues."

But the paradoxical fact is that, while the Fascist faith revolted from the Liberal Society and totally denied the idea of Economic Man, yet the development of this faith and the techniques it employed to triumph were, in truth, devastatingly logical fulfillments of doctrines born in the brain of the Liberal. Most obviously, the reverent conception of the supreme national state was bred in a context of intellectual and political conditions which the Liberal faith had produced: the essential foundation for the power-politics of Fascism was laid when the Liberal emancipated all political authority from the governance of religious ethics. More ironically and more specifically, it was the Liberal of the West who had made articulate his passion for national freedom, throughout the nineteenth century, by his enthusiastic support of the causes of German and especially Italian national unification. It seemed indeed as if the seeds scattered in central and Eastern Europe by the French Revolution bore their fruit in these national forces of the twentieth century which rose to strike down the legacy of that same Revolution as it had taken form in the Western states.

This connection and interaction had even deeper historical roots. It has been traced back to the time of the Reformation by one of America's most noted Protestant scholars, who has observed that "German fascism has developed upon a soil of Lutheran Protestantism in which Christian pessimism about the sinfulness of man was allowed to express itself without restraint and with such a degree of consistency that all significant distinctions between justice and injustice in the social order were obscured. . . . The highest possibility in corporate life was not justice but coerced order and peace. . . . Lutheran pessimism therefore produces a political ethic remarkably similar to the secular pessimism of Thomas Hobbes. . . . The Lutheran Reformation is therefore that particular locus in the history of Christendom where the problem of justice is most clearly disavowed. It is therefore no accident of history that Nazi pessimism, with its glorification of force as the principle of order, its unqualified affirmation of the state, its disavowal of all concepts of justice and its rejection of all universal standards of morality, should grow upon this soil."[12] . . . The princes of the world are gods, the common people are Satan: those phrases had not ceased echoing.*

* Hitler's own reflections on this phase on his country's history are illuminating. "The Church," he explains, "did not seem to feel with the German people, but seemed unjustly to take sides with its enemies. The root of the evil was . . . that the head of the Catholic Church was not in Germany, a fact which accounted for the concerns of our nationality." (*Mein Kampf*, p. 139.)

In the active operation of its political technique, Fascism made ingenious use of arts developed originally by the Liberal Society, two of which were outstanding. The first of these was the dynamism of the Fascist state—its ceaseless, inner energy which, finding some Liberals in a devout mood, has provoked them to the suspicion that it is an essentially amoral, acquisitive energy which has no end but its own endless pursuit of power. But was this, in any fundamental sense, a new social phenomenon? Rather it seems to have been anticipated in all essential particulars by two equally striking phenomena in the Liberal Society. In the first place, the energizing economic principle of Liberalism had been the announced belief that the good society would be realized through the ceaseless pursuit of material wealth—through a dynamic acquisitiveness which, as medieval thinkers had warned, would, when ungoverned by any ethical purpose or orientation, literally become infinite. It would seem that what the Liberal had here exalted in economic terms was simply converted by the Fascist into the more evident terms of power-politics: in one case, economic acquisitiveness, in the other instance political conquest, neither dedicated to a transcendent end, neither circumscribed by a moral purpose, both self-sustaining and self-justifying pursuits which knew no objective beyond their own gratification.

In the second place, the dynamism of the Fascist state was foreshadowed by Liberalism in the character of the techniques used by the bourgeoisie to perpetuate its class dominion: compromise with rebellious forces from below, expedient concessions to proletarian protest when the central economic citadel seemed in danger—an entirely capricious policy of dealing with hostile forces as the exigencies of the moment dictated, all dedicated to the single end of securing economic power. Was this a fundamentally distinct policy from that invoked by Fascism in the arena of international politics—the policy of threat, judicious compromise, transient pledges of good faith, and all that made the Fascist technique so powerful? In one case a class secured its estate against hostile classes;

in the other case a nation triumphed over hostile national forces—both succeeding by the same dynamic political technique.

There was, in addition to this issue of the dynamic state, a second and more graphic method by which Fascist political technique exploited an art developed by the Liberal: the doctrine of national "self-determination." The most striking example of this came in 1938, when Nazi Germany had pointed its guns in threat toward the border of Czechoslovakia. Beyond that border were 3,500,000 Germans in the Sudetenland. Their leader, Konrad Henlein, and the ruler of the German Reich were as eloquent as any of the nineteenth century nationalists in deploring the maltreatment of these people . . . "oppressed in an inhuman and intolerable manner . . . brutally struck . . . pursued like wild beasts for every expression of their national life." With a Wilsonian ring in his voice, Hitler concluded an oration in these words: "And I say that if these tortured creatures cannot obtain rights and assistance by themselves, they can obtain both from us. An end must be made of depriving these people of their rights. . . . I demand that the oppression of 3,500,000 Germans in Czechoslovakia shall cease and be replaced by the free right of self-determination."[13] . . . What could the distracted Liberal answer?

Revealing as all these instances are, however, they but reflect the larger and fundamental fact: the correspondence between Fascism and Liberalism in their denial of the reality of moral values and absolute ethical disciplines. The Liberal was sincerely shocked by such statements of the Fascist as: "We shall never approach history impartially, but as Germans"[14]—or this: "The captious emphasis laid on the 'liberty of the Church,' imperceptibly slipping over to the 'value of Liberty,' is calculated to make the Church a haunt of all treasonable elements. . . . A Church devoid of the State and thrown upon mass favor would be used by the masses as a concessioned gathering-place for rebellion. . . . The German

Faith movement poses the question: How far does Christianity agree, how far does it disagree with our Kind? . . . We cannot kneel down before a God who pays more attention to the French than to us!"[15] . . . But, shocked though the Liberal might be, had not the Liberal Faith movement posed the same question long before: How far does Christianity agree, how far does it disagree with our kind?*

The unvarnished truth of the matter is that the strength and resourcefulness of Fascism ultimately rests on a freedom from self-confining ethical absolutes which the Liberal faith had applauded centuries before. That denial, never made complete in the Liberal Society, of moral precepts binding on society as much as on the individual is made total by the Fascist faith. "We do not know of or recognize," the Fascist proclaims, "truth for truth's sake or science for science's sake. . . . For Fascism such things do not exist as a philosophy independent of race; a culture without a nation . . . knowledge which has no end but itself.[16] . . . It [propaganda] has not to search into truth as far as this is favorable to others, in order to present it then to the masses with doctrinary honesty, but it has rather to serve its own truth uninterruptedly.[17] . . . Our moral consciousness is nothing but a deployment of our self-consciousness as natural beings. . . . Formerly we were in the habit of saying: *this is right or wrong*; today we must put the question accordingly: *What would the 'Führer' say?*"[18]

Damn the absolute! William James had cried. And Adolph Hitler damned it.

* "Trying to produce order at the Vatican is a fault into which we Germans have unfortunately often fallen. . . . From the standpoint of the Reich it would have been most desirable if there had been, not one Pope, but at least two or, if possible, many more. They would have fought one another. The people must be wrested from the churches and their priests. Their influence must be permanently broken in the same way as the harmful influences of astrologers, soothsayers and similar swindlers. Our National Socialist world picture stands far above the teachings of Christianity."

These words (reported in *Time*, March 2, 1942) came from the lips of Martin Bormann, who succeeded Rudolph Hess as the third ranking Nazi after Hess's famed flight to England. But, with the proper names slightly changed, they could just as well have been spoken by Voltaire or others of the Enlightened, Fouché or other molders of French Revolutionary nationalism.

Dazed and distracted, the Liberal is walking among the ruins of the City which he built on sand.

His own tradition has confused itself in his mind, even though he is still unaware of the greater anomalies and contradictions in his creed. He is uncertain yet as to the true foundation for the rights of man he has been applauding for more than a century; he turns to utilitarianism and sees the logical dangers of so frail a base for freedom as social expediency; he turns to the doctrine of natural law and natural rights and finds little more than the mist that confused the actual and the ideal in the mind of the Enlightened Liberal. He is no more sure of his own inheritance of economic theory; he looks back to Ricardo and finds that one of the earliest apostles of economic liberalism denied the spontaneous harmony of individual and class interests in a freely competitive economy; he looks back to John Stuart Mill and learns that this great Liberal political philosopher, by inventing the dichotomy of "higher" and "lower" pleasures, implicitly conceded the existence of a social criterion that transcended simple utility—but what that criterion could be the Liberal cannot discover. In the contemporary world, he sees around him fellow-Liberals everywhere being forced to admit ever increasing supervision by the state of the private domain of business enterprise—concessions which, however casual or isolated, signify the ultimate invalidation of the Liberal's basic economic premises.

His troubles projected into the arena of immediate international issues, the Liberal finds that the statesmanship which has followed his principles has become a monument to ineptitude. He sees the course of international politics dominated by men who give no consistent manifestation of being rational or of themselves being profoundly impressed with the idea that the principles of virtue are graven on the hearts of all men. He sees that his faith in the natural harmony of conflicting economic forces within the state has become translated into a Liberal mirage of spontaneous harmony among states— a harmony which needs no abridgment of national sovereignty nor the secure binding of any firm international pacts: a mirage of harmony by which the individual Western nations of Europe were hypnotized into inaction in the face of the Fascist advance.

In an effort to meet and refute the Fascist indictment of the Liberal Society on an intellectual or philosophic level, the Liberal emerges no more successful. Facts too manifestly sustain the Fascist charge that the social and economic structure of the Liberal state belies its gospel of freedom and equality. And groping for weapons with which to retaliate, the Liberal finds them to be not in his own, but in the Christian arsenal. To indict Fascism for its corruption of moral absolutes, to cry out against its subversion of religion to secular objectives, to denounce the unprincipled acquisitiveness of the Fascist faith —can the Liberal do any of these things and still retain a vestige of intellectual integrity? Can a society that is Christian but little more than to the extent that it refrains from persecution of the practice of the Christian religion—can this society indict another as pagan?

Returning in desperation to a realm in which he might hope to be more competent, the Liberal's final solutions to economic maladjustments springing from his own social order themselves indict an order which must have recourse to such expedients. Forced at last to concede that economic progress is not automatic, the Liberal, to accelerate the pace of slackening business enterprise, advances such remedies as could emerge only from a mind distracted by the rising consciousness of its own limitations. He pays men not to produce—thus implicitly abandoning confidence in that energizing force which he had promised would bring the good society. Or— echoing Malthus—he prays men not to reproduce.

The exhilarating triumph of the French Revolution seems long distant—that time when men cheered and hoped and were filled with a new sense of power, that time

> When France in wrath her giant limbs upreared,
> And with that oath, which smote air, earth, and sea,
> Stamped her strong foot and said she would be free. . . .

But in the year 1940 France lay prostrate. And, echoing ever louder through the years, had come the cry of the poet who had written in 1798 words first whispered, then passed about, finally shouted as the brute falsehoods of the Liberal faith became manifest—shouted ever louder, by the great unwashed, by angered humanity . . .

> Are these thy boasts, Champion of human kind?
> To mix with Kings in the low lust of sway,
> Yell in the hunt, and share the murderous prey;
> To insult the shrine of Liberty with spoils
> From freemen torn; to tempt and to betray?
>
> The Sensual and the Dark rebel in vain,
> Slaves by their own compulsion! In mad game
> They burst their manacles and wear the name
> Of Freedom, graven on a heavier chain!*

So has ended the day of the Liberal Society. Unable longer to hypnotize the masses of humanity with the loud, false promise of the omnicompetence of productive power; betrayed and frightened by the ever more apparent contradictions in his own creed; threatened with destruction by forces which refuse to genuflect at the shrine of the Natural Harmonies; petulantly exclaiming, as the simplest explanation of Fascism for the lazy mind, that it is one more monumental proof of the ignorance and credulity of the masses, while still speaking hollow phrases about the innate rights and the innate dignity of all men . . . the Liberal has become that most pitiable of social animals: one grown cynical of either the truth or the efficacy of the faith he professes.

* Coleridge, *France, An Ode.*

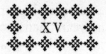

XV

The Faith of Democracy

THE great question presented by the work of Machiavelli had been: was it only coincidence that the same sweeping creed which had converted religion into an instrument of the state also had converted men into instruments of the state— that the same faith which dethroned morality also dethroned humanity? The answer to that question, apparent at various times in the course of the Liberal experience, was uncompromisingly given by Fascism. The reason that this was the answer was to be found in the meaning of democracy.

The faith of democracy is a faith in the essential worth of all men and the essential equality of all men—deriving from men's creation in the image of God and their equality in the final judgment before their Creator: a faith which asserts the consequent inalienable right of all men to share in the benefits of social organization, in just proportion to their recognition of the obligation to contribute to the well being of that society and of fellow men. It is a faith which takes man as its central figure, his freedom as a moral agent as its central fact, his infinite value and infinite latent potentialities as its central truth. It then dedicates itself to the fullest possible assertion, the clearest possible articulation of those infinite potentialities: to which end all institutions and all social forms must be but as instruments.

Thus conceived, democracy and Liberalism stand separated by a wide and deep gulf.* Democracy's base is religious and

---

* Discussions which may clarify further this dichotomy are to be found in Mumford, L., *Faith for Living*, and Hayes, C. J. H., *A Generation of Materialism*. The former writer uses the distinction of "ideal liberalism" and "pragmatic liberalism," while Hayes distinguishes between "ecumenical liberalism" and "secular liberalism." Neither of these analyses is by any means following the same line of distinction drawn here, but what these writers call "ideal" or "ecumenical" Liberalism may, in the broadest sense, be applied to what is here discussed as "democracy."

specifically Christian in essence; Liberalism's is secular. Democracy knows no age but is the unattained ideal to which some men of all times have made contribution and pledged allegiance; Liberalism is the intellectual progeny of the modern era. Democracy knows no classes and casts its definitions in terms of men, not social groups; Liberalism's roots are middle-class, and its branches and foliage that aspire to be catholic quickly wither. Democracy is bound to no single economic structure and views all economic machineries as but instruments; Liberalism has become little more than the ethos and rationale of capitalism, and the perpetuation of that economic system it has conceived as an end in itself. Democracy speaks of a man subject to the discipline of moral absolutes, working toward a destiny that is spiritual; Liberalism knows no such man. Democracy is dedicated to a goal which signifies the positive fulfillment of the demands and the potentialities of man's nature; Liberalism conceives of little more than that freedom which means immediate removal of those ideal or institutional forces constricting men in their unfettered exercise of "natural" rights and their undisciplined pursuit of self-interest.

Amid the disintegration and collapse of bourgeois Liberal Society, in the face of the rushing force of Fascism, the most menacing threat to what is best in the cultural and political tradition of the West is the possible implication of the democratic faith in the Liberal disaster. The immediate and compelling necessity is that the faith of democracy, far from being thus confused and disabled, be infused with new and sustained energy.

In the mediation between the world of immediate social facts and the ideal democratic tradition, it was for long believed by many that Socialism could assume the burden of the task. The creed of which Karl Marx was the great prophet inspired the greatest mass movement to sweep Europe since the early days of Christianity. It claimed freedom from the hard, artificial national categories of Liberalism; it inspired men of all nations with a virile sense of social justice; it evolved a system of historical and economic study which, to many, seemed revealing, often profound, and essentially true. But the evolution of Socialism in many particulars has told a tragic and disappointing story.

The theoretical structure of Marxism has assumed most of the characteristic signs of a religious faith, encircled with a wall of dogmatism by comparison with which the doctrines of Christianity seem less rigid, less authoritarian in tone. The term "dialectical materialism," as one writer expresses it, has "become something like the sacred syllable *Om* to the Hindus."[1] The conception of immutable economic laws over which men have no ultimate control has been little more than a reiteration of divine-laws doctrine, cast now in the mold of the new science. Faith in the inevitability of bourgeois disaster and proletarian triumph has bred a Marxist self-assurance and intolerance beside which the Liberal's confidence in the power of free economic enterprise often seems meek. A class-predestination doctrine has evolved which has often served to take the place of militant and immediate social action. Many times men of the laboring classes have been asked by the Marxist faith to accept social injustices in the cause of ultimate Marxist victory in a not too specific future: an enjoinder which is of no finer substance than the Liberal injunction to the working masses to stand by the system of free enterprise until the bright and inevitable day dawns when there shall be freedom and justice for all.

In the colder domain of fact, Marxist prognostication has proved false. Wealth has not become concentrated in the hands of increasingly fewer numbers, however true this may be of control and management; nor has the material misery of the laboring masses constantly increased. The only Marxist victory won in the century after the *Communist Manifesto* came counter to all prescriptions of Marxian dialectic—in a far from industrialized nation in which the "inevitable" decline of the bourgeoisie, which Marx had outlined with such precision, could never have taken place because the country had never witnessed anything approaching bourgeois triumph.

In the two great international crises of the early twentieth century, the Marxist theory of history and society unraveled in pitiful fashion. In the World War of 1914, the Socialists of all nations, almost unanimously, abandoned their allegiance to a faith that claimed to be supra-national and took up arms in their respective nations with the zeal of patriots. At the end of the war, when Marxism triumphed in the Russian Revolution, it quickly froze into nationalistic form—and those who denounced this development were hunted around the earth with a mad zeal matching the most fanatical religious persecution. In the World War that began in 1939, international political Marxism threw off the last torn shreds of intellectual integrity. Having insisted for years on the patently untrue proposition that Fascism was a determined last-stand of the capitalistic economy, the one Communist state in the world then signed a pact with the state it thus regarded as the embodiment of economic tyranny, thereby permitting that state to achieve its most fabulous military triumphs. For the period while that pact endured, Communists around the world assailed the Western powers as embodiments of capitalism and perpetrators of the greatest imperialistic outrages. Then, when the legions of Hitler were suddenly turned upon the Communist state, once again Fascism became the bourgeois menace, while Russia took her stand beside the Western nations this time. And the magic alchemy of Marxian dialectic was again invoked to convert the struggle into a class war in which the liberation of the world proletariat was indissolubly linked with Russian military victory.

Antedating and transcending in importance this intellectual and moral degeneration, however, was the signal and vital flaw of the whole Marxian system of thought. Marx had been much more perceptive than most of his contemporaries in his understanding of the character of capitalistic society. In interpreting his times, he had, with great acumen, traced almost all social phenomena to an economic basis. But what he failed to realize was that he was only dissecting Economic Man—not observing the constant forces of social change. Every age is decisively characterized by its own peculiar conception of man's nature and destiny; the nineteenth century's Liberal Society thought and worked in terms of Economic Man; hence the understanding of that age and that society was obtainable only through a knowledge of the determining economic forces. Marx and his disciples failed completely to perceive this fact: that he could see the economic to be decisive in the world about him *because it was in economic terms that men about him defined their own nature—the economic factor in man's society was not per se decisive.* Having thus confused the anatomy of Economic Man with the pattern of human history, the Marxist faith was committed to error and ultimate disillusionment.

The essential vitality of the Marxist movement and its intelligent, incisive understanding of the economic energies of the Liberal Society—these were facts which the Western world could neither ignore nor destroy. But the patent errors of traditional Marxism's analysis and the intellectual dishonesty of many of its apostles—these were facts which, by the advent of the War of 1939, signified clearly that historic Marxism would have to undergo serious reorientation if it ever were to take a decisive part in shaping the historic future of the West. Only when thus refined, and only when divested of its mystical presumption to explain all facts and forces of the universe, the Marxist technique of economic analysis, in conjunction with other and more profound forces, could contribute to the forging of that future.

This history of the Liberal Society itself demonstrates that its weaknesses have not been merely in its publicized political or economic doctrines, but actually in its religious and ethical premises—for the former have been only the translation of the latter into a different idiom. The philosophical technique by which the Liberal faith triumphed first proved victorious in the realms of religion and ethics, and from these victories was deduced the political and economic creed. Therefore there exists no justification for assuming that recurrence of the disasters to which the Liberal Society has led can be prevented simply by the recasting of its political theories. Alone sufficient can be more radical action, for the same philosophical premises, allowed to survive behind the verbal veil of a new political vocabulary, will continue to give birth to the same ideological offspring.

The truly crucial importance of this cannot be overemphasized. For so long as the issue is assumed to be simply one involving announced political doctrines, so long are critics of the Liberal faith burdened with the fear of seeming to attack all the generous, humane, vacuous and innocuous platitudes associated with the word "liberal." It is not in this generalized, amorphous character that Liberalism can or should be attacked, for the effort would be quixotic and the result insignificant. It is against the specific, ultimate philosophical definitions and axioms that the attack must be launched. It is the Liberal faith's very definition of man which must be the issue.

The importance of this can be simply illustrated. Who can or would bluntly attack the Liberal's aversion to political tyranny? Yet that aversion, and the doctrines on which it rests, have not proved strong enough to prevent the rise of the greatest political tyranny the Western world has ever known. Grief has not come because the Liberal opposed tyranny. It has come because he could not explain *why* he opposed it— *why* the dignity of the individual is indestructible, why the very fallibility of all descendants of Adam (and not the infallibility of the mysterious "common man") makes arbitrary power a dangerous threat to that dignity.

It is to these basic principles that the battle must be carried—to the realm of the faith and the will and the reason which have built the Liberal Society. And for that darkened reason, for that weakened will, for that now uprooteu faith, there needs to be substituted a clearer reason, a stronger will and a deeper faith.

Men who turn to the Church to find these things cannot expect to have at their disposal a political machine geared to competition on the ward and precinct level of politics; nor can they expect to discover a perfectly unified and harmonious institution which, in one or a few exuberant testimonies of belief, will reshape the minds of men and the course of human history. Men who see in the Church, on the basis of its past intellectual tradition, the logical and powerful propagator of that redefinition of man which the collapse of the Liberal faith demands, yet must be willing honestly to face difficult obstacles—a fact which is the eternal price of any political or intellectual position that is neither vacuous nor innocuous. The degree to which the Church can succeed in this task—which is nothing less pretentious than the reinvigoration of democracy—can be measured by the frankness with which these problems are faced, the courage with which their solution is undertaken.

The problems are not small. Inherent in an institutional structure so elaborate as the Church is a slowness to translate will into action, a tenacious clinging to inherited habits of thought. Yet more serious, no matter how profound be the ideal contradiction between the principles of such an institution and those of the world around it, it is from the existing economy, whatever be its form, that financial strength must be drawn—a fact which does not reinforce the vigor of the Church's revolt from the Liberal Society or its capitalistic ordering of economic life. There follows quickly from this a too frequently apathetic view of the social issues involved in the uncritical perpetuation of Liberal economics: an over-anxious tendency to sharpen the edge of the spiritual sword when Marxism is attacked, an often perceptible softening of the blows when Liberalism is the issue.

Not only has much of the institutional strength of the Church thus been subject to atrophy, but also much of its intellectual resources have been wasted in an empty effort to inspire mankind to rally to the banner of medievalism. With regard to the persistence of religious or ethical precepts, this effort is intelligent and obligatory for any institution which does not admit the refashioning of moral standards according to the capricious prescriptions of any given historical moment. But, profound as were many of the central truths of the medieval social gospel, it is grossly unrealistic to assume that these truths need no recasting to govern new social and economic realities. To ignore the past five centuries because so much of them has been sheer heresy, because so much of the whole period has been pharisaical in its social gospel and pagan in its morality—to do this is to forget that five hundred years of human experience cannot be removed from man's legacy by pronouncement of a papal encyclical: to disregard the fact that any modern synthesis comparable to the work of Aquinas must embrace, not seek to repudiate, the material triumphs of science. What the Church faces, in short, is the task of succeeding in the twentieth century in that which it failed to achieve in the sixteenth and in the eighteenth centuries: to restate the Christian tradition to the modern age—in Archbishop Ireland's words—in terms of things that it feels and in language that it understands.

While atrophy and waste can play such threatening roles, vanity too has its part—the vanity of intellectual power. The very consciousness of Church leaders of the potential force and the inherent strength of their institution's intellectual tradition—this very realization easily lends itself to becoming a vitiating, enervating influence in the form of the self-assurance which it can inspire. Power imposes a double responsibility—not only to use it wisely and discreetly, but also to use it affirmatively and constructively. However strong be the doctrines of Aquinas, a voice that was stilled in the thirteenth century cannot be heard in New York and London today. Silent, introspective self-satisfaction on the part of the inheritors of that tradition can condemn it to eternal silence. Only the voice of the present can, in the last analysis, be audible to the present—and he who has not the courage to speak need never ask why he is not heard.

Finally, this triumvirate of imperilling tendencies must be joined by one other—expediency. When in 1869 Bishop von Ketteler warned the leaders of the Church to heed and to heal the social question, he did so "because it is indissolubly bound up with her mission of teaching and guiding mankind." He did not say: "because it is indissolubly bound up with the protection of our own estate." For the issue is one of principle, and the issue is lost if it be treated as a matter of expediency. If ever leaders of the Church direct their appeal to the working masses as a self-interested political device, then a binding moral obligation is being perverted and exploited as a political tactic of self-defense. The price of such distortion can only be ultimate failure.

These are some of the grave issues which men of the Church must have the moral and intellectual strength to face with clear vision. These men must be unwilling to accept the cheap solution that the problems do not exist. They must, above all, themselves be willing to pay the penance for the historical misjudgments and institutional sins of the Church, by acknowledging their existence and laboring for their expiation.

While thus working to fortify the Church in its task of restoring moral and intellectual strength to the democratic tradition, men themselves can find strength in this knowledge: that it is the only historic institutional force which can be expected to be able to succeed in that task. It stands as the most virile moral authority in the contemporary world. It has been the only historic institution defiantly and valiantly insistent on the social applicability of Christian ethics. It has never compromised principle with the creed of the Liberal Society, nor allowed doctrines of the Liberal faith to be insinuated into the body of Church philosophy. It has never welcomed or abetted the exaltation of sovereign national states and itself stood forth as the only supra-national power when war struck the Western world in 1939.

Not merely fidelity to its own principles but also the almost inescapable pressure of historical necessity qualify the Church for the work of the present. The wide popular base of its institutional structure is the laboring masses, from the wheat-fields of central Europe and the vineyards of Spain to the mills and factories of New York and Chicago. Its celibate hierarchy can never be stifled by the baneful influence of inherited power and must constantly draw its blood and strength from the peoples of the world.

Intellectual or political association with a landed aristocracy has become an historical impossibility; and between the ethic, the world-perspective, of the bourgeoisie and that of the Church, there never has been and there never can be compromise or alliance. The Liberal Society in which today the laboring masses have lost faith is the same social order whose philosophical foundations the Church has never ceased attacking.

There no longer remains doubt that the forecast of Manning is coming true: "The future will call forth into the light of reason the social state of the world of labor." There remains only one great central question: whether that social state will be called into existence by a creed which again accepts the Liberal definition of man, or whether the realization will come in time that that definition must be destroyed and replaced by another; whether that social state marks only a precarious shift in the center of gravity of political power, or whether the true objective is the building of a Christian democratic society.

For the Church, in proclaiming its answer to this question, there is but one response to give, clear, inescapable, and expressed in these words by a man of the Church: "When a culture begins to disintegrate, it is important to realize that some things are not worth saving. The status quo cannot be maintained. When the visitation came from Jerusalem, God did not say, 'Fight! Defend!' but 'Flee, and go not back for thy coat. Let it perish.'

"Our hope rises from below, from those whose wants are

too many, whose rights too few, those whom Edmund Burke contemptuously called 'the great unwashed.' "[2]

Effective intellectual and spiritual rehabilitation of a world distracted by the inward collapse of its own faith; creative construction of new and stronger social ideals which can stand above the mutable and the contingent; development of foundations to men's beliefs which are not chance persuasions or casually inherited habits of thought, but are made of a tough and durable intellectual fiber . . . movement in these directions is movement toward the building of a Christian democratic society.

They are movements, not fixed objectives. They are basic strategic axioms in the ceaseless battle against social injustice —they are not guarantees of quick or complete victory, for victory, in the realm of the spiritual is rarely quick and never complete. They are human labors to be undertaken while that endless, tense interplay of the ideal and the real continues through all human affairs. Taken together as a whole they constitute a broad vision of men fighting the endless war against social evil, men working toward the good society. Taken individually, they come to mean these things. . . .

I. Effective reassertion of spiritual values and ethical disciplines, defining not only man's character and destiny but also his rights and duties in life with his fellow men.

This means much more than the enunciation of pious ethical precepts and rules of conduct. It means the reinstitution of the moral and spiritual basis for the dignity of man. That basis will be the same as that to which Bellarmine pointed in saying: We are all equal and have value only as do pennies—in bearing the image of the King.

It was on this issue that the Liberal faith collapsed most disastrously. To speak of man's rights and worth as deriving from "nature" quickly came to appear, even to the Liberal, like nothing more substantial than rhetoric. Neither could there be found any enduring basis for belief in an innate human dignity in the vast scientific treasury of learning. Man, as conceived by the masters of science, was "little more than a chance deposit on the surface of the world, carelessly thrown up between two ice ages by the same forces that rust iron and ripen corn."[3] What dignity could inhere in such a product of capricious natural forces? To a man like Bertrand Russell it is apparent that there is none—and he exclaims that there is no philosophy which can endure which does not maintain "that man is the product of causes which had no prevision of the end they were achieving; that his origin, his growth, his hopes and fears, his loves and beliefs, are but the outcome of accidental allocations of atoms; that no fire, no heroism, no intensity of thought and feeling can preserve an individual life beyond the grave; that all the labors of all the ages, all the devotion, all the inspiration, all the noonday brightness of human genius are destined to extinction in the vast depth of the solar system, and that the whole temple of man's achievement must inevitably be buried beneath the debris of a universe in ruins. . . ."[4] To man conceived by the scientist in these terms, in a world conceived in these terms, could there attach any innate worth?

When the Liberal sought to found his faith in human dignity on what seemed the solid rock of utilitarianism, the result was more disastrous than ever. That it was so was not strange, as any Liberal who read Bentham with some perception could readily have understood. If the sanction of utility could support any doctrine firmly, it should have done so for the most elementary conception of freedom. But, hypnotized by the criterion of "pleasure" and "pain," Bentham could not denounce even slavery in unqualified terms: if, in fact, as many would derive "pleasure" from slavery as derived "pain," it would be an institution neutral in character—while if the masters outnumbered the slaves, it would be a social advantage. Thus Bentham reasoned: "If slavery were established in such proportions that there would be but one slave for each master, I might hesitate before pronouncing on the balance between the advantage of one and the disadvantage of the other. It might be that all considered the sum of happiness by that arrangement would almost equal the sum of pain."[5] As one critic remarked pungently and accurately, on the same principle one could defend and vindicate a majority cannibalism.[6] When the Liberal considered this doctrine to fortify his ungrounded faith in human dignity, it was manifest how frail the entire structure of his thought had become.*

The final, simple fact was this: that when the Liberal came to talk in rapturous phrases about "the dignity of man," he was showing reverent regard for a doctrine which had no rational foundation, no unshakable support, in his own faith. The doctrine of the dignity of man, in short, has no intelligible validity when not fortified by the substance of Christian philosophy: to deny the latter and invoke the former was, for the Liberal, to try to replant a branch of the tree he had torn up by its roots. The Enlightenment had essayed a similar task when it tried to make logically comprehensible the concept of natural law and natural rights, once severed from their historic religious basis. *No more than the conception of Natural Law can the belief in the dignity of man satisfy the rational requirements of common sense, once it is detached from its Christian foundation.*

There remains yet a second issue involved in the reaffirmation of moral disciplines: a clean, clear and courageous statement of the doctrine of social sin. The word "sin" has long been without popularity in the most highly regarded Liberal circles: it sounds pietistic and doctrinaire, absolute and authoritarian. Moreover, application of such a doctrine to the affairs

* Another example will clarify the discussion. Max Lerner, one of the more intelligent Liberal writers of twentieth century America, in the foreword to his first book, writes of something he calls "democracy": "I happen to care for it not because of any moral perfection it may have, but because it is by and large the best instrument I know for giving us the kind of world we want to live in." Having thus dismissed moral dimensions from his consideration of the good society, he proceeds, in his first chapter, to expand upon "the richness of human life . . . the dignity of the individual and the sanctity of human life." These are strange words—"dignity" and "sanctity"—to be used by one who scorns any discussion of "moral perfection." Yet these pious words are the vital core of his own faith—and they have no intelligible foundation in his own structure of thought. It is this type of thinking which, as the subtitle of his book states, is regarded as constituting "militant democracy"! (Cf. *It Is Later Than You Think*, p. ix and p. 22.)

of society would reinstate that ethical discipline, in market place and political forum, which the sixteenth century so successfully banished.

But however inimical to Liberal habits of thought, such a doctrine has a clear and necessary function—which is essentially twofold. First, it would establish a standard by which men could measure forces like Fascism, evaluate them by constant principles, and be unafraid to condemn the evil in them by calling it by its true name. Secondly, it would erect a like standard of social conduct by which men, viewing the mechanics of their own social organizations, could come to realize the intimate relevancy of moral principles to the affairs of economic and political life. Equipped with such a standard, men could come to understand clearly that manufacture of poisonous foods and drugs is murder; that fraudulent deception of the consuming community is theft; that failure to protect laborers against the hazards of their occupation is manslaughter; that self-interested stock manipulation and dishonest financial statements are larceny; that hiring and hurling children into factories, mills and mines is abduction and slavery; that political graft, corruption of officials, and perversions of popular referendums constitute, under a presumably popular government, acts of treason; that investiture of corporations with personality and individuality is deceit.

All this constitutes the necessity for the reassertion of spiritual values and ethical disciplines, at once rendering vital and intelligible the belief in the dignity of man, and condemning openly all that militates toward the corruption of that dignity.

II. Clear distinction of social ends and social means, defining the proper role of man-made institutions in a Christian society.

Here a new direction of thought would stipulate two developments. It would abandon the fantasy of Helvetius: men of genius, like men of morality, cannot be legislated into existence by Liberal senates. And—again reversing the characteristic position of the Enlightenment—it would abandon the doctrine of political quietism and affirm the role of civil government in terms not of a passive guardian of individual rights, but of an active agent for social well being.

In at once circumscribing and projecting the functions of the state, there is no contradiction of thought. For in the realm of ends, of cultural values and of things that pertain to man's spiritual life—in this sphere government's just function can be no more than the negative one of removing impediments, opening paths among which the individual must choose and pursue on his own initiative. There is no morality in compulsion, no moral act which is not volitional. For the state to attempt to do man's moral and spiritual work for him would be to contradict and to abrogate the objective by the method.

It is in the realm of means—the sphere of man-made political and economic institutions, the sphere of material advance—it is here that man's state must be an active agent. Here the state's task, more than that of any other social agent, is to harness the vast institutional equipment of society as the collective means to an end which man finds in a realm transcending the plane of political and economic forms.

In wider terms, this doctrine signifies the affirmation of man himself as the supreme end of social action, and the corollary recognition that all his institutions are only mutable, contingent instruments for that social action. In the economic sphere, it must follow that institutions like private property and irresponsible corporate enterprise will cease to be regarded as social forms which are their own justification: they may be social goods, but they are not so in and of themselves—they have to prove their value in terms of serviceability to men. Not only characteristic institutional forms, but also the whole sphere of economics will be reassessed and reintegrated into a wider frame of values. The world of business enterprise no longer can claim privileged exemption from obedience to moral ends. Like fire, it is invaluable as a servant, terrible when it becomes the master of men.

As in economics, so likewise in politics will the transformation become evident under a new definition of social means and ends. The confused identification of the faith of democracy and the political system of representative government is as essentially false an inversion of values as exaltation of an autonomous and supreme sphere of business enterprise. The democratic faith expresses a doctrine of man's nature, worth, and destiny—and it is not equatable with any given political methods. Because it realizes the threat implied in uncontrolled and unresponsive government, it deems it *expedient*, on the basis of past historical experience, to adhere to some pattern of representation; and on the basis of future experience, men may change that pattern, choosing among geographical, numerical, industrial, vocational, and similar forms. Such fluctuation would not be aberration from the authentic tradition of democracy—it would be the *fulfillment* of that teaching . . . that teaching which denies investiture of any man-made social institutions—political or economic—with the quality of immutability or immortality . . . demanding that men, largely through the agency of the state, govern and nourish the institutional growth of their society in the light of their own needs and final ends, not in regard to terms laid down by those institutions explaining and exalting their own existence.

III. Reaffirmation of man's moral freedom, together with recognition of his ineradicably political and social nature.

The movement toward a Christian democratic society can heed no creeds whose gospel is fatalism or which posit any immutable determination of man's destiny by historical forces beyond his control. Such creeds may assume the form of a scientific determinism which binds man's God to unchanging natural laws, a Marxist determinism which promises inevitable triumph to a class elite, a Fascist determinism which proclaims certain victory for a national elite, or a Liberal determinism pronouncing the inevitability of poverty and misery as the unchanging lot of the laboring masses. All such doctrines must be pronounced false; only that can be accepted which recognizes man as a free moral agent capable of either edifying or wasting a future which is his own to build.

Along with this will be recognition of the fact that morally free man yet can satisfy his needs—moral, mental and material—only in that life in which he works with fellow men in civil society. Only in such cooperative existence, living the *communis vita*, can man's nature realize itself and his potentialities become articulate. Such a social existence can spring not from communal performance of tasks imposed by an authoritarian state, but basically from common consciousness and appreciation of the moral purpose with which society is endowed. That consciousness established, society's institutional texture will assume a variegated pattern of religious, cultural, educational, and vocational associations. The immediate task will be to multiply these associations mediary between the individual and the state, associations whose model will be the family, associations saving men from the social extremes of either atomism or totalitarianism.

With an assertion of man's moral freedom and the working toward a social organization approximating the ideal of a *communitas communitatum* in which that freedom can find its fruitful exercise and expression—with this, men can once again talk with John of Salisbury of "the assured certainty of life."

IV. Recognition that man is a religious animal.

In the Liberal's world of relatives, men have insistently demanded absolutes. When the Liberal tried to strip society of all paraphernalia of religion, men endowed the instrumental mechanics of social life with the properties of final truths of a religion. Liberalism, Marxism, Fascism: all three, while seeking to destroy previous faiths, have been compelled to construct new faiths from the substance of their doctrines. In the case of Marxist and Fascist deification of class and nation respectively, the issue is self-evident. With Liberalism, even after the Enlightenment's worship of Nature became an intellectual pastime of the past, men still continued to think in terms of final, all-justifying ends. In the process which the psychologist has called "reification," men endowed the institutional equipment of their society with the properties of innate virtue and immortality. The political machinery of representative government, the corporation whose legal life was not earth-bound but could thrive long after its founders had died, the system of private property—all such things, in varying degrees to men of varying character and temperament, came to be consecrated as ends in themselves. When the object of regard was the nation, almost all the rituals, observances and overtones of thought were present which were associated with a religion. And it was in vain that the pragmatist called upon men to use their institutions, not to venerate them.

The fact was that the Liberal and the pragmatist could not destroy in man's nature the psychological and spiritual imperative which demanded some object to accept as an absolute, all-vindicating end and reason. The impulse of faith had been disassociated from traditional religion—but it continued to demand articulation. To find that articulation men inevitably came to consecrate the instrumentalities of social organization as ends in themselves. And the pragmatist's dream of a world-without-ends proved a shallow failure.

This was probably the most profound lesson of the whole Liberal adventure: the undefeatable and undying need within men for a faith. When the validity of the whole religious realm was challenged by the Liberal, he removed the logical province in which the impulse of faith might express itself. The experience that followed revealed this truth: *Only when the impulse of faith is permitted its logical spiritual expression can it be assured that men will conceive their political and economic institutions as means and not ends. Hence only that social organization can be truly pragmatic which is circumscribed by a religious definition of its meaning and purpose.*

From the standpoint of the Church, there is sound historic precedent for this affirmation of a pragmatic view of social institutions within the framework of its social philosophy. In the thirteenth century, at a similar time of intellectual crisis in the history of the West, a much more sweeping amalgamation was made by Thomas Aquinas in his theological reconciliation of reason and faith. To thinkers before him—men like Augustine and Tertullian—reason and faith had seemed inexorably inimical to one another. But in the system of Aquinas reason was conceived to fortify faith and faith to fulfill reason, just as the natural order was the manifestation of divine power and not the refutation of the divine.

In a similar all-embracing coherence, pragmatism and traditional Catholic social philosophy can be seen to fuse. Like reason and faith, they can be viewed as complementary parts of a single whole, each supporting and fulfilling the other, each stimulating those conditions in which the other can be most effective and articulate. It is not an integration made by the forced grafting of elements foreign to each other, but an integration brought to life by the fulfillment of each through the other. The essentially pragmatic view of social institutions is implicit in the Church's social doctrine, although it has not always been clearly enunciated. It springs logically from the Church's insistence that man comes before all social institutions, not excluding even the supreme institution of the state: that all such institutions are but tools by which men must work out their destiny: that all things of this world are but contingent, flexible, mortal instruments in the attainment of an end that is spiritual. In terms of politics, Leo XIII expounded such a pragmatism years ago with the statement: "The right to rule is not necessarily . . . bound up with any special mode of government. It may take this or that form, provided only that it be of a nature to insure the general welfare." In the simple words of Saint Paul: "Examine all things and keep only what is good."[7]

Through a synthesis conceived and carried out along these broad lines, the Church can succeed in the twentieth century where it failed in the sixteenth and in the eighteenth.

In this fashion, a clearer, more perceptive vision of the democratic faith can take form.

The immediate necessity is that democracy cease to be accepted as a sentimental mood, an inherited persuasion, for which men can advance no rational foundation. Caught in the net of his own axioms, the Liberal has become chronically incapable of either defending or explaining the democratic tradition. He refers his argument to "the dignity of man": but to define that dignity he must employ a language he does not understand. He categorically states that democracy is the absolutely true and just social faith; but he has long since himself condemned the reality or the validity of any absolute, and no amount of empirical study can yield scientifically verified proof for his pronouncement. He eloquently condemns the Fascist threat to the democratic faith; but he finds the essence of that threat to be the very denial of moral absolutes which he himself has propelled. By a process of attrition, the base to the democratic faith has been worn away to a point that leaves the whole like an inverted pyramid.

The faith of democracy can be made lastingly strong alone by the faith of the Church—can be firmly fortified alone by the social principles of that faith. Those principles alone, in their affirmation of the reality of absolute truth, can extricate democracy from the quicksand of philosophic relativism—and therewith give to democracy the categorical, immutable value which attaches to it as the only social philosophy logically springing from the heart of Christianity. They alone can restore substance to the phrase, the dignity of man—that dignity intelligently definable only in terms of the Christian conception of man's creation, nature and destiny. They alone can salvage men's belief in democracy from the crumbling edifice of the Liberal Society. They alone can banish the false, enervating illusion of social utopia, affirm the eternity and endless fury of the human fight for freedom and justice, and prevent democracy from ever becoming a static faith whose disciples believe its promise to be fulfilled and hence exhausted. They alone can make and keep democracy a militant faith, by projecting its aims on the scale of the *infinite*—the infinite worth of the human personality, the infinite latent potentialities of all men which, never to be fully realized on earth, democracy must seek ever to make more real and articulate.

The faith of democracy, so conceived and so dedicated, can long endure.

NOTES

Part I · The Genesis of the Liberal Society

CHAPTER II

1. R. H. Tawney, *Religion and the Rise of Capitalism* (Harmondsworth: Penguin Books, 1938), p. 29.
2. John of Salisbury, *Policraticus*, Book V, Ch. II. All the quotations from John of Salisbury are taken from *The Statesman's Book of John of Salisbury*, tr. by John Dickinson (New York: Alfred Knopf, 1927).
3. E. Gilson. *The Unity of Philosophical Experience* (New York, 1937), p. 50.
4. St. Thomas Aquinas, *Summa Theologica*, tr. by Fathers of the English Dominican Province (London, 1915), Part II, First Part, Third Number, Question XCIV, Article ii.
5. John of Salisbury, *op. cit.*, Book V, Ch. II.
6. *ibid*, Book VII, Ch. XVII.
7. *ibid*, Book VII, Ch. XXV.
8. *ibid*, Book VI, Ch. XXV.
9. Cf. J. Maritain, *An Introduction to Philosophy* (London, 1930), p. 131.
10. This and immediately preceding quotations are cited by F. S. Nitti, *Catholic Socialism* (New York, 1895), pp. 64-69.
11. St. James, v., 1-5.
12. Cited by B. Jarrett, *Social Theories of the Middle Ages* (London, 1926), p. 154.
13. Cited *ibid*, p. 156.
14. Aquinas, *op. cit.*, Part II, Second Part, Second Number, Question LXXVII: "Of Cheating, Which Is Committed in Buying and Selling."
15. *Patrologiae Latinae Tomus* CLXXXVII (1861), *Decretum Gratiani, Pars Prima, Distinctio* LXXXVIII, c. xi.
16. Cf. Tawney, *op. cit.*, p. 49.
17. Gratian, *op. cit.*
18. E. Salin, article on Usury: *Encyclopedia of Social Sciences*, Vol. XV, pp. 193-197.
19. Aquinas, *op. cit.*, Part II, Second Part, Second Number, Question LXVI: "Theft and Robbery."
20. Jarrett, *op. cit.*, p. 148.
21. Cited by Nitti, *op. cit.*, p. 66.
22. Tawney, *op. cit.*, pp. 69-71.

CHAPTER III

1. Cited by H. Pirenne, *Medieval Cities* (Princeton, 1939), p. 86.
2. H. Pirenne, *Economic and Social History of Medieval Europe* (New York, 1937), p. 52.
3. H. Pirenne, *Medieval Cities*, p. 212.
4. *ibid*, p. 103.
5. E. P. Cheyney, *The Dawn of a New Era* (New York, 1936), p. 2.
6. Francis Bacon, *The Advancement of Learning*, Book I (p. 29 in 1898 edition, notes by F. G. Selby).
7. H. Pirenne, *Economic and Social History of Medieval Europe*, p. 51.
8. H. Pirenne, *Medieval Cities*, p. 213.

9. *ibid*, p. 214.
10. Robert Crowley, *Select Works*, p. 11: "Of Allayes."
11. Thomas à Kempis, *The Following of Christ*, Ch. III, Book First.
12. Cited by J. H. Robinson, and H. W. Rolfe, *Petrarch, the First Modern Scholar and Man of Letters* (New York and London, 1898), p. 40.
13. Thomas à Kempis, *op. cit.*, Book First, Ch. I.
14. Cited by E. Gilson, *The Unity of Philosophical Experience* (New York, 1937), p. 6.
15. Letter to Lapo of Castiglionchio, in F. Schevill, *The First Century of Italian Humanism* (New York, 1928).
16. George Santayana, *Poems*: "On a Volume of Scholastic Philosophy" (Charles Scribner's Sons, 1928).

CHAPTER IV

1. Erasmus, *Adagia*: cited by R. H. Tawney, *Religion and the Rise of Capitalism* (Harmondsworth: Penguin Books, 1938), p. 82.
2. H. J. C. Grimmelshausen, *Simplicissimus the Vagabond* (New York, 1934), p. 39.
3. Machiavelli, *The Prince*, Chapter XV.
4. *ibid*, Chapter XVIII.
5. *ibid*, Chapter XVIII.
6. *ibid*, Chapter VI.
7. Cited by R. Roeder, *The Man of the Renaissance* (New York, 1935), p. 288.
8. Machiavelli, *op. cit.*, Chapter XXVI.
9. Cited by P. Smith, *The Age of the Reformation* (New York, 1920), pp. 594-595.
10. Martin Luther, *Works*, "An Open Letter to the Christian Nobility of the German Nation Concerning the Reform of the Christian Estate" (Philadelphia, 1931), Vol. II, pp. 66 and 70.
11. *ibid*, Vol. I, p. 263: "A Treatise on Good Works."
12. *ibid*, Vol. IV: "On Trading and Usury."
13. J. H. Robinson, *Readings in European History* (New York, 1908-09), Vol. II, pp. 71-73.
14. The phrase is Tawney's, *op. cit.*, p. 103.
15. Cited by E. P. Cheyney, *The Dawn of a New Era* (New York, 1936), p. 185, footnote.
16. Cited by R. Ergang, *Europe from the Renaissance to Waterloo* (Boston, 1939), p. 228.
17. H. J. Laski, *The Rise of Liberalism* (New York: Harpers, 1936), pp. 50-51.
18. Bossuet, *Histoire des Variations des Eglises Protestantes*, Livre V: in *Oeuvres* (Paris, 1852), Vol. IV, p. 67.
19. J. Strachey, *The Coming Struggle for Power* (New York, 1935), p. 29.
20. Luther, *op. cit.*, Vol. II, pp. 314-317.
21. *ibid*, Vol. IV, p. 54: "Treatise on Usury." The translation of Luther's words here used, however, is from Tawney, *op. cit.*, p. 101.
22. Tawney, *op. cit.*, p. 87.
23. Luther, *op. cit.*, Vol. II, pp. 134-135: "Open Letter to Christian Nobility of German Nation."
24. *ibid*, Vol. IV, pp. 249-250: "Against the Robbing and Murdering Hordes of Peasants."
25. *ibid*, pp. 252-253.

26. Tawney, *op. cit.*, pp. 138-139, to which passage the remarks immediately following are indebted.
27. F. A. Gasquet, *Henry VIII and the English Monasteries* (London: Bell, 1906), pp. 476-477.
28. *Star Chamber Proceedings*, Henry VIII, Vol. VI, No. 181: in R. H. Tawney and E. Power, *Tudor Economic Documents* (London, 1924), Vol. I, p. 21.
29. G. O'Brien, *An Essay on the Economic Effects of the Reformation*, p. 50.
30. Luther, *op. cit.*, Vol. IV, p. 49.
31. John Calvin, *De Usuris*. Cited by Troeltsch, *The Social Teaching of the Christian Churches* (London, 1931), Vol. II, p. 642, footnote.
32. R. H. Tawney, Foreword to *The Protestant Ethic* [M. Weber] (London: Allen and Unwin, 1930), p. 3.
33. Cf. Tawney, *Religion and the Rise of Capitalism* (Harmondsworth: Penguin Books, 1938), p. 111.
34. *ibid*, p. 135.
35. Laski, *op. cit.*, p. 83.
36. Cf. *ibid*, p. 58.
37. *ibid*, p. 59.
38. *ibid*, p. 63.
39. Bacon, *The Advancement of Learning*, Book I.
40. Montaigne, *Essays*. Cited by Laski, *op. cit.*, pp. 66-67.
41. Cited by P. Smith, *History of Modern Culture* (New York, 1930-34), Vol. I, p. 424.
42. Cf. Laski, *op. cit.*, pp. 88-89.

Part II · The Making of the Liberal Society

CHAPTER V

1. Letter to Boccaccio, in F. Schevill, *The First Century of Italian Humanism* (New York, 1928).
2. Cited by J. H. Randall, Jr., *The Making of the Modern Mind* (New York: Houghton Mifflin, 1926), p. 220.
3. Cited *ibid*, p. 221.
4. Francis Bacon, *The Advancement of Learning*, Book I.
5. A. N. Whitehead, *Science and the Modern World* (New York, 1939), p. 83.
6. Newton, *Principia*, Book III.
7. Leonardo, *Notebooks* (ed. by E. McCurdy), p. 55.
8. Cited by Randall, *op. cit.*, p. 240.
9. Descartes, *Discourse on Method*, Part II.
10. Construction of Descartes' thought as "mathematicism" is made by E. Gilson, *The Unity of Philosophical Experience* (New York, 1937), Chapter V.
11. Descartes, *op. cit.*, Part VI.
12. *ibid*, Part IV.
13. Augustine, *Soliloquies*, Book II, Chapter I: cf. Gilson, *op. cit.*, pp. 155-157.
14. Descartes, *op. cit.*, Part I.
15. *ibid*, Part I.
16. Cited by E. A. Singer, *Modern Thinkers and Present Problems* (New York, 1923), p. 13.
17. Diderot, *Oeuvres* (Paris, 1875), Vol. I: *Pensées Philosophiques*, VI, p. 129.
18. Descartes, *op. cit.*, Part VI.

19. Diderot, *op. cit.*, Vol. II: *Pensées sur L'Interprétation de la Nature*, IV, p. 11.
20. Pope, *Essay on Man.*
21. Holbach, *Système de la Nature* (Paris, 1821), Chapter XIV (pp. 409-410 in new edition of 1821), Vol. II.
22. *ibid*, pp. 420-421.
23. Marlowe, *Tamburlaine.*
24. Bossuet, *Histoire des Variations des Églises Protestantes*, Livre V: in *Oeuvres*, Vol. IV, p. 75.
25. Cited by R. R. Palmer, *Catholics and Unbelievers in Eighteenth Century France* (Princeton, 1939), p. 81.
26. Cited *ibid*, p. 139.
27. Cited by R. R. Ergang, *Herder and the Foundations of German Nationalism* (New York, 1931), p. 217.
28. Cited by K. Martin, *French Liberal Thought in the Eighteenth Century* (Boston, 1929), p. 96.
29. Pascal, *Pensées*, tr. by W. F. Trotter, p. 23, note.
30. Pope, *op. cit.*
31. Montesquieu, *Persian Letters* (London, 1923), Letter XLVI.
32. Cited by Martin, *op. cit.*, p. 129.
33. Cited by P. Smith, *History of Modern Culture* (New York, 1930-34), Vol. II, p. 501.
34. Cited by Martin, *op. cit.*, p. 131.
35. Montesquieu, *op. cit.*, Letter XXIX.
36. *ibid*, Letter XXIX.
37. *ibid*, Letter XXXVI.
38. Cited by Martin, *op. cit.*, p. 145.
39. Holbach, *op. cit.*, Vol. II, Chapter IV: cf. pp. 144-159.
40. Abbe Nonnotte, *Dictionnaire Philosophique de la Religion* (Paris, new edition of 1774), Vol. II, p. 366.
41. Cf. Palmer, *op. cit.*, p. 98, and N.-S. Bergier, *Le Déisme réfuté par lui-même*, Vol. I, pp. 127-135.
42. Diderot, *op. cit.*, Vol. I: *Pensées Philosophiques*, I & III, pp. 127-128.
43. Helvetius, cited by Palmer, *op. cit.*, p. 187.
44. Cited by K. S. Pinson, *Pietism as a Factor in the Rise of German Nationalism* (New York, 1934), p. 45.
45. The following discussion paraphrases C. L. Becker, *The Heavenly City of the Eighteenth Century Philosophers* (New Haven, 1935), pp. 30-31.
46. Diderot, *Oeuvres*, Vol. XIX, pp. 463-465.
47. Cited by Smith, *op. cit.*, Vol. I, p. 419.
48. Diderot, *op. cit.*, Vol. I: *La Promenade du Sceptique*, p. 183.
49. Holbach, *op. cit.*, Chapter VII, pp. 257-260.

CHAPTER VI

1. Richard Steele, *The Tradesman's Calling*, pp. 1, 4; cited by R. H. Tawney, Religion and the Rise of Capitalism (Harmondsworth: Penguin Books, 1938), p. 216.
2. Cited by M. Weber, *The Protestant Ethic and the Spirit of Capitalism*, Chapter IV, note 25.
3. Tawney, *op. cit.*, pp. 221-222.
4. R. Crowley, *Select Works (The Voyce of the Last Trumpet).*
5. Arthur Young, *An Inquiry into the State of the Public Mind among the Lower Classes* (London, 1798), p. 6.

6. Arthur Young, *The Farmer's Tour Through the East of England*, p. 361.
7. Young, *The State of the Public Mind* (London, 1771), p. 25.
8. In J. O. W. Haweis, *Sketches of the Reformation and Elizabethan England taken from the Contemporary Pulpit*, p. 277.
9. The quotation is from an essay on Bolingbroke of that title by Carlton J. H. Hayes, included in *Essays in Intellectual History*.
10. H. St. John Bolingbroke, *Works*, Vol. II, p. 379.
11. Cited by Hayes, *op. cit.*, p. 200.
12. *ibid*, pp. 196-197.
13. Cited by D. Ogg, *Europe in the Seventeenth Century* (New York, 1938), p. 298.
14. K. S. Pinson, *Pietism as a Factor in the Rise of German Nationalism*, p. 26.
15. Cited *ibid*, p. 185.
16. Milton, *Areopagitica* (New York, 1927), pp. 35-36.
17. Cf. H. J. Laski, *The Rise of Liberalism* (New York: Harpers, 1936), pp. 61 and 142-145.
18. *Letter to the Archbishop of Lyons*, cited *ibid*, p. 190.
19. Hobbes, *Leviathan* (Oxford, 1881), Part I, Chapter II.
20. Locke, *Essay Concerning Human Understanding*, Book II, Chapter I.
21. Helvetius, *A Treatise on Man (De L'Homme)*, Vol. II, Sec. X, Ch. I.
22. Helvetius, *Essays on the Mind (De L'Esprit)*, Essay III, Ch. XXII.
23. Locke, *Essay Concerning Civil Government*, Ch. IX. Cf. also Ch. V.
24. Laski, *op. cit.*, p. 127.
25. Cited *ibid*, p. 129.
26. Voltaire, *Philosophical Dictionary*, art. on Government, Sec. VI.
27. Cited by K. Martin, *French Liberal Thought in the Eighteenth Century* (Boston, 1929), p. 140; and H. N. Brailsford, *Voltaire* (New York, 1935), p. 126.
28. Cited by Martin, *op. cit.*, p. 140.
29. *Dictionnaire Encyclopédique*, Vol. VIII, art. on *Représentants*.
30. *ibid*.
31. Diderot, *Oeuvres*, Vol. III, *Essai sur les Règnes de Claude et de Néron*, Book II, Sec. XXXVI.
32. E. Burke, *Thoughts and Details on Scarcity*, p. 2.
33. *ibid*, pp. 6 and 13.
34. *ibid*, p. 18.
35. *ibid*, pp. 3 and 35.
36. *ibid*, p. 32.
37. Cited by Laski, *op. cit.*, p. 219.
38. Adam Smith, *The Theory of Moral Sentiments*, Part II, Sec. III, Ch. III.
39. *ibid*, Part VI, Sec. II, Ch. I.
40. Smith, *Wealth of Nations*, Vol. I, p. 421.
41. *ibid*, Vol. I, p. ii: cited by Laski, *op. cit.*, p. 225.
42. Laski, *op. cit.*, p. 207.
43. Quesnay, *Dialogues sur les travaux des artisans*, p. 192: cited *ibid*, p. 209.
44. Du Pont de Nemours, *Origines et Progrès d'une Science nouvelle*: cited by J. H. Randall, Jr., *Making of the Modern Mind*, p. 324.
45. Martin, *op. cit.*, p. 230.
46. Cited *ibid*, p. 234.
47. Hume, *Essays*, II, p. 94.
48. Rousseau, cited by Martin, *op. cit.*, p. 198.
49. C. L. Becker, *The Heavenly City of the Eighteenth Century Philosophers*, p. 130.
50. Diderot, *Oeuvres*, Vol. XVIII (*Lettres à Falconet*), pp. 100-101.

51. Cited by Brailsford, *op. cit.*, p. 108.
52. Gibbon, *Decline and Fall of the Roman Empire*, Vol. I, p. 430.
53. Cited by Randall, *op. cit.*, p. 383.

CHAPTER VII

1. F. C. Palm, *The Middle Classes: Then and Now* (New York, 1936), p. 74.
2. Cited *ibid*, p. 78.
3. Cf. K. Martin, *French Liberal Thought in the Eighteenth Century* (Boston, 1929), pp. 259-260.
4. Cf. H. J. Laski, *The Rise of Liberalism* (New York, 1936), p. 116.
5. Lewis Roberts, *The Treasure of Traffic* (1641), cited by Laski, *op. cit.*, p. 117.
6. Cf. Laski, *op. cit.*, pp. 122-123.
7. Cited by E. Bernstein, *Cromwell and Communism* (London, 1930), p. 105.
8. Cited *ibid*, p. 164.
9. Macaulay, *The Battle of Naseby*.
10. Cf. S. E. Morison and H. S. Commager, *The Growth of the American Republic* (New York, 1937), Vol. I, p. 41.
11. Cited *ibid*, p. 60.
12. Cf. C. A. and M. R. Beard, *The Rise of American Civilization* (New York: Macmillan, 1937), Vol. I, p. 302.
13. For elaboration of this, cf. L. Hacker, *The Triumph of American Capitalism* (New York, 1940), pp. 182-195.
14. This and all succeeding quotations from the Convention are from S. E. Morison, *Sources and Documents: 1764-1788* (Oxford, 1923).
15. Morison and Commager, *op. cit.*, Vol. I, p. 163.
16. Cf. Morison, *op. cit.*, pp. 321-322.
17. Thomas Paine, *Common Sense*.
18. Cf. Martin, *op. cit.*, p. 86.
19. Cited by Laski, *op. cit.*, p. 255.
20. Abbe Sieyès, *Qu'est-ce que le Tiers État?* (Paris, 1789), pp. 9-14.
21. Cited by Martin, *op. cit.*, p. 256.
22. Cited *ibid*, pp. 256-257. (From Postgate, *Revolution 1789-1906*, pp. 41-44.)
23. Cited by Laski, *op. cit.*, p. 262.
24. Locre, *La Législation Civile de la France*, Vol. XVI, p. 499 (for statement of Lahary), cited by Laski, *op. cit.*, p. 259. Glasson, *Le Code Civil et la question ouvrière*, p. 68: cited by Laski, *op. cit.*, p. 261.
25. R. M. Johnston, *The French Revolution* (New York, 1909), pp. 101-102.
26. Cited by A. Aulard, *Christianity and the French Revolution* (Boston, 1927), p. 102.
27. Cited *ibid*, p. 103.
28. Cited *ibid*, p. 104.
29. Cited *ibid*, p. 125.
30. Cf. *ibid*, pp. 106-107.

CHAPTER VIII

1. Cf. J. P. Mayer (ed.), *Political Thought: The European Tradition* (New York, 1939), p. 460.
2. P. B. de Villemert, *Pensées philosophiques sur la nature, l'homme et la religion*, Vol. I, p. 112: cited by R. R. Palmer, *Catholics and Unbelievers in Eighteenth Century France*, p. 196.

3. Cited by Palmer, *op. cit.*, p. 200.
4. Cited by K. Martin, *French Liberal Thought in the Eighteenth Century* (Boston, 1929), p. 54.
5. John Dryden, *Religio Laici*, lines 93-98.
6. *ibid, The Hind and the Panther*, lines 62-71.
7. Goldsmith, *The Deserted Village*.
8. *ibid.*
9. Cf. Aquinas, *Summa Theologica*, Part II, First Part, Question XCI, Article II.
10. N. S. Bergier, *Quelle est la source de toute autorité?*, p. 44: cited by Palmer, *op. cit.*, pp. 198-199.
11. Descartes, *Discourse on Method*, Part III.
12. Cited by H. N. Brailsford, *Voltaire* (New York, 1935), p. 218.
13. Cited by C. L. Becker, *The Heavenly City of the Eighteenth Century Philosophers* (New Haven, 1935), p. 119.

Part III · Liberal Society and Church Militant

CHAPTER IX

1. Rousseau, *Social Contract*, Book I, Chapter VI.
2. *ibid*, Book I, Ch. VIII.
3. *ibid*, Book I, Ch. IX.
4. *ibid*, Book II, Ch. IV.
5. *ibid*, Book I, Ch. VI.
6. *ibid*, Book I, Ch. VII.
7. Cited by B. Russell, *Freedom versus Organization 1814-1914* (New York, 1934), p. 89.
8. Cited by V. Pareto, *The Mind and Society* (New York, 1935), Vol. III, p. 939.
9. Bentham, *Deontology* (London, 1834), Vol. I, p. 59.
10. Bentham, *Manual of Political Economy*, Ch. I.
11. Bentham, *Deontology*, Vol. I, pp. 10-11.
12. *ibid*, Vol. I, p. 161.
13. *ibid*, Vol. I, pp. 11-12.
14. Edition of 1834, London: Longman, Rees, Orme, Brown, Green & Longman.
15. Malthus, *Principles of Population*, Chs. I, V, VII.
16. Ricardo, *Principles of Political Economy*, Ch. V, Sec. XXXVII.
17. E. A. Hooton, *Up from the Ape* (New York, 1931), p. 67.
18. Ricardo, *op. cit.*, Ch. V.
19. Spencer, *Social Statics*, Ch. XXV.

CHAPTER X

1. Tennyson, Locksley Hall.
2. L. Mumford, *Technics and Civilization* (New York: Harcourt Brace, 1934), p. 51.
3. Cf. *ibid*, pp. 81-96 for extended and brilliant elaboration on this discussion.
4. For statistics on the course of population in this period, cf. J. L. and B. Hammond, *The Rise of Modern Industry* (New York, 1937), pp. 222-223.

5. This and the immediately following citations from the committees will be found in J. F. Scott and A. Baltzley, *Readings in European History Since 1814* (New York, 1934), pp. 78-94.

6. For detailed discussion of what follows, cf. L. Mumford, *The Culture of Cities* (New York: Harcourt Brace, 1938), Ch. III.

7. Cf. *ibid*, pp. 171-173.

8. Hammond, *op. cit.*, p. 232.

9. Cited by Mumford, *The Culture of Cities*, p. 168.

10. Cited by D. C. Somervell, *English Thought in the Nineteenth Century* (London, 1929), p. 80.

11. W. Bagehot, *The English Constitution* (New York, 1920), Introduction, p. xviii.

12. T. B. Macaulay, *Speeches, Parliamentary and Miscellaneous*, Vol. I, p. 39.

13. *ibid*, p. 73.

14. *ibid*, p. 392.

15. *ibid*, p. 12.

16. *ibid*, p. 391.

17. *ibid*, p. 13.

18. *ibid*, p. 72.

19. *ibid*, pp. 21 and 26.

20. *ibid*, Vol. II, p. 207.

CHAPTER XI

1. Cited by S. E. Morison and H. S. Commager, *The Growth of the American Republic* (New York, 1937), Vol. II, p. 1.

2. Cited *ibid*, p. 16.

3. C. A. and M. Beard, *The Rise of American Civilization* (New York: Macmillan, 1937), Vol. II, p. 99.

4. For revealing statistics on the comparative wealth of New and Old World dynasties, cf. F. Lundberg, *America's Sixty Families*, pp. 6-7.

5. L. Mumford, *The Golden Day* (New York: W. W. Norton, 1926), pp. 158-159.

6. Cited by Morison and Commager, *op. cit.*, Vol. II, p. 16.

7. Cited *ibid*, p. 33.

8. Cited by Beards, *op. cit.*, Vol. II, p. 110.

9. Cited *ibid*, p. 175, Vol. II.

10. *ibid*, Vol. II, p. 177.

11. Cf. M. Josephson, *The Politicos* (New York, 1938), p. 602.

12. Beard, *op. cit.*, Vol. II, p. 198.

13. Cf. *ibid*, p. 192.

14. Sherwood Anderson, *Poor White* (New York: B. W. Huebsch, 1920), pp. 129-133.

15. Cited by V. L. Parrington, *Main Currents in American Thought* (New York, 1930), Vol. III, pp. 58-59.

16. *Theodore Roosevelt, An Autobiography* (New York, 1929), p. 163.

17. For the cases indicated, cf. J. R. Commons and J. B. Andrews, *Principles of Labor Legislation* (New York, 1936), pp. 9, 14, 113, 140, 149, 238, and 284. Cf. also W. Anderson, *American Government* (New York, 1938), pp. 978, 1010, and 1015.

18. Cited by Morison and Commager, *op. cit.*, Vol. II, p. 171.

19. For instances, cf. Commons and Andrews, *op. cit.*, pp. 80, 139, 145, 168-186, 388 and 405.

20. Cf. Lincoln Steffens, *Autobiography* (New York, 1931), p. 565.

21. *ibid*, p. 372.
22. *ibid*, p. 417.
23. Cf. Josephson, *op. cit.*, pp. 488 and 637.
24. Cited *ibid*, p. 419.
25. Cited *ibid*, p. 517.
26. Cf. *ibid*, p. 426.
27. Frederick T. Martin, cited by Morison and Commager, *op. cit.*, Vol. II, p. 218.
28. Cited by Josephson, *op. cit.*, p. 641.
29. Roosevelt, *op. cit.*, pp. 279-283.
30. Cited by Josephson, *op. cit.*, p. 526.
31. Anderson, *op. cit.*, p. 114.
32. Cited by Beards, *op. cit.*, Vol. II, p. 385.
33. For much of this discussion the author is indebted to the Beards' extraordinary chapter on *The Gilded Age*: *op. cit.*, Vol. II, Ch. XXV.
34. For the classic elaboration of this theme, cf. Thorstein Veblen, *The Theory of the Leisure Class* (New York, 1935), especially Chs. III, IV, VI and XIV.
35. Letter to Roosevelt, cited by Roosevelt, *op. cit.*, p. 300.
36. This and the following quotations on the gospel of wealth, unless otherwise noted, are from R. H. Gabriel, *The Course of American Democratic Thought* (New York: Ronald Press, 1940), pp. 157 and 147.
37. Cited *ibid*, p. 147.
38. Cited *ibid*, p. 149.
39. Cited by Morison and Commager, *op. cit.*, Vol. II, p. 152.
40. Cited *ibid*, p. 164.
41. William James, *Pragmatism* (New York, 1907), p. 51.
42. Cf. Mumford, *op. cit.*, Chapter IV, and for the quotation from Moncure Conway, cf. p. 163.
43. *ibid*, p. 188.
44. James, *op. cit.*, p. 123.
45. Whitman, *Democratic Vistas*.

CHAPTER XII

1. Thomas More, *Utopia*: cited by W. B. Guthrie, *Socialism Before the French Revolution* (New York, 1907), p. 95.
2. Cf. R. Fulop-Miller, *Leo XIII and Our Times* (New York, 1939), pp. 29-30.
3. Cited by J. Morley, *Life of William Ewart Gladstone* (New York, 1903), Vol. II, p. 520.
4. The phrase is used in reference to the Syllabus by E. L. Woodward, in *Three Studies in European Conservatism* (New York, 1930).
5. Cited by Fulop-Miller, *op. cit.*, p. 81.
6. Cited by Morley, *op. cit.*, Vol. II, p. 508.
7. Cf. the witnessed account, here followed, in P. Leto, *Eight Months at Rome During the Vatican Council* (London, 1876), pp. 1-6.
8. Cited by Fulop-Miller, *op. cit.*, p. 22.
9. Cited by Morley, *op. cit.*, Vol. II, p. 512.
10. Cited *ibid*, Vol. II, pp. 514 and 516.
11. Cited by Fulop-Miller, *op. cit.*, pp. 7-8.
12. Cited *ibid*, pp. 14, 24 and 34.
13. *Immortale Dei*, Paragraph V.
14. *ibid*, Paragraph V.

15. *Rerum Novarum*, Paragraphs II, XIX, XXVI, XXVII, XXIX, XXX, XXXII, XXXVI, XXXVII.
16. In J. A. Ryan and J. Husslein, *The Church and Labor* (New York, 1924), p. 9.
17. Cited by J. C. Harrington, *Catholicism, Capitalism, or Communism* (St. Paul, 1926), pp. 30-31.
18. Cf. Ryan and Husslein, *op. cit.*, pp. 40-41.
19. Cited by F. S. Nitti, *Catholic Socialism* (New York, 1895), p. 346.
20. For detailed narrative of this cf. *ibid*, pp. 336-344.
21. Manning, *The Dignity and Rights of Labour* (London, 1934), pp. 38-39.
22. *ibid*, p. 68; and cited by Nitti, *op. cit.*, p. 377.
23. Manning, *op. cit.*, pp. 62 and 68.
24. Cited by Nitti, *op. cit.*, pp. 319 and 323.
25. *Quadragesimo Anno*, Paragraphs III, XXV, XLIX, LIII, LVII, LIX, LXII, LXXV, LXXXII, LXXXIII, LXXXVIII, CV, CVI, CVIII, CIX.

Part IV · The Crisis of the West

CHAPTER XIII

1. Cited by R. R. Ergang, *Herder and the Foundations of German Nationalism* (New York, 1931), p. 84.
2. Cited *ibid*, p. 85.
3. Cited *ibid*, p. 86.
4. Cited by K. S. Pinson, *Pietism as a Factor in the Rise of German Nationalism* (New York, 1934), p. 75.
5. Cited by Ergang, *op. cit.*, p. 117.
6. Cited *ibid*, p. 206.
7. Cited *ibid*, p. 154.
8. Cited *ibid*, p. 182.
9. Cited *ibid*, p. 246.
10. Cited *ibid*, p. 122.
11. Cited *ibid*, p. 252.
12. The following discussion is drawn almost in entirety from C. J. H. Hayes, *Essays on Nationalism* (New York, 1926), Essay IV.
13. H. Nicolson, *Peacemaking: 1919* (New York: Harcourt Brace, 1939), pp. 31-32.
14. John Maynard Keynes, cited *ibid*, pp. 41-42.
15. Cited *ibid*, p. 196.
16. Cited *ibid*, p. 201.
17. Cited *ibid*, p. 61.
18. From Nicolson's diary, *ibid*, p. 241.
19. *ibid*, p. 78.
20. Cf. point by point narration, *ibid*, pp. 43-44.
21. *ibid*, p. 188.

CHAPTER XIV

1. G. Niemeyer, *Law without Force: The Function of Politics in International Law* (Princeton, 1941), p. 69.
2. *ibid*, p. 71.
3. L. Mumford, *Technics and Civilization* (New York: Harcourt Brace, 1934), p. 54.

4. Cf., for example, F. H. Allport, *Institutional Behavior*, pp. 10-11.
5. A. Carrel, *Man the Unknown* (New York: Harpers, 1935), pp. 291 and 296-299.
6. Cf. R. M. MacIver, *Society* (New York, 1931), Chapters III, VI, and XIV-XVII.
7. F. J. C. Hearnshaw, cited by L. Woolf, *After the Deluge* (New York, 1931-40), pp. 137-138.
8. H. G. Wells, *The Outline of History*, p. 1170.
9. The phrase is Mumford's: cf. *Faith for Living*, p. 121.
10. P. F. Drucker, *The End of Economic Man* (New York: John Day, 1939), pp. 66-67.
11. Hitler, *Mein Kampf* (New York, 1939), p. 199.
12. R. Niebuhr, *Christianity and Power Politics* (New York: Charles Scribner's Sons, 1940), pp. 49-51.
13. Cited by W. Millis, *Why Europe Fights*, pp. 220-221.
14. *Die Deutsche Schule*, cited by H. F. Armstrong, *We or They* (New York, 1937), p. 10.
15. W. Stapel, H. Schwartz and E. Bergmann: cited by A. Kolnai, *The War Against the West* (New York, 1938), pp. 230 and 249; and Armstrong, *op. cit.*, p. 21.
16. E. Krieck and P. Orano, cited by Armstrong, *op. cit.*, pp. 11-12.
17. Hitler, *op. cit.*, p. 236.
18. P. Krannhals and H. Frank, cited by Kolnai, *op. cit.*, pp. 29 and 279.

CHAPTER XV

1. M. Nomad, *Apostles of Revolution* (Boston, 1939), p. 87.
2. Monsignor Fulton J. Sheen: address to New York Circle of the International Federation of Catholic Alumnae, *New York Herald Tribune*.
3. C. Becker, *The Heavenly City of the Eighteenth Century Philosophers* (New Haven, 1935), p. 14.
4. Cited *ibid*, pp. 13-14.
5. Cited by V. Pareto, *The Mind and Society* (New York, 1935), Vol. III, p. 942, note.
6. *ibid*.
7. Cf. above, p. 287.

SPECIAL ACKNOWLEDGMENTS

WHILE listing below most of the works that have been used in the writing of this book, I wish to acknowledge a special debt to the following men and studies:

R. H. Tawney (*Religion and the Rise of Capitalism*): for his analysis of the foundations of medieval social thought and his keen perception of the problem of the relationship of ethics and economics.

Harold J. Laski (*The Rise of Liberalism*): for the most astute analysis of the bourgeois rationale that I have read.

John H. Randall, Jr. (*Making of the Modern Mind*), and Samuel Morison and Henry Commager (*The Struggle for American Civilization*): for invaluable guides to the source materials of the times with which they dealt.

Charles and Mary Beard (*The Rise of American Civilization*): for their unsurpassed study of America's "gilded age."

Kingsley Martin (*French Liberal Thought in the Eighteenth Century*) and Carl Becker (*The Heavenly City of the Eighteenth Century Philosophers*): for two brilliant studies of the Enlightenment.

Lewis Mumford (*Technics and Civilization*, and *The Culture of Cities*): for his study of the development of the industrial age.

Peter Drucker (*The End of Economic Man*): for his penetrating, honest study of the roots and meaning of Fascism.

. .

THE following bibliography is not and could not be exhaustive. The publications included are those which are of particular relevance, either because of the author's debt to them or because of their being immediately germane, at least in some essential aspects.

Primary sources of signal value throughout are included in the first list. Following that the critical bibliography—almost entirely of secondary sources—is organized by chapters.

Aquinas, St. Thomas. *Summa Theologica*, tr. by Fathers of the English Dominican Province. R. and T. Washbourne: London, 1915.

Bentham, Jeremy. *Introduction to the Principles of Morals and Legislation.* London: Pickering, 1823.
    Deontology. London: Longman, 1834.

Bossuet, J. B. *Oeuvres.* Paris, 1852.

Burke, E. *Thoughts and Details on Scarcity.* London: Rivington, 1800.

Descartes, R. *Discourse on Method.*

Diderot, D. *Oeuvres Complètes.* Paris, 1875.

Encyclicals:
    The Pope and the People. London: Catholic Truth Society, 1929. (Texts of selected social encyclicals from Leo XIII to Pius XI).
    Quadragesimo Anno. Oxford: Catholic Social Guild, 1934.

Helvetius, C. A. *Treatise on Man*, tr. by W. Hooper. London: Albion, 1810.
    Essays on the Mind. London: Albion, 1810.

Hitler, A. *Mein Kampf.* New York: Reynal and Hitchcock, 1939.

Hobbes, T. *Leviathan.* Oxford, 1881.

Holbach, P. H. d'. *Système de la Nature*, Paris, 1921.

Hume, David. "Dialogues Concerning Natural Religion," in *The English Philosophers from Bacon to Mill*, ed. by E. A. Burtt. New York, Modern Library.

James, William. *Pragmatism.* New York: Longmans Green, 1925.

John of Salisbury. *Policraticus*, tr. by J. Dickinson. New York: Alfred Knopf, 1927.

Lenin, V. I. *State and Revolution.* New York: International, 1932.

Locke, John. "Essay Concerning Human Understanding" and "Essay Concerning Civil Government," in *The English Philosophers from Bacon to Mill*, ed. E. A. Burtt. New York, Modern Library.

Luther, M. *Works*, 8 vols. Philadelphia: A. J. Holman, 1931.

Macaulay, T. B. Speeches: *Parliamentary and Miscellaneous*, 2 vols. London: Vizetelly, 1853.

Machiavelli, N. *The Prince and The Discourses.* New York, Modern Library.

Marx, Karl. *Capital.* New York, Modern Library.

Nonnotte, Abbé. *Dictionnaire Philosophique de la Religion.* Paris, 1774.

Rousseau, J. J. *The Social Contract.*

Smith, A. *Wealth of Nations.* New York, Modern Library.
    Theory of Moral Sentiments. London: War, Lock Co.

Voltaire, François. *Philosophic Dictionary* (in *Works*). New York: St. Hubert Guild, 1901.

Young, A. *Farmer's Tour.* London: Strahan, 1771.
    State of the Public Mind. London: Richardson, 1798.

CRITICAL BIBLIOGRAPHY

Part I · The Making of the Liberal Society

CHAPTER II: DEATH MASK OF A SOCIETY

Coker, F. W. *Readings in Political Philosophy.* New York: Macmillan, 1938.

Farrell, W. *A Companion to the "Summa,"* 3 vols. New York: Sheed and Ward, 1939-41. Volume II (*The Pursuit of Happiness*) of immediate value to understanding of Catholic social thought.

Hearnshaw, F. C. (ed.). *The Social and Political Ideas of Some Great Medieval Thinkers.* London: Harrap, 1926.

Jarrett, B. *Social Theories of the Middle Ages.* London: Benn, 1926. One of the best summaries.

McIlwain, C. H. *The Growth of Political Thought in the West.* New York: Macmillan, 1932. Excellent on Later Middle Ages.

Power, E. *Medieval People.* Harmondsworth (England): Penguin Books, 1939. Finely written sketches of typical lives of the Middle Ages: peasant, prioress, merchant, etc.

Tawney, R. H. *Religion and the Rise of Capitalism.* Harmondsworth (England): Penguin Books, 1938. First chapter on the medieval background as fine as the rest of the work.

Von Gierke, O. *The Development of Political Theory,* tr. by Bernard Freyd. New York: Norton, 1939. A classic.

CHAPTER III: THE REVOLT OF ECONOMICS

Cheyney, E. P. *The Dawn of a New Era.* New York: Harpers, 1936. Good on the economic changes, weaker on cultural change. Excellent bibliography.

Heaton, H. *Economic History of Europe.* New York: Harpers, 1936. One of the pioneer texts in economic history. Well written and well organized.

Huizinga, J. *The Waning of the Middle Ages.* London: Arnold, 1937. Vastly superior to Cheyney on the cultural evolution in the period (ca. 1250-1450) which they both cover. As the titles imply, the two works have contradictory interpretations of the same era.

Kerr, A. B. *Jacques Coeur.* New York: Scribners, 1927. Life of most famous merchant prince of the middle ages.

Mumford, L. *The Culture of Cities.* New York: Harcourt, Brace, 1938. First chapter on the medieval town presents original, though not always substantiated, interpretation of factors propelling disintegration of medieval world.

Pirenne, H. *Economic and Social History of Medieval Europe,* tr. by I. E. Clagg. New York: Harcourt, Brace, 1937.
Medieval Cities, tr. by F. D. Halsey. Princeton: Princeton University Press, 1939.

Mohammed and Charlemagne, tr. by B. Miall. New York: Norton, 1939. . . . These three works contain the substance of the work of one of the greatest scholars in the field, including his original and much-disputed theory of the ending of the ancient world through the on-slaught of Islam.

CHAPTER IV: THE CALDRON OF THE SIXTEENTH CENTURY

Grimmelshausen, H. J. C. *Simplicissimus the Vagabond*, tr. by A. T. S. Goodrick. New York: E. P. Dutton, 1924. Classic literary picture of Germany in the period of the Thirty Years War.

Hearnshaw, F. J. C. (ed.). *The Social and Political Ideas of Some Great Thinkers of the Renaissance and the Reformation*. London, Harrap.

Hobson, J. A. *Economics and Ethics: A Study in Social Values*. New York: Heath, 1929. Part II excellent in discussion of the economic ethics of the Reformation.

McGiffert, A. C. *Protestant Thought Before Kant*. New York: Scribners, 1936. Emphasizes almost exclusively theological development.

O'Brien, G. *An Essay on the Economic Effects of the Reformation*. London: Burns, Oates and Washbourne, 1923. Written from Catholic viewpoint.

Robinson, J. H. *Readings in European History*, 2 vols. New York: Ginn, 1908-1909.

Roeder, R. *The Man of the Renaissance*. New York: Viking, 1935. Studies of four lawgivers: Savonarola, Machiavelli, Castiglione, Aretino. Scholarly and brilliantly written.

Smith, P. *The Age of the Reformation*. New York: Holt, 1920. Balanced and careful work. Concluding chapter on the many interpretations of the Reformation good summary. Exhaustive bibliography.

Tawney, R. H. *Religion and the Rise of Capitalism*. (Cf. Chapter II above.) Finest short study of the relationship of Protestantism and capitalism. As author himself notes (in preface to 1937 edition), there is a serious omission in the absence of discussion of Catholic social thought in post-Reformation period. Despite this, work is invaluable in this field.

Troeltsch, E. *The Social Teaching of the Christian Churches*, tr. by O. Wyon. London: Allen and Unwin, 1931. The only extensive (2 vols.) treatment of the subject in English, by one of the greatest scholars of Protestantism.

Protestantism and Progress, tr. by W. Montgomery. New York: G. P. Putnam, 1912.

Weber, M. *The Protestant Ethic and the Spirit of Capitalism*, tr. by T. Parsons. London: Allen and Unwin, 1930. The pioneer work upon which Tawney built. Detailed (100-page appendix of notes) and thorough, lacking the literary flourishes of Tawney's work.

CHAPTER V: PHILOSOPHERS IN ARMS:
THE NEW WORLD OF IDEAS

Becker, C. L. *The Heavenly City of the Eighteenth-Century Philosophers.* New Haven: Yale University Press, 1935. Brilliant exposition of the thought of the Enlightenment in the context of Christian tradition. Source material voluminously quoted throughout.

Brailsford, H. N. *Voltaire.* New York: Holt, 1935.

Maritain, J. *Three Reformers: Luther, Descartes and Rousseau.* New York: Scribners, 1936. Three essays by one of the most notable Catholic thinkers of the twentieth century.

Marlowe, Christopher. *The Plays of Christopher Marlowe.* New York: E. P. Dutton, 1924.

Martin, K. *French Liberal Thought in the Eighteenth Century.* Boston: Little Brown, 1929. From Bayle to Condorcet, the best single-volume exposition of the subject. Broader in scope than Becker's work.

Montesquieu. *Persian Letters*, tr. by J. Davidson. London: G. Routledge, 1923.

Mumford, L. *Technics and Civilization.* New York: Harcourt, Brace, 1934. See below: Part III, Chapter X.

Palmer, R. R. *Catholics and Unbelievers in Eighteenth Century France.* Princeton: Princeton University Press, 1939. Contains much previously unexplored material on the defense of the Church's doctrines against the attacks of the Philosophes. In broad outline, it owes much to Becker's work, but in detail it cuts entirely new ground—and cuts it well.

Pope, Alexander, *Selected Poems*, ed. by L. I. Bredvold. New York: F. S. Crofts, 1926.

Randall, J. H. *The Making of the Modern Mind.* New York: Houghton Mifflin, 1926. Exceptional compendium of material from primary sources, making it valuable reference text. Somewhat infatuated with the mechanical triumphs of science, but not so extremely as other works dealing with similar material.

Smith, P. *History of Modern Culture*, 2 vols. New York: Henry Holt, 1930-1934. Like Randall, contains good selection of primary-source material. Rather uninspiringly written, and divided too categorically into convenient chapters.

Spinoza, B. de. *The Philosophy of Spinoza*, ed. by Joseph Ratner. New York: Modern Library, 1927. With life of Spinoza and introduction by the editor.

Voltaire. *Philosophical Dictionary*, ed. and tr. by H. I. Woolf. New York: Alfred Knopf.

Whitehead, A. N. *Science and the Modern World.* New York: Macmillan, 1939. Something of a modern classic. Chapters on place of mathematics in the history of thought, "the century of genius," and the eighteenth century are succinct and authoritative.

CHAPTER VI: THE LIBERAL FAITH:
CIVITAS HOMINIS

In addition to most of those listed under Chapter V, the following:

Laski, H. J. *The Rise of Liberalism*. New York: Harpers, 1936. A Marxist critique of the Liberal Society. It states incisively, often brilliantly, the historic weaknesses of the Liberal faith.

Milton, John. *Areopagitica*. New York: Everyman's Library.

Ogg, D. *Europe in the Seventeenth Century*. New York: Macmillan, 1938.

Perkins, J. B. *France Under Louis XV*. New York: Houghton Mifflin, 1897.

CHAPTER VII: MEN IN ARMS:
THE NEW WORLD OF FACTS

Acton, Lord J. E. E. *Lectures on the French Revolution*. London: Macmillan, 1910. Twenty-two readable lectures: numbers one, two, eleven and twenty especially good. At times a little dogmatic.

Aulard, A. *Christianity and the French Revolution*, tr. by Lady Frazer. Boston: Little Brown, 1927.

Beard, C. A. and M. R. *The Rise of American Civilization*, 2 vols. New York: Macmillan, 1937. Its interpretation of the American Revolution has largely been followed in the text above. Strong economic emphasis, though far from being narrowly Marxist.

Bernstein, E. *Cromwell and Communism*, tr. by H. J. Stenning. London: Allen and Unwin, 1930. By a noted Marxist. Fair selection of source material. Otherwise weak; dogmatic in interpretations, no bibliography.

Brinton, C. *The Anatomy of Revolution*. New York: Norton, 1938. Most conspicuous of several recent attempts at a comparative study of revolutions. Avoids extremes, but all highly speculative. Bibliography excellent.

Corey, L. *The Crisis of the Middle Class*. New York: Covici Friede, 1935. Marxist interpretation; from bourgeois revolutions to rise of Fascism. Superficial and hopelessly infatuated with what the author calls "the Marxist Enlightenment."

Federalist, The. New York: Modern Library, 1941. Invaluable for understanding of the times and issues revolving about the American Constitution.

Fisher, S. G. *The Struggle for American Independence*, 2 vols. Philadelphia: Lippincott, 1908. Still one of the best histories of the period; one of the first to break away from the overly-patriotic historical eulogies to America so conspicuous in the latter part of the nineteenth century.

Gottschalk, L. *The Era of the French Revolution*. New York: Houghton Mifflin, 1929.

Hacker, L. *The Triumph of American Capitalism*. New York: Simon and Schuster, 1940.

Johnson, R. M. *The French Revolution*. New York: Henry Holt, 1909. Compact summary. Well written and well organized.

Morison, S. E. *Sources and Documents*: 1764-1788. New York, Oxford, 1923.

Morison, S. E. and Commager, H. S. *The Growth of the American Republic*. New York, Oxford, 1937. More detailed than the Beards' work, and more organized in text-book fashion. Sums up the latest scholarship in a flowing literary style. The critical bibliography is exhaustive and excellently organized.

Palm, F. C. *The Middle Classes: Then and Now*. New York: Macmillan, 1936. Moving from medieval times to the New Deal in America, its most useful chapters are four dealing exclusively with literature. Absence of footnotes or bibliography unfortunate.

Roustan, M. *The Pioneers of the French Revolution*. Boston: Little Brown, 1926.

Sieyès, Abbé E. J. *Qu'est-ce que le Tiers Etat?* Troisieme edition, Paris 1789. One of the most influential pamphlets in all history. Succinct summary of Liberal outlook and aims at dawn of French Revolution: in revealing this, worth many times its length in pages of secondary sources. Is significant also as a reflection of lower clergy's position before the Civil Constitution of the Clergy.

Tocqueville, A. de. *The Old Regime and the Revolution*, tr. by J. Bonner. New York: Harpers, 1856. One of the earliest works to perceive: (a) the reality behind the facade of words that had formerly concealed the true results of the French Revolution, i.e. administrative centralization; and (b) the religious character of the French Revolution.

CHAPTER VIII: THE MOUNTAINS MADE LEVEL

In addition to those books listed under Chapters V-VII, the following:

Davis, Jerome. *Capitalism and Its Culture*. New York: Farrar, 1935.

Dryden, John. *Poems*, ed. by B. Dobree. New York: Everyman's Library, 1934.

Goldsmith, Oliver, in: *The Poems of Johnson, Goldsmith, Gray and Collins*, ed. by T. M. Ward. London: G. Routledge.

Mayer, J. P. (ed.). *Political Thought: The European Tradition*. New York: Viking, 1939. Thorough and stimulating survey from the Greek city-state to the Fascist state. Articles by the editor, Tawney, R. H. Crossman, C. J. S. Sprigge and others. By nature of organization, however, lacks continuity at points.

Ruggiero, G. de. *The History of European Liberalism*, tr. by R. G. Collingwood. London: Oxford, 1927. Largely nineteenth century, but short background chapter on Enlightenment. The only extended historical treatment of the subject in English.

CHAPTER IX: THE RATIONALE OF THE NEW ORDER

Babbitt, I. *Rousseau and Romanticism.* New York: Houghton Mifflin, 1930. Severely critical.

Mill, John Stuart. *Autobiography.* New York: Holt, 1874. An illuminating reflection of the men utilitarianism produced—in the person of the elder Mill, described at length.

Utilitarianism; On Liberty; and *Representative Government*: in one volume. New York: Everyman's Library, 1931. Revealing not only as an exposition of Mill's ideas, but also as the best indication of the profound change that overtook the utilitarian faith between the time of Bentham and the second Mill.

Pareto, V. *The Mind and Society,* 4 vols., ed. and tr. by A. Livingston and A. Bongiorno. New York: Harcourt, Brace, 1935. Pareto's massive attempt to reduce all social action to basic drives and "derivatives." His constructive theory aside, his volumes contain a wealth of illustrative material, excellently organized. Vol. III contains some of the most incisive criticism of the utilitarian doctrines anywhere written.

Ratzlaff, C. J. *The Theory of Free Competition.* Philadelphia: University of Pennsylvania Press, 1936.

CHAPTER X: THE TITAN OF INDUSTRIALISM

Bagehot, W. *The English Constitution.* New York: Appleton, 1920. One of the classic interpretations—and one of the classic representations of nineteenth century Liberalism.

Chase, Stuart. *Men and Machines.* New York: Macmillan, 1929. Popular interpretation of effects of technology. Scarcely a scholarly work, but provocative at points.

Hammond, J. L. and B. *The Rise of Modern Industry.* New York: Harcourt, Brace, 1937. In this, along with their specialized work on the town and village laborer at the turn of the nineteenth century, the Hammonds offer the best introduction to the machine age in English.

Hayes, C. J. H. *Political and Cultural History of Modern Europe,* 2 vols. New York: Macmillan, 1937.

Mumford, L. *Technics and Civilization.* New York: Harcourt, Brace, 1934. *The Culture of Cities.* New York: Harcourt, Brace, 1938. More interpretive than the work of the Hammonds, these two books of Mumford, following the path of his master—Patrick Geddes, are brilliant studies in urban and industrial sociology. Well written, with thorough bibliographies.

Russell, B. *Freedom versus Organization*: 1814-1914. New York: Norton, 1934.

Scott, J. F., and Baltzly, A. *Readings in European History Since 1814.* New York: F. S. Crofts, 1934.

Somervell, D. C. *English Thought in the Nineteenth Century.* London: Methuen, 1929. Excellent blend of political, religious, scientific and literary trends. No bibliography and index microscopic.

Woolf, L. *After the Deluge.* Harmondsworth (England): Penguin Books, 1937. A stimulating attempt to analyze the "communal psychology" of the nineteenth century. Unfortunately, written too close to the World War of 1914, which then recent experience colors much of the work.

CHAPTER XI: THE GREAT LIBERAL ADVENTURE

Anderson, Sherwood. *Poor White.* New York: B. W. Huebsch, 1920.

Anderson, W. *American Government.* New York: Holt, 1938.

Beard, C. A. and M. R. *The Rise of American Civilization.* (See above, Part I, Chapter VII.) Probably finest part of entire work is delineation of American character in the era of triumphant big business.

Bowers, C. G. *The Tragic Era.* New York: Cornwall, 1929. Lively and fluent account of Reconstruction Era. Carried a little too far on the wave of sentimental reaction which, in some historical circles, has led to glorifying pre-Civil War aristocracy of the South.

Commons, F. R., and Andrews, F. B. *Principles of Labor Legislation.* New York: Harpers, 1936. A monumental work. Balanced and careful to avoid emotional overtones. An elaborate critical bibliography.

Gabriel, R. H. *The Course of American Democratic Thought.* New York: Ronald Press, 1940. Explores a field that has been but barely touched yet.

Josephson, M. *The Politicos.* New York: Harcourt, Brace, 1938. With his earlier work, *The Robber Barons,* this constitutes one of the best introductions to the detailed political technique of the Liberal Society.

Lynd, R. S., and H. M. *Middletown, A Study in American Culture.* New York: Harcourt, Brace, 1929. The first of the famous pair of studies of Muncie, Indiana, "typical" American town. An urban microcosmus of the Liberal Society. This first volume lacks much of the interpretation that went into *Middletown in Transition,* hence more objective, duller.

Millis, W. *The Martial Spirit.* Cambridge: Riverside Press, 1931. The first sane narration of the Spanish-American War. Summary example of American society in a militant fever—often led headlong by industrial and journalistic barons.

Morison, S. E., and Commager, H. S. *The Growth of the American Republic.* (See above, Part II, Chapter VII.)

Mumford, L. *The Golden Day.* New York: Norton, 1926. The finest short study of "American literature and culture." The discussion of mid-century pragmatism is unsurpassed.

Myers, Gustavus. *History of the Great American Fortunes.* New York: Modern Library, 1936. The classic investigation, still valuable after thirty years.

Parrington, V. L. *Main Currents in American Thought,* 3 vols. New York: Harcourt, Brace, 1930. The most scholarly and exhaustive work on the subject, ranking beside the volumes of Van Wyck Brooks, and more concerned with political thought than the latter. The untimely death of Parrington has left many of the most important chapters still in outline form.

Roosevelt, T. *Autobiography*. New York: Scribners, 1929. With Steffens' autobiography, in many respects the most valuable autobiographical work of the era. With irrepressible gusto and egotism, Roosevelt sketches the political scene in detail: his own comments and digressions succinct and shrewd.

Steffens, L. *Autobiography*. New York: Harcourt, Brace, 1931. Best first-hand account of political corruption and sabotage of popular will.

Veblen, T. *The Theory of the Leisure Class*. New York: Viking, 1935. The highly original, often profound analysis of one of America's greatest social thinkers.

CHAPTER XII: THE CHURCH MILITANT

Binkley, R. C. *Realism and Nationalism*: 1852-1871. New York: Harpers, 1935. Though major part of this work is concerned with political and diplomatic events, the early chapters on Science, Materialism and the Church are germane to this work.

Corrigan, R., S. J. *The Church and the Nineteenth Century*. Milwaukee: Bruce, 1938. Excellent summary of theme, with not easily available material on numerous Catholic social workers. Not strong in its theoretical discussions. Appendix contains text of Syllabus of Errors.

Dorlodot, Canon. *Darwinism and Catholic Thought*, tr. by Rev. E. Messenger. London: Burns, Oates and Washbourne, 1922. Detailed Catholic effort to state relationship of new science and traditional Catholicism, by the director of the Geological Institute at the University of Louvain.

Fulop-Miller, R. *Leo XIII and Our Times*. New York: Longmans Green, 1937. By a non-Catholic, a sympathetic treatment. Probably the most balanced and most scholarly treatment of the subject in single-volume compass. Poorly documented.

Guilday, P. (ed.). *The Catholic Church in Contemporary Europe*. New York: Kennedy, 1932. With an introduction by Carlton J. H. Hayes.

Kenyon, R. (ed.). *The Catholic Faith and the Industrial Order*. London: Allan, 1931. Summary of the work of the Anglo-Catholic Summer Schools of Theology 1928-1930. Detailed analysis of the immediate implications of industrialism and mass production, but very little material dealing with theoretical or philosophical background.

Leto, P. (pseudonym of F. Nobili-Vitelleschi). *Eight Months At Rome During the Vatican Council*. London: Murray, 1876. Writing under the name of a famous Catholic dissenter from orthodoxy of the Renaissance period, the author gives detailed description from personal observation. Author's personal opinions aside, the work is valuable for its thorough narration of the elaborate events.

MacCaffrey, J. *History of the Catholic Church in the Nineteenth Century*, 2 vols. St. Louis: Herder, 1910. The most judicious work on the subject from a Catholic standpoint. Well documented, but rather uninspiringly written. A satisfactory work in this field yet remains to be written.

Manning, H. E., Cardinal. *The Dignity and Rights of Labour*. London: Burns, Oates and Washbourne, 1934. Short work containing some of Manning's best articles. Along with *Quadragesimo Anno*, required reading for understanding of Catholic social theory.

Mathew, D. *Catholicism in England*. New York: Longmans Green, 1936. Good 400-year survey, from a Catholic stand. Bibliography poor.

Morley, J. *The Life of William Ewart Gladstone*, 3 vols. New York: Macmillan, 1903. The second volume contains thorough account of Gladstone's view of the decree of Papal Infallibility.

Nell-Bruening, O. von, S. J. *Reorganization of Social Economy*. New York: Bruce, 1937. The finest extended analysis and interpretation of the social encyclicals, especially *Quadragesimo Anno*. Substantial bibliography and appendix, containing the three most notable encyclicals.

Nitti, F. S. *Catholic Socialism*, tr. by M. Mackintosh. New York: Macmillan, 1895. Summarizes under its title the "radical" tradition in Christian thought from the time of the early Church founders. Though often loose in its interpretations, the work contains a mine of material on Catholic social movements in Europe, probably nowhere else available in English.

Ryan, J. A., and Boland, F. J. *Catholic Principles of Politics*. New York: Macmillan, 1940.
Ryan and Husslein, J., S. J. *The Church and Labor*. New York: Macmillan, 1924. . . . These two works are the best summaries by American prelates. The latter, a compendium of articles by different authors, is especially valuable.

Sencourt, R. *The Genius of the Vatican*. London: Cape, 1935.

Vidler, A. R. *The Modernist Movement in the Roman Church*. Cambridge: University Press, 1934. Scholarly treatment by a non-Catholic.

Walsh, H. H. *The Concordat of 1801*. New York: Columbia University Press, 1933. Exceptionally fine. Should be read along with Pius IX's *Quanta Cura* for an excellent summary of the modern problem of church-state relations.

Watt, L. *Catholic Social Principles*. London: Burns, Oates and Washbourne, 1934. Short commentary on *Rerum Novarum*.

Woodward, E. L. *Three Studies in European Conservatism*. New York: Smith, 1930. The third study is on the Church in the nineteenth century. Most reliable in account of clashes with Cavour and Bismarck.

GENERAL

Arnold, T. *The Symbols of Government*. New Haven: Yale University Press, 1935.
> *The Folklore of Capitalism*. New Haven: Yale University Press, 1937.
> . . . These two books contain the most sane, realistic critique of modern Liberal society that America has produced. Occasionally too flippant, but more often brilliant.

Belloc, H. *An Essay on the Restoration of Property*. New York: Sheed and Ward, 1936.
> *The Servile State*. London: Constable, 1927. . . . Two representative works of one of the most notable contemporary Catholic writers. On critical side, good. On constructive side, picture of distributist state shallow.

Berdyaev, N. *The Meaning of History*. New York: Scribners, 1936. *The Fate of Man in the Modern World*. New York: Morehouse, 1935. The former work is Christian thought in the best vein. The latter work is an attack on industrialism *per se*, more than a little lost in its own metaphysical complications.

Bonn, M. J. *The Crisis of Capitalism in America*, tr. by W. Ray. New York: John Day, 1932. A German economist's objective treatise on America in the Great Depression. One of the best of its kind.

Briefs, G. A. *The Proletariat*. New York: McGraw Hill, 1937.

Carrel, A. *Man the Unknown*. New York: Harpers, 1935.

Crossman, R. H. S. *Plato Today*. New York: Oxford, 1939. An interesting restatement of Platonic social thought in twentieth-century terms, by one of England's most astute young Socialists. Final chapter on democracy excellent.

Dawson, C. *Religion and the Modern State*. New York: Sheed and Ward, 1938. Short statement by noted English Catholic apologist.

Deploige, S. *The Conflict between Ethics and Sociology*, tr. by C. C. Miltner. St. Louis: Herder, 1938. Exceedingly thorough statement of Catholic thought, made particularly in reference to the work of Durkheim and Levy-Bruhl.

Eliot, T. S. *The Idea of a Christian Society*. New York: Harcourt, Brace, 1940. Lucid statement by Anglo-Catholic, but at some points little more than a literary exercise.

Fanfani, A. *Catholicism, Protestantism and Capitalism*. New York: Sheed and Ward, 1930. Short but well rounded study of interrelationships of the three. By a Catholic. Should be read with Tawney's work (see above, Part I).

Gilson, E. *The Unity of Philosophical Experience*. New York: Scribners, 1937. By perhaps the greatest Catholic thinker of the early twentieth century. Brilliantly and cleanly written, living proof that such subjects can be made intelligible to the unversed, yet be fortified with real scholarship.

Gras, N. S. B. *Business and Capitalism*. New York: F. S. Crofts, 1939. An elaborate effort to show, by juggling terms, that capitalism always has been—and presumably always will be. Dubious.

Green, T. H. *Lectures on the Principles of Political Obligation*. New York: Longmans Green, 1937. Contains some of the most incisive criticism of natural-rights and state-of-nature thinking that has ever been penned. Green strongly influenced the thought of Laski, as the latter has acknowledged.

Hobhouse, L. T. *Liberalism*. New York: Henry Holt. Home University Library. Sympathetic treatment, well done.

Joad, C. E. M. *Guide to the Philosophy of Morals and Politics*. New York: Random House. Author is professor of philosophy at University of London. Otherwise sound survey marred by weakness of inadequate bibliographical references.

Laski, H. J. *The State in Theory and Practice*. New York: Viking, 1938. *Democracy in Crisis*. Chapel Hill: University of North Carolina Press, 1935. . . . The first states the abstract conclusions to *The Rise of Liberalism*, lacking the historical background. The second is the most succinct summary of Laski's philosophy, here with Marxist strain very pronounced. Always stimulating.

Lerner, M. *It Is Later Than You Think*. New York: Viking, 1939. Not far from Laski's position, less effectively stated.

Maritain, J. *Scholasticism and Politics*, tr. by M. Adler. New York: Macmillan, 1940.
—with Wust, P., and Dawson, C. *Essays in Order*. New York: Macmillan, 1931.

Nicolson, H. *Peacemaking: 1919*. New York: Harcourt, Brace, 1939. The best single volume on Versailles—in its widest implications.

Niebuhr, R. *Christianity and Power Politics*. New York: Scribners, 1940. By one of the outstanding Protestant scholars America has produced. Discussion of German heritage from the Reformation most suggestive part of work.

Sheen, F. J. *Liberty, Equality and Fraternity*. New York: Macmillan, 1939.

Tawney, R. H. *The Acquisitive Society*. New York: Harcourt, Brace, 1920. Brilliant short exposition of the theory of the functional society. Interesting to compare with *Quadragesimo Anno*.

SOCIALISM AND COMMUNISM

Hook, S. *Towards the Understanding of Karl Marx*. New York: John Day, 1933. One of the clearest and best introductions in English. Sympathetic: by a Marxist. Discussion of historical materialism exceptionally good.

Kropotkin, P. *Memoirs of a Revolutionist*. New York: Houghton Mifflin, 1930. Though protagonist not a Marxist, excellent material on the revolutionary movements of the nineteenth century. Interesting to compare with Jan Valtin, *Out of the Night* (New York: Alliance, 1941).

Laidler, H. *Socializing Our Democracy*. New York: Harpers, 1935. *History of Socialist Thought*. New York: Crowell, 1938. The second is a competent, thorough and objective survey—one of the best convenient compendiums of information on Socialism.

Lyons, E. *Assignment in Utopia*. New York: Harcourt, Brace, 1937. A Marxist experiences disillusion in Soviet Russia. It is probably the best available summary of the aftermath of the Russian Revolution. Vigorously denounced by Marxist periodicals.

Morris, William. *Selected Writings*, ed. by G. D. H. Cole. New York: Random House, 1934. Contains the humane Socialist dreams of the most conspicuous Socialist of the late nineteenth century. Approached from artistic and cultural viewpoint. Far cry from harsh dialectic.

Nomad, M. *Apostles of Revolution*. Boston: Little Brown, 1939. Study and story of great nineteenth century revolutionists: Blanqui, Marx, Bakunin—to Stalin. Very critical. Well documented and excitingly written.

Rosenberg, A. *Democracy and Socialism*, tr. by G. Rosen. New York: Knopf, 1939. An effort to define "democracy." Best in its narrative discussions of the proletarian revolutions of the nineteenth century.

Strachey, J. *The Coming Struggle for Power*. New York: Modern Library, 1935. The noted English Socialist's analysis of the "crisis of capitalism." Condescending toward all religious forms and institutions.

FASCISM

Armstrong, H. F. *We Or They: Two Worlds in Conflict*. New York: Macmillan, 1937. Among the first to avow the inevitability of war with Fascism.

Ascoli, M., and Feiler, A. *Fascism for Whom?* New York: Norton, 1938. By an Italian and a German refugee, the work does not yield to hysterics. A detailed, penetrating analysis. Excellent on the distinction drawn between Italian Fascism and German Nazism. Unfortunately shallow in tracing historical backgrounds beyond 1900. No bibliography.

Barnes, J. S. *Fascism*. New York: Holt, 1931. Dispassionate, brief appraisal. Unusually long discussion of the Fascist *weltanschauung*.

Drucker, P. *The End of Economic Man*. New York: John Day, 1939. By all odds, the most intelligent and stimulating treatment of the meaning of the Fascist revolt from the Liberal tradition. Integrates the rise of Fascism with the whole cultural heritage of the West, with amazingly wide and deep perspective. The discussion of "The Failure of the Christian Churches" contains much merited criticism, some unmerited.

Kolnai, A. *The War Against the West*. New York: Viking, 1938. By an Austrian Catholic Socialist. Most detailed of all the analyses here cited, with best selection of source material. Serious flaw in conversion of Fascism into a simple last-stage defense mechanism of declining capitalism. Fascism signifies, represents, threatens a great deal more than that.

INDEX

Abailard, Peter, 27
Act of Supremacy (1534), 37
Act of the Six Articles (1539), 37 n.
Adams, Thomas, 78
Aeterni Patris, 213
Aldrich, Thomas Bailey, 188
Alembert, Jean LeRond d', 131 n.
Alva, Duke of, 30
Amalfi, 18
America, 179, Chap. XI, *passim*. See *also* United States of America
Anderson, Sherwood, cited, 186
Anglican Church, *see* Church of England
Anti-Council of Free Thinkers, 211
Aquinas, *see* Saint Thomas Aquinas
Arnauld, 60 n.
Arnold, Matthew, 177
Articles of Confederation, 113
Ashley Commission, 169
Augsburg, Peace of (1555), 36

Babylonian Captivity, 25
Bacon, Sir Francis, 23, 50, 58, 99
Bagehot, Walter, 174
Balfour, Arthur James, 231
Barbarossa, 30
Bardi (family), 128
"Barebone's Parliament," 106
Baudeau, Nicolas, 94
Bayle, Pierre, 84
Beard, Charles and Mary, cited, 184
Becon, 42
Beggars Lesson, The, 79
Bellamont, Richard Coote, Earl of, 113
Bellarmine, Robert, Cardinal, 204, 221, 265
Bentham, Jeremy, 151, 266
Bentley, Elizabeth, 167, 168
Bergier, Nicolas, 72, 139
Bismarck, Otto von, 205, 210
Black Death, 25
Board of Trade, London, 113
Bodin, Jean, 96
Boissy d'Anglas, François-Antoine, 122
Bolingbroke, Lord, 81-82, 131 n., 227
Bormann, Martin, 254 n.

Bossuet, Jacques-Bénigne, 38, 67, 126, 134
Bourgeoisie, *see* Middle class, Cities, Merchant class
Brahe, Tycho, 58
Brougham, Lord, 174, 176
Bruges, 19
Bruno, Giordano, 62
Burke, Edmund, 87, 91-92, 95
Business enterprise, 183-89, 191, 255; autonomy of, 129, 189, 218, 269
Butler, William, 116
Byron, George Gordon, Lord, 177

Calvin, John, 3, 80, 198
Calvinism, 73, 78, 103, 124, 248; ethics of, 44-47, 130
Capital, 21, 188-89. *See also* Business enterprise, Private property, Financial class
Capitalist society, 247
Carlyle, Thomas, 177
Carnegie, Andrew, 184, 193, 200
Carolingian Empire, 18
Catholic Church, *see* Church, the (Roman)
Cavour, Camillo di, 206
Chanut, 59
Charles VIII of France, 29
Chartists, 177
Chénier, Marie-Joseph, 126, 127
Christian God, attack on, 56, 65-66, 72, 125-27, 130-31, 134, 203; defense of, 67, 132-41
Church, the (Roman), 25, 31, 38-40, 64-68, 70, 228, 263-65, 272-73; attack on, 124-27, 128; counterattack of, 132-41, Chap. XII, *passim*
Church lands, 37, 43, 47, 124
Church of England, 37, 43, 105, 112
Cities, growth of, 18 ff.; freedom of, 20; medieval, 20; confederation of, 20; nineteenth century industrial, 170-72
Civil Code, 123
Civil Constitution of the Clergy, 124
Civil War, American, 180, 181, 182
Clemenceau, Georges, 231, 233
Cleveland, Grover, 193

Clews, Henry, 200
Code Civil, see Civil Code
Coleridge, Samuel Taylor, 177, 257 n.
Colonies, American, 110-13
Commerce, see Trade
Committee of Public Safety, 123, 126
Communism, 246. See also Marxism
Communist Manifesto, 260
Conciliar Movement, 25
Concordat of 1801, 123
Concordat of 1855 (Austrian), 210
Condillac, Etienne de, 86
Condorcet, Antoine-Nicolas de, 100
Confessions (Rousseau), 148
Congress of the Confederation, 114
Constantinople, 17, 18
Constitution, the Federal, 114, 116-17
Constitution of 1791, 121
Constitution of the Year III, 122
Constitutional Convention, 115-18
Consumption economy, 12, 22, 45
Conwell, Russell, cited, 199
Copernican revolution, 58
Copernicus, 49
Cornwallis, Lord, 113
Corporations, 184-85, 188, 190, 191
Corruption, political, 191-94
Cortes, 21 and n.
Council of Nicea, 209
Council of Trent, 209
Crabtree, Mathew, 167
Cromwell, Oliver, 3, 106-10
Crowley, Robert, 42, 79
Czechoslovakia, 253

Danton, Georges-Jacques, 121
Darboy, Georges, Archbishop, 209
Darwin, Charles, 201, 240
Darwinism, 205
Decretum (Gratian), 13
De Revolutionibus Orbium Celestium, 58
Deism, 68-71, 72, 74, 82, 126, 240
Democracy, 150, 258-59, 262, 265, 270, 273-74
Deontology, 155
Descartes, René, 58, 59-61, 63, 69, 140
Deschamps, 209
Determinism, 270
Dictionnaire encyclopédique, 90, 98
Diderot, Denis, 50, 62, 63, 72, 74, 87, 90-91, 92, 97, 99, 131 n., 171
Diggers, 108

Discourse on Inequality, 147
Döllinger, Johann Joseph Ignaz, 205, 210 n., 212
Douglass, Frederick, cited, 183
Drake, Sir Francis, 30
Drogheda, 106
Dryden, John, 135
Dupanloup, Félix-Antoine-Philibert, Bishop, 209
DuPont de Nemours, Pierre-Samuel, 95
Dürer, Albrecht, 29

Economic Man, 56, 160, 203, 218, 219, 235, 249, 250, 262
Economics, 160; and ethics, see Ethics; and politics, 189-96, 238-40, 269-70; and religion, 39, 134
Economic theory, of Middle Ages, see Medieval society; change in, 22-24, 48-49; of Luther, 41-42; of Calvin, 44-47; of Puritans, 78-80, 105; of Adam Smith, 92-94; of Physiocrats, 95; of Constitutional Convention, 115-16; of French Revolution, 120-23; of Bentham, 154-56; of the Church, 218, 220-21; of industrial nineteenth century, Chap. X, passim, 190; of Marxism, 247, 261-62
Elizabeth of England, 106
Ellis Island, 188
Emancipation of slaves, see Slavery
Encyclicals, papal, 206, 213, 219, 220
England, 36, 42-44, 78-82, 105-11, 165-70, 205
England, Church of, see Church of England
Ephémérides, 94
Equality, 147-48
Estates General, 21 and n., 119-20
Ethics, of middle ages, 6 ff., 13-15; change in, 22-23; in the Prince, 32; weakened by Reformation, 44; of eighteenth century, 73; of Puritans, 78-80; of Bentham, 152; of Liberalism, 235, 243; rejected by Fascism, 254; Christian, 267-68; and economics, 10-16, 17-18, 26, 44-47, 111 and n., 129, 130, 140, 198-201, 235, 268

Factory, the, 170
Fascism, 246, 249-54, 256, 258, 261, 271

Federalist Papers, The, 116
Feudalism, 3; decline of, 21 ff.
Financial class, 21, 181-82, 196. *See also* Merchant class, Middle class
First Crusade, 18
Flanders, 18-19
Flaubert, Gustave, 211
Florence, 31
Fontenelle, Bernard le Bovier de, 99
Fouché, Joseph, 125, 226, 254 n.
Fourier, Charles, 87
Fourteen Points (Wilson's), 230, 232
Fourteenth Amendment, 183, 191
France, 37-38, 205, 256-57. *See also* French Revolution
Francke, Sebastian, 83
Franco-Prussian War, 212
Franklin, Benjamin, 88, 127
Frederick Henry, 104
Frederick the Great, 70, 124, 134
Freedom, *see* Liberty
French Revolution, 120-27, 205, 251, 256
Fréron, Elie, 68 and n.
Fugger (family), 128

Galileo, 3, 58, 62
Gallicanism, 82, 123
Geddes, Patrick, cited, 172
Genoa, 18
George, David Lloyd, *see* Lloyd George, David
German unification, 251
Germany, 205, 225, 245; Nazi, 253
Gerry, Elbridge, 115
Ghent, 19
Gibbon, Edward, 205
Gibbons, James, Cardinal, 217
Gierke, Otto Friedrich von, 7 n.
Gladstone, William, 208, 210-11
Glasson, Ernest Désiré, cited, 123
Glorious Revolution, 109
Goldsmith, Oliver, 136
Gooder, Sarah, 167, 169
Gospel of wealth, 198-200, 252
Government, 214, 268-69; of United States, 183, 185, 188-89
Graft, *see* Corruption
Gratian, 6 n., 13
Great Schism, 25
Gregory XVI, Pope, 205 n.
Guglielmo of Apuleia, 18

Hamann, Johann Georg, 72
Hamilton, Alexander, 116
Hanna, Mark, 194
Harrison, William Henry, 193
Hartley, David, 86
Harvard College, 114
Hawkins, Sir John, 30
Hayer, 67
Hayes, Carlton J. H., cited, 258 n.
Hecker, Isaac Thomas, 217
Heloise, 27
Helvetius, Claude-Adrien, 87, 98, 152 n., 268
Henlein, Konrad, 253
Henry, Patrick, 117-18
Henry VIII, of England, 36, 106
Henry of Prussia, Prince, 114
Herder, Johann Gottfried, 68, 88, 205, 225-27, 237
Hess, Rudolf, 254
Hitler, Adolf, 245, 251 n., 253, 254
Hobbes, Thomas, 66, 86
Holbach, Paul-Henri, Baron d', 64, 71, 72, 206
Holy Alliance, 238
Hopkins, Mark, 199
Howe, William, Lord, 113
Huguenots, 37, 47, 85
Humanity, 85, 97-98
Hume, David, 50, 66 n., 71, 96
Hundred Years War, 25
Huntington, Collis P., 192
Hutten, Ulrich von, 35, 37

Immaculate Conception, doctrine of, 206-7
Immigration, 183-84, 185, 188
Imperialism, 179, 229, 238
Individualism, 49, 72, 93, 111, 131-32, 148-50, 155, 213, 219, 243-45
Industrialism, 159, Chap. X, *passim*, 181-82, 184, 186-89
Industrial Revolution, 162, 165-67
Ineffabilis Deus, 206, 219
Instrument of Government, 107
Interstate Commerce Act, 191 and n.
Interstate Commerce Commission, 194-95
Ireland, John, Archbishop, 217, 264
Iron Law of Wages, 157
Islamic empire, *see* Moslem empire
Italian unification, 251
Italy, 205-6

Jacapone da Todi, 26
James, William, cited, 201
Jansenism, 83
Jefferson, Thomas, 88
Jesuits, 71
John of Salisbury, 8, 9, 10, 23, 26, 33, 204, 221, 271
Joseph II, of Austria, 226
Jus mercatorum, 20
Just price, 13

Kant, Immanuel, 50, 99
Kepler, Johannes, 58, 61
Kershaw, Patience, 167, 169
Ketteler, William Emmanuel von, 209, 216-17

LaBeaumelle, Laurent Angliviel de, 68
Labor, organized, 188-89, 191, 217
Laboring-classes, 90-91, 123, 140, 156-58, 167-72, 174, 176, 177, 188-89, 214-19, 247, 260, 264
Lafayette, Marquis de, 231
Lahary, Judge, cited, 123
Laissez-faire, 40, 92, 154
Lamennais, Félicité de, 205
Latimer, Hugh, 42, 198
Law of Love and Love as Law, The, 199
Lawrence, William, Bishop, cited, 200
Laws, as defense of capitalism, 191, 218
League of Nations, 238-39
Leibniz, Gottfried Wilhelm, 58, 88
Leo XII, Pope, 205 n.
Leo XIII, Pope, 8 n., 205 n., 208, 212-16, 220, 273
Leonardo, *see* Vinci, Leonardo da
Lepeletier de Saint-Fargeau, Louis-Michel, 125
Lerner, Max, 267 n.
Lessing, Gotthold Ephraim, 88
Lettres sur les Anglais, 89
Levellers, 108
Lever, Thomas, 42, 198
Leviathan, 86
Liberalism, as faith, 4, 56; attacked by Church, 132-37, 206-8, 216, 219-21; philosophy of, 138-41, 145-51; and industrial capitalism, 159-60, 161-67; in America, Chap. XI, *passim*; and nationalism, 227-

28, 237-40; and science, 240-43; its view of man, 243-44; its political tactics, 244-45; its optimism, 245-47; and Marxism, 247-49; and Fascism, 250-54; and democracy, 258-59. *See also* Liberal Society
Liberal Society, 127, 129-30, and *passim*; social policy of, 173-79; philosophy of, 234-36; collapse of, 236 ff., 255-57, 265-68, 274. *See also* Liberalism
Liberty, 24, 125, 126, 147-48, 154, 243, 245; medieval concept of, 9-10; middle class demand for, 18-20, 23-24
Lille, 19
Lloyd George, David, 231
Locke, John, 50, 84, 86, 87, 88-89, 92, 98, 132, 176
Lowell, James Russell, 180
Luddites, the, 177
Luther, Martin, 3, 29, 35, 40-42, 47, 73, 80, 102, 130

Macaulay, Thomas Babington, 175, 176, 178, 215
McCosh, James, cited, 198
MacHale, John, 209
Machiavelli, Niccolo, 3, 29, 31, 32-33, 34, 47, 93, 227, 258
Madison, James, 115
Malthus, Thomas Robert, 156-57, 256
Man, dignity of, 61-62, 265, 268, 270, 274
Manning, Henry Edward, Cardinal, 209, 210, 217-19
Marat, Jean-Paul, 125
Marston Moor, 106
Marx, Karl, 13, 46, 247, 259
Marxism, 124, 247-49, 260-62, 271
Mathieu, François Désiré, 209
Mazarin, Giulio, Cardinal, 83, 138
Mazzini, Giuseppe, 206, 227
Medici (family), 128
Medieval society, Chap. II, *passim*; values of, 6 ff., 15; organic unity of, 8-9, 11-12, 14; economic theory of, 10-16, 17-18; social ideals of, 13-15, 263; decline of, 25 ff.
Medieval synthesis, 15, 213. *See also* Medieval society

Mercantilism, 48, 74, 92, 102, 105, 110

Merchant class, 19 ff., 103-5, 109, 111, 128. *See also* Middle class, Financial class

Mercier de la Rivière, 94, 95

Metz, 30

Middle Ages, society of, *see* Medieval society

Middle class, 173-77, 237; rise of, 3, 19 ff., 46 ff., 78, 89, 100, 140; ethics of, 78, 155, 198-201; revolution in England, 107-10; revolution in America, 112-14; political desires of, 115-18; in French Revolution, 120-23; triumph of, 159-60, 173; political techniques of, 190-96; culture of, 196-98. *See also* Merchant class, Financial class, Mercantilism, Business enterprise, Industrialism, *and* Economic theory

Mill, John Stuart, 255

Milton, John, 84

Mirabeau, Honoré-Gabriel, 94, 120

Montaigne, Michel de, 50, 59, 66

Montesquieu, Charles de Secondat, Baron de, 69, 70-71, 80 n., 87, 127, 150

More, Sir Thomas, 50, 204, 221

Morellet, André, Abbé, 92

Moret, Chevalier de, 120

Morris, William, 177

Moser, Friedrich Carl, 83

Moslem empire, 17, 18

Mumford, Lewis, cited, 163-64, 182, 258 n.

Munich, Pact of, 234

Mystery of the Universe, 61

Mysticism, 26

Naples, 18

Naseby, 106

National Assembly (French), 120, 124, 125

National Convention (French), 126

Nationalism, 3, 36, 82, 104, 225-29, 233, 236-38, 251. *See also* National state

National state, 21, 47-48, 81, 227, 239-40, 250. *See also* Nationalism

Natural law, 138-39. *See also* Nature

Natural man, 96, 160-61

Natural religion, 132-33

Natural rights, 149-51, 243, 255, 267. *See also* Natural law

Natural selection, 159

Nature, 58-59, 63-64, 73, 74, 76-77, 97, 163, 240. *See also* Natural law, Natural rights

Nature of man, 248, 249, 258 ff., 265

Negro, the, 182-83

Netherlands, 84, 102-5

New Atlantis, 51

Newman, John Henry, Cardinal, 209

Newton, Sir Isaac, 58, 59, 63, 64

Nicholas V, Pope, 29

Nicolson, Harold, cited, 230

Nominalism, 26

Nonnotte, Abbé, 67

North, Frederick, Lord, 113

Ockham, William of, 26

Old régime, 100

Olney, Richard, 194

Ordre essentiel, 94

Orlando, Vittorio, 231

Ozanam, Frédéric, 215

Paine, Thomas, 118, 184

Pantheism, 62

Papacy, 25, 71

Papal Infallibility, 209-10

Paris (Peace Conference, 1919), 230, 231-32

Parliament (English), 21 and n., 106-7

Party system, American, 192 ff.

Pascal, Blaise, 69, 75-76

Paxton Boys, 113

Peasants' Revolt, 42

Pecci, Joachim, *see* Leo XIII, Pope

Persian Letters, 80 n.

Peruzzi (family), 128

Pessimism, 251

Petrarch, Francesco, 26, 27, 57 and n., 152

Petty, Sir William, 84

Philip II, of Spain, 104

Philosophes, 68, 89, 90, 119, 131 n., 139, 156; political technique of, 98

Physiocrats, 94, 216

"Piepowder" courts, 20

Pietism, 82, 83

Pisa, 18

Pittsburgh, 184

Pius VII, Pope, 205 n.
Pius VIII, Pope, 205 n.
Pius IX, Pope, 205 n., 206-9, 212
Platt, Charles, Senator, 198
Poitiers, 36
Policraticus, 9
Political theory, 269-70; sixteenth century, 29, 32-34; seventeenth and eighteenth century, 81, 88-92; of Constitutional Convention, 115-18; relation to religion, 131; of Rousseau, 146-50; nineteenth century, 150; of Bentham, 154; of entrenched middle classes, 175-77, 178, 189-96, 235, 244; of Leo XIII, 214
Politiques, 37-38, 70
Pope, Alexander, 138
Population trends, 156-58, 166
Pragmatism, 201-2, 203, 273
Prescot, 106
Pride's Purge, 106
Principia (Newton), 58
Private property, 88, 115, 147, 175-77; medieval attitude toward, 14-16; right of, 121, 123, 124, 198-200
Profit economy, 22, 44-47; medieval attitude toward, 10-12
Progress, doctrine of, 98-100, 133, 245-46, 248
Property rights, *see* Private property
Protestantism, 198
Protestant Revolution, *see* Reformation
Psychology, 86-87, 242
Pufendorf, Samuel, 84
Puritan Revolution, 105, 106
Puritans, 78-82, 105-10
Puritan tradition, 111

Quesnay, François, 87, 94, 95
Qu'est-ce que le Tiers Etat?, 120

Rabelais, François, 50
Railroads, 185
Reason, 71, 73, 74, 97, 124, 125, 126
Rebellion, right of, 9, 89
Reformation, the, 31-48, 73, 129-31, 251
Reform Bill of 1832, 173, 176
Regulators, 113

Reichstag, 21 and n.
Relativism, 243
Religion, and economics, 39, 105-6, 198-201; of individual, 130, 271-72; and political theory, 131; natural, *see* Natural religion
Renaissance, the, 29-30, 56-57
Republican Party, 183, 184
Rerum novarum, 220
Revolution, American, 113
Revolution, French, *see* French Revolution
Revolution, Glorious, *see* Glorious Revolution
Revolution, Industrial, *see* Industrial Revolution
Revolution, Protestant, *see* Reformation
Revolution, Puritan, *see* Puritan Revolution
Revolution, Russian, *see* Russian Revolution
Revolution, social, *see* Social revolution
Revolution of the Church, 127-28
Revolution of the State, 128
Ricardo, David, 156, 157-58, 255
Ricciardi, President, 210
Richelieu, Cardinal, 83, 138
Robespierre, Maximilien de, 121, 126
Rockefeller, John D., cited, 199
Roosevelt, Theodore, 189, 194
Rousseau, Jean-Jacques, 3, 72, 87, 99, 126, 127, 131 n., 146-50, 243
"Rump" Parliament, 106
Ruskin, John, 177
Russell, Bertrand, 266
Russia, 261
Russian Revolution, 261

Sadler Committee, 167
Saint Ambrose, 11
Saint Anselm, 26
Saint Antonio, 12
Saint Augustine, 26, 60
Saint Basil, 11, 204
Saint Bonaventura, 26 and n.
Saint Clement, 15
Saint James, Epistle of, 11
Saint Jerome, 10
Saint John Chrysostom, 11
Saint Paul, 204, 273

Saint-Pierre, Abbé Charles-Irénée de, 99

Saint Thomas Aquinas, 10, 12, 13, 14, 26, 62, 139, 204, 213, 221, 263, 272, 273

Salisbury, John of, *see* John of Salisbury

Schleiermacher, Friedrich Ernst Daniel, 226

Schopenhauer, Arthur, 211

Science, 240-43; renaissance of, 3, 49-50; growth of modern, 57-64; and social philosophy, 131, 163, 241-43

Second Reform Bill, 174, 176

Secularization of society, 22-28, Chap. IV, *passim*, 65-66

Self-determination, national, 253

Sensationalist psychology, 86-87

Seruantes Lesson, The, 79

Shays, Daniel, 114, 183

Sherman, James Schoolcraft, 193

Sherman Anti-Trust Act, 191 and n.

Siéyès, Abbé, 120

Simplicissimus, 30

Sin, 267-68

Slavery, 112, 178; emancipation from (United States), 182-83, 191

Smith, Adam, 41, 50, 87, 92-94, 95, 132

Social contract, 111, 147-49

Social Contract, The, 147, 148

Social flux, American, 196-98

Socialism, *see* Marxism

Social philosophy, 267-71, 272-73; of Liberalism, 87-92, 133-35, 178, 242-44; and science, 131; of nineteenth century, 156-59; of the Church, 213-19, 220-21

Social reform, 194-95, 214-15

Social revolution, 108, 112-14

Social welfare, 47, 73, 76, 153, 178, 214

Sociology, 243

Spain, 138

Spencer, Herbert, 156, 158-59, 171, 191

Spinoza, Baruch, 66 n., 86

Stamp Act, 110

State, function of, 269

State, national, *see* National state

Steffens, Lincoln, 192

Stevens, Thaddeus, 183

Stockwood, J., 80

Strossmayer, Joseph Georg, 205, 209, 212

Stuart England, 105, 107

Suarez, Francisco, 204, 221

Sudetenland, 253

Sugar Act, 110

Suleiman, 30

Summa Moralis, 12

Summa Theologica, 12

Supreme Being, 126. *See also* Deism

Swift, Jonathan, 135

Syllabus of Errors, 206, 207-8, 210

Table Oeconomique, 94

Tawney, R. H., cited, 15

Tea Act, 110

Temple, Sir William, 84

Tertullian, 26

Theft, medieval definition of, 10-11, 199 n.

Theology, medieval, 10

Theory of Moral Sentiments, 92

Third Estate, 120

Third French Republic, 205

Thirty Years War, 104

Thomas à Kempis, 26

Thouret, President, 124

Thrasymachus, 240

Toleration, religious, 84-85, 227

Toul, 30

Townshend Acts, 110

Trade, 18-19, 162-63

Treatise on Christian Liberty, 40

Turgot, Anne-Robert-Jacques, 99

Twentieth Ecumenical Council, *see* Vatican Council

United States of America, 166. *See also* America

Usury, 13, 35, 45

Utilitarianism, 98, 151-56, 244, 266

Utopia, 50

Vanini, Lucilio, 68

Vatican, the, 207, 209, 220

Vatican Council, 206, 208-12, 219

Venice, 18, 19

Verdun, 30

Versailles, 101

Versailles, Treaty of, 231-33

Vinci, Leonardo da, 58, 59

Vittoria, Francis of, 204
Voltaire, 3, 50, 67, 68, 70, 71, 72, 75, 87, 89-90, 98, 99, 124, 127, 131 n., 140, 180, 254 n.

War, as economic asset, 103-5
War, Thirty Years, *see* Thirty Years War
War, World, 1914, *see* World War of 1914
War, World, 1939, *see* World War of 1939
Wars of religion, 30, 36
Wars of the Roses, 25
Weimar, 225
Wells, H. G., 246

Western expansion, 185-86
Westphalia, Treaty of, 104
Wexford, 106
Whitman, Walt, cited, 202
William III, of Orange, 109
William the Silent, 104
Wilson, Woodrow, 230-32
Windthorst, Ludwig, 205
Wolsey, Thomas, Cardinal, 83
World War of 1914, 229, 261
World War of 1939, 261

Yeomans Lesson, The, 79
Yorktown, 113
Young, Arthur, 79-80, 218
Ypres, 19

the Christian tradition, natural law had been clearly defined by St. Thomas Aquinas in the thirteenth century: it was construed as signifying the participation by man in the Eternal Reason, the reflection in things of nature and nature's laws of the Eternal Law.[9] It was thus an essentially theological and normative conception. Similarly with the idea of Christian natural rights—rights that derived immediately from the nature of man's creation and destiny.

To the Philosophes of the Enlightenment, however, natural law meant something vastly different: it signified those universally valid precepts governing nature which were discovered not from prior religious premises, but from empirical scientific study. But this signification was never completely accepted, because the old associations of natural law persisted. The Enlightenment's failure clearly to distinguish ideal from actual, in interpreting the "Natural," followed from this basic confusion of the normative and empirical, theological and scientific, constructions of the term, Natural Law. From this confusion stemmed the weakness of the Enlightened's foundation for natural rights—for *they were derived from a nature stripped of spiritual meaning.* "How, indeed, could these [rights] be founded," Bergier asked, "on a nature that arose by chance from chaos?"[10] It was a pertinent question, which received no audible response. The summary, simple fact—whose importance would not be evident for many years to come—was this: *the concept of Natural Law, integral to most of the philosophy of the Enlightenment, was, in essence, normative, religious and Christian: dissociated from its religious foundation, it defied common sense.*

To recognize the importance of this critical failure of Liberal thought, however, cannot detract from the ingenuity of the general philosophic technique which brought to Liberalism intellectual success. In an age when the cloak of religion could not be quickly tossed aside, men had succeeded in their initial circumvention of philosophic obstacles through the simple and frank *equation* of the prescriptions of Christianity and the exigencies of profitable business enterprise. Victory in the realm of ethics then came, with pronouncement of the equivalence of the dictates of virtue and the impulses of desire. Finally, into the all-important realm of social doctrine, the identical philosophic technique was invoked triumphantly to equate pursuit of self-interest and perpetuation of social well being. Audaciously conceived and masterfully employed, the philosophic technique of Liberalism was an unqualified success.

With the mountains thus made level, men turned to the even, level philosophical plane extended, by Descartes, indefinitely before their wondering eyes. "All that is necessary to right action is right judgment," he revealed, "and to the best action the most correct judgment."[11] Or, as Voltaire had explained, "Authority bade men believe, instead of telling them to be just."[12] Thus was the issue drawn and the hopeful answer implied. Would not men, *without* faith, belief or moral sanction, be just? Could not the good society be realized by leaving unharnessed the forces and energies that flow from the innate goodness of man?

In concrete terms, the hope for Liberal success stemmed from its promise of material gain and economic conquest to be won by the triumphant middle class. That promise and program indicated at once what were to be the two great forces ultimately to challenge the foundations of the Liberal Society. One, the Church: uncompromisingly assailing a faith the gospel of which was the salvation of man through economics. The second, the laboring masses: the descendants of the yeomen of Yorkshire, the peasants of the Vendée, the frontiersmen of the Piedmont—they who had fought to bring to pass the Liberal Society, only to see its citadels occupied by men whose hopes were not their hopes, whose faith was not their faith.

But for now—for the great, triumphant present—there is only buoyant confidence: immediate, profound certainty that humanity's days of bondage are past. Inscribed by Priestley and waving victoriously from all the newly-conquered citadels of power, the banner reads: "Whatever was the beginning of this world, the end will be glorious and paradisaical, beyond what our imagination can now conceive."[13]

For OURS shall be the Kingdom, and the Power, and the Glory.